The Art of Fieldwork

Second Edition

Malinowski explicitly discussed the difference between his data and those used by his predecessors. Indeed, in some respects much of his work has to be seen as an intellectual battle waged against his predecessors and many of his contemporaries, the successful outcome of which was to raise ethnographic fieldwork itself to a professional art.

—Max Gluckman
Introduction to *The Craft of Social Anthropology*, 1967, p. xiii

The Art of Fieldwork

Second Edition

Harry F. Wolcott

ALTAMIRA
PRESS

A Division of Rowman & Littlefield Publishers, Inc.
Walnut Creek • Lanham • New York • Toronto • Oxford

AltaMira Press
A division of Rowman & Littlefield Publishers, Inc.
1630 North Main Street, #367
Walnut Creek, CA 94596
www.altamirapress.com

Rowman & Littlefield Publishers, Inc.
A wholly owned subsidary of The Rowman & Littlefield Publishing Group, Inc.
4501 Forbes Boulevard, Suite 200
Lanham, MD 20706

PO Box 317
Oxford
OX2 9RU, UK

British Library Cataloguing in Publication Information Available

Library of Congress Cataloging-in-Publication Data

Wolcott, Harry F., 1929-
  The art of fieldwork / Harry F. Wolcott.— 2nd ed.
    p. cm.
  Includes bibliographical references and index.
  ISBN 0-7591-0796-3 (hardcover : alk. paper) — ISBN 0-7591-0797-1 (pbk. : alk. paper)
  1. Ethnology—Field work. 2. Ethnology—Methodology. 3. Ethnology—Philosophy. I. Title.
  GN346.W65 2005
  305.8'00723—dc22
                                2004011387

Printed in the United States of America

♾™ The paper used in this publication meets the minimum requirements of American National Standard for Information Sciences—Permanence of Paper for Printed Library Materials, ANSI/NISO Z39.48-1992.

Cover design inspired by Ben Hill.

CONTENTS

CONTENTS

PART I
FIELDWORK CONTEXTS

CHAPTER ONE
INTRODUCTION

By all means the move to increase the general research sophistication of ethnographers should be encouraged. But at the same time, it would be tragic to lose what some converts call "soft," "unscientific," or "fuzzy" research. Much of the world we seek to understand has just those characteristics, including our own involvement in it as researchers.

—Michael H. Agar
The Professional Stranger, pp. 245–46

Without the continued grounding in the empirical that scientific aspects of our tradition provide, our interpretive efforts may float off into literary criticism and into particularistic forms of history. Without the interpretive tradition, the scientific tradition that grounds us will never get off the ground.

—Roy A. Rappaport
Comment on "Cultural Anthropology's Future Agenda," p. 76

This book is about fieldwork and the art of doing it. My purpose is to encourage fieldworkers past, present, and future to reflect on how fieldwork is an artistic undertaking as well as a scientific one. While I intend to bolster the artistic side of fieldwork, I do not intend to diminish its scientific side. I do look at artists and how they go about their work, but I do so for the sake of analogy, to gain a perspective on what fieldworkers do that is like what artists do. That includes how both field-worker and artist are also "moved about" by the worlds in which they work.

I will not argue that fieldwork is art, any more than I believe that fieldwork is science. One often hears it described with cautious phrases that implicate both art and science, locating it tenuously between them: art as well as science; a "strange" or "gentle" science; a "rigorous" art; an activity requiring the artistic rendering of behavior systematically observed. The nexus between fieldwork and data collection is a central issue to be considered. So, too, is the relationship between the scientific aspects of the fieldwork tradition on the one hand and what anthropologist Evans-Pritchard has described as the "imaginative insight of the artist which is required in interpretation of what is observed" (1952:82) on the other.

Underscoring the complementarity of art and science has a certain appeal, especially in recognizing that fieldwork is not only science or that it should not be restricted by the canons of science. But the case on behalf of science has been better served than the case for fieldwork as art. So you may find me pushing for the artistic dimensions of fieldwork as though I am redressing a wrong or correcting an imbalance. The notion that art and science are contradictory may have originated with Nietzsche (who considered art as the highest form of human activity), but Americans are noted for thinking in dualities, and the art-versus-science dichotomy is well institutionalized in everyday thinking. It is amply reinforced by the existence of parallel but differentially revered (and funded) agencies like the National Science Foundation and our two national endowments, one for the arts, the other for the humanities. An international journal, *Leonardo,* is devoted exclusively to the arts/sciences/technology dialogue. I have not set out to address the issues underlying that dialogue.

Fieldwork is taken here to refer to a form of inquiry in which one immerses oneself personally in the ongoing social activities of some individual or group for the purposes of research. My position is that fieldwork of this sort is best regarded as its own thing, neither as wildly creative as art sometimes may appear nor as characteristically systematic as science is reputed to be. Rather than leaving it hanging somewhere between the two because it is discernibly neither, fieldwork deserves a place of its own, an activity incorporating elements of both art and science yet slightly apart, in the way one might envision three interlocking rings. Fieldwork always combines elements of art and science. In the hands of any individual fieldworker, however, one or the other usually receives greater emphasis, and a text presented as a scientific account or an artistic rendering ought to be satisfyingly so.

Collecting data can be done scientifically, but fieldwork consists of more than collecting data. Whatever constitutes that elusive "more" makes all the difference. That needs to be stated emphatically, for a crucial aspect of fieldwork lies in recognizing when to be unmethodical, when to resist the potentially endless task of accumulating data and to begin searching for underlying patterns, relationships, and meanings.

Portrait of the Author as a Not-So-Young Man

No one kind enough to commend me for something I have written, either as a result of, or about, fieldwork, has gone so far as to suggest that I am an artist—and you aren't an artist until someone says you are. On the other hand, I would never deny unabashed efforts to approach my work artistically, and I count on practiced skills in writing to produce text intended to be both interesting and readable. Nor have I felt much urgency about defending the research I have done as science. I have endeavored to tell it like it is; my lack of preoccupation with doing good science does not necessarily leave me doing bad science, either.

My purpose is to examine how fieldwork not only invites but requires something of an artistic approach. How can we capitalize on that potential? And how, like other art forms, including the fine arts, does fieldwork exhibit satisfactions, constraints, conceits, and deceits comparable to the art world? After all, artists live and work in a real world, too. What can we learn from examining that world?

I confess that I am not an artist, and I do not look for anyone to argue the contrary. Yet in ways both cultural and cultured, art plays a significant role in my life, not merely in terms of what I enjoy and appreciate aesthetically, but in what I have been able to create, in spite of the absence of any recognizable talent. I like to think there is something of the artist in me, some capacity not only for appreciating but for creating, just as I assume there is something of the artist in you, and in everyone.

For example, the home in which I now live is a home I designed myself. That may, of course, speak more for my sense of space than for my artistic capacity, for even professional architects are inclined to set themselves apart from other artists. Whatever the case, the house is the handsomest one, aesthetically as well as practically, that I will ever have or need, and I feel a sense of artistic pride in the accomplishment. In the past sixty or more years I have taken thousands of photographs, admittedly amateur in nature but certainly including some splendid ones. I have written several books, the kind that earn me the cautious accolade of "a writer on academic subjects" rather than the more imposing one of "author," but even academic writing is something of an art. I have been a regular theatergoer for six decades, a concertgoer for five, and an opera buff for almost that long.

Like most Americans, I learned too early and too well that as an ordinary layman—and I have endeavored to retain that status by avoiding those art-, music-, and literature-appreciation courses and programs constantly placed in my path—I am not expected to understand or fully appreciate "real" art. But I also realize, as part of this understanding, that I am forgiven for recognizing what does and does not appeal to me personally so long as I keep my opinions to myself. None of these activities alone, nor all of them collectively, makes an artist out of me or links me in a recognizable way to an art world. It is not unknown for people to take photographs, go to concerts, or sometimes even design their own homes. Probably the best case I can make on behalf of art in my life would fit under a broad category of appreciation for what one might call "the art of living." (While I was writing the first edition of this book, someone was writing that one. See Sartwell 1995.)

Among the activities I include in the art of living, I have conducted and reported fieldwork. We have no special category for the artistic fieldworker, and if we did, I am not sure I would want to be known as one—the words seem ill suited for each other. Nor am I likely to be singled out as a scientific fieldworker. I have endeavored to make my fieldwork accounts careful and accurate, but I have also endeavored to make them reflective and deeply human. The longer I have been doing fieldwork, the more important this latter activity seems to become.

Although I doubt that I will advance the cause of scientific fieldwork in what follows, neither do I mean to diminish that effort or to argue against fieldwork's becoming more scientific in the future, as it most surely will. My argument is that fieldwork can become more artful at the same time, with the important reminder that, in its own ways, art is every bit as rigorous and systematic as science. I do not argue on behalf of a "soft" or "fuzzy" approach to fieldwork; I only argue against a fieldwork in which there is no allowance for fuzziness or ambiguity when there is so much fuzziness and ambiguity around. I argue on behalf of an approach that keeps humans always visibly present, the researcher as well as the researched.

Where there is the ever-present temptation to play art against science, one might give more than passing thought to the philosophical notion that science itself is but an art form, one among many aspects of art rather than the complement to it. But science, or more accurately the technology derived from it, has come to take the upper hand. We look to science in support of programs and policies calling for swift action, with a bias toward intervention and treatment based on what can be done rather than judgments about what is worth doing. Fieldwork evolved out of a different tradition, one based on "naturalistic" observation over extended periods of time with as little intervention as possible and an underlying premise that other systems, other ways of knowing and doing, are worthy of sustained efforts to understand. Not everything needs to be counted and measured, or changed and "improved," to conform to our standards, our ways. Artists portray. That also is what fieldwork is all about.

About the Title and Contents

The title *The Art of Fieldwork* is intended to convey two central ideas: first, that this is a book about fieldwork; second, that its focus is not on scientific techniques but on whatever else fieldwork entails in addition to technique. Out of curiosity, when I began working on the first edition, I searched on the phrase "The Art of . . ." in our library's then newly computerized card catalog. I was dazzled to discover that the university had 1,516 entries that began that way. And that did not include books with compound titles from "A" to "Z" or "Z" to "A," such as *Zen in the Art of Archery* or *Zen and the Art of Motorcycle Maintenance*. For this edition, now with the help of a librarian, I searched the Library of Congress collection. We found 7,734 titles!

On both occasions, I was relieved to discover that no one had yet written *The Art of Fieldwork*, yet distressed to discover long after I was committed to it that my title was so undistinguished. It is, however, a proper title for what follows. I assume that it immediately won some readers, including new recruits willing to take up the call, but may have lost others concerned about their image and status as scientists.

I hope to present the case well enough that those who regard field-work as requiring both art and science will find further support on behalf of strengthening its artistic dimensions and potential. Fieldwork is not merely a blend of the two; it is a mode of inquiry in its own right. My hope is that even those not inclined to emphasize artistic aspects might be induced to reflect on whether being regarded as scientists is all that critical, whether they may have internalized too rigid a view of how scientists themselves actually go about their inquiries. Would anything be lost if we were to insist that *fieldwork is fieldwork*, and only that? What might be lost were we completely to lose sight of fieldwork's artistic potential? Should we endeavor to suppress evidence of imagination or emotion in our own work, or should we be encouraging our colleagues and our students (especially our students) to see the critical role such elements play in the mind-work that accompanies fieldwork? Read any particularly unimaginative studies lately? Are they our model?

I am challenged by the notion of and delighted by the phrase "the art of fieldwork." I wish I could claim the idea for the title as my own. It came in correspondence with Robert Trotter at Northern Arizona University some years ago. Like many of his colleagues in the social sciences, Trotter is an anthropologist who found himself drawn almost too exclusively to the scientific side of fieldwork, both by the kind of research he was conducting (folk healing and minority health problems, including AIDS research) and by the academic company he keeps. In writing I was doing at the time, I sought his help in tracking adaptations of the so-called rapid or time-effective data-gathering techniques like Rapid Rural Assessment that have been finding their way into fieldwork practice. Applied anthropologists in particular see themselves as facing the reality that, if traditional fieldwork takes so long to accomplish, someone else will be called whenever a short time is all the time available.

Trotter's response directed me toward the kind of resource I was seeking (for example, van Willigen and Finan's 1991 bulletin *Soundings*). He went on to note how his own work was making increasing use of such time-effective techniques: lots of data, quickly gathered and fed into computer programs already instructed as to how the analysis is to proceed.

Analysis seems to be winning at the present time, because it is safer than interpretation. It is harder to get sued for analysis; you take fewer risks, reap fewer benefits. [Robert Trotter, personal communication, April 1993]

His comment prompted a further note of reflection: The way he was conducting fieldwork somehow seemed to lack a ring of ethnographic authenticity:

How systematic can we become before we destroy the type of understanding that we are fundamentally seeking through ethnography? We have not had a good book on ethnography, and how it can be approached, for a number of years.

That is not to say there are no books on the topic, he hastened to add, but that the books we have are too "cookbook oriented," or focused too exclusively on systematic approaches. To illustrate: H. Russell Bernard's books on qualitative research, authored and edited texts alike (e.g., 1994b, 1998, 2000, 2001), are examples of very good but very systematically oriented introductions to fieldwork. What we do not have, Trotter observed, is a book on the art of ethnography.

The art of ethnography? An idea began to form. But why focus exclusively on ethnographic research when qualitatively oriented researchers in many fields conduct field-based studies. How about *The Art of Fieldwork* instead? Voilà! A book idea is conceived, title and all, to be devoted to exploring dimensions of fieldwork not well served by a preoccupation with data-gathering alone.

This book is devoted to that exploration. Most of the discussion turns on an examination of what it is about fieldwork that resembles what artists do and how what artists do differs from (and is similar to) what scientists do.

Many of my references and examples come from cultural anthropology, my discipline of orientation. An ethnographic bias toward cultural interpretation will be evident throughout. Anthropology and sociology are where fieldwork got its start, and it helps to keep before us the cross-cultural and comparative basis on which the anthropological approach was founded. The cross-cultural aspect of fieldwork has become especially problematic for those being introduced to, or encouraged to pursue, qualitative approaches in settings totally familiar. My illustrations include research conducted in settings not all that different from other too-familiar settings in which researchers find themselves today.

About Art

Ultimately, of course, each researcher must strike a working balance to draw appropriately on both art and science in conducting any particular study. Although I intend to make a case for the art of doing fieldwork, even to proselytize on its behalf, I also subject such efforts to critical examination. Art worlds have their own problems and peculiarities, and fieldworkers share some remarkably similar concerns with them. As well, we engage in some "darker" arts that need to be examined.

Part I, "Fieldwork Contexts," takes a look at art and art worlds to provide perspective for what follows. Part II addresses what I call "The Fieldwork Part of Fieldwork," including both its basic arts and these darker arts. The conceptual aspects undergirding fieldwork are dealt with separately in the chapters that comprise part III, "Fieldwork as Mindwork." In part IV, "Fieldwork as Personal Work," I first inventory some satisfactions accruing to the fieldworker. Finally, I examine three of my own studies to render an appraisal and suggest a quality that can only be contributed from the artistic side, a quality that I call the "art of discretion."

I do not see the relationship between art and science as a zero-sum game in which one side must lose in order for the other side to win. As fieldwork gets better—or, better stated, as we get better at it—my hope is that we will find ourselves doing better art and better science without becoming too possessed about whether or not we are doing either. Since more attention seems to be going toward measuring and counting, I turn attention here to the flip side of the argument to ponder, What counts? The real genius in fieldwork lies in knowing how to answer that seemingly simple question.

No succinct, unifying concept or definition of art emerges in these pages. I did not start out with one. I have such faith in the power of writing that I firmly believed a definition would emerge. But that never happened. Instead, I look at some facets of art, ranging from how, viewed as a social institution, art works in its unique ways, to suggestions for pursuing fieldwork more artfully. That led to a working definition stated in terms of what artists seek to do, rather than what art is. I should caution that the definition is well suited to my purposes, although it may lack qualities that would make it universally noteworthy:

> Art is achieved when the addition of an idiosyncratic human touch in any production, whether performance or artifact, is recognized by a discriminating audience as achieving an aesthetic quality exceeding what is expected by the exercise of craft skill alone.

That the definition of art remains somewhat ambiguous throughout these pages proved discomforting at first, especially since I did seem to be playing it off against the powerful forces of science. Yet science thrives on that same ambiguity—it has come to mean too much to too many who accept its findings too uncritically as our Ultimate Salvation, our Truth, our reliable Western Way of Knowing. Science does indeed offer a way to know the physical world, including the physical bodies, human and otherwise, in that world, but it is not the only way.

Fieldwork involves the study of human beings in social interaction. The physical properties of those beings can explain only part of what goes on in everyday discourse. Measurement data and probabilities do not take on significance until the samples become large enough to support claims of representativeness. Fieldwork involves research in which the numbers are small, the relationships complex, and although we can detect patterns, nothing occurs exactly the same way twice. The artistic challenge is to preserve, convey, and celebrate that complexity, even to the point of messing science up the way humans seem capable of doing. If, as Jerome Kirk and Marc Miller suggest (1986:49), a fieldworker must be "ready to look a fool for the sake of science," the questions addressed in these pages is, What should a fieldworker be willing to do for the sake of art? And how far can one go?

art, Art, the Arts, the Fine Arts

Although most fieldworkers seem pleased to have their endeavors recognized as art, they are not at all pleased when the complementary, yet uncomplimentary, suggestion is made (whether stated or implied) that their work is not scientific or, far worse, that it is patently unscientific. A century of effort, after all, has been devoted to making fieldwork more scientific, an "artful science," as Ivan Brady characterizes it.

The ability to do successful fieldwork does indeed include the capacity for systematic work, but it also requires a sensibility that recognizes when systematic data are not called for, or are not all that are called for. Michael Agar, quoted in the first epigraph, is anything but a soft or fuzzy ethnographer, but he warns against fieldworkers who are unaware that they themselves have a soft, fuzzy, unscientific side. Similarly, Roy Rappaport reminds us that without the interpretive tradition, we would be grounded forever by our own solid, empirical grounding. Perceived thus, science is perhaps best recognized as a critical aspect of the art of fieldwork. That is a different view from one that holds science to be kingpin in the fieldwork endeavor.

Fieldwork can also be regarded as a "fine" art in the sense that it can be achieved and reported brilliantly. But it is not a fine art in the sense we customarily associate with music, painting, sculpture, architecture, and so forth. Great fieldworkers can produce great studies, but they are not recognized as great artists. Come to think of it, academics in general are not regarded as artists; the roles seem antithetical. And fieldwork is by definition an academic undertaking, to be judged by standards of academic competence. Academic performance can be likened to artistic performance, but it is rarely confused with it. The course I pursue looks for comparisons with art and the work of artists without making the least suggestion that fieldwork is art.

Art has multiple meanings. Some of those meanings can be examined for the light they shed on fieldwork contexts, some for their more direct bearing on fieldwork practice, some for the meaning they give to activity itself. Let me begin by sampling a range of meanings, emphasizing those of special relevance for this discussion. I am guided in this review by my trusty second edition of the *Random House Dictionary*:

- Art may express what is beautiful, appealing, or of more than ordinary significance.

- Art may refer to "a class or collection of objects" subject to aesthetic criteria, as in reference to paintings as an art form, or to a museum of art that houses such a collection.

- Art may refer to a field, genre, or category recognized as one of the arts, as in dance as an art.

- Art may refer to the fine arts collectively, sometimes with architecture singled out separately, as in a school or college of fine arts and architecture.

- Art may refer to any field using the skills or techniques of art (particularly in graphic design), such as industrial art or computer graphics.

- Art may refer to the principles or methods governing any craft, or to the craft or trade using them, as in the art of baking, the art of quilting.

- Art may refer in general to skilled workmanship or execution, or to skill in conducting any human activity, as, for example, the art of observing, an activity critical to participant observation. Thus, art can be a component of craft.

- Art may refer to a branch of learning or specialized study, especially one of the fine arts (e.g., music) or the humanities (e.g., philosophy, literature) or to such studies more generally (e.g., the humanities collectively, the liberal arts).

- Art may refer to trickery, cunning, or artificiality in behavior.

Taken in reverse order, these various definitions form an ascending scale, from craftiness, to craft in everyday skills, to recognized craft skills, to the artful representation associated with the fine arts. Since fieldwork aims at representation, it cuts across these various meanings without having to become confused with the restricted meaning of the fine arts or denying fieldworkers the possibility of achieving fine art in their inquiries.

For example, the completed accounts that result from fieldwork are sometimes recognized for achievement of more than ordinary significance. We can, and do, identify or debate our own shelf of classics, models for others to admire and emulate. There is no danger of our classics being confused with The Classics, but we have our fieldwork exemplars, those we more or less agree among ourselves to be masterpieces.

And we, too, stumble over distinctions between art and craft. Fieldwork is likened as often to a craft as to an art, and social anthropology itself has been portrayed as a craft (Epstein 1967). Fieldwork can also involve deception or foster misunderstanding, so this aspect also needs to be addressed. I use the term *darker arts* to identify some pressing issues confronting fieldworkers along these lines and devote an entire chapter to the topic (chapter 6).

For perspective, and before I become too involved with fieldwork itself, let me begin by turning attention to works of art and the work of artists. The two chapters that make up part I deal with similarities between the work of artists and the work of fieldworkers. Since that is a dominant theme of the book, it seemed natural to begin there. You are free of course to skip ahead to chapter 4, "Fieldwork versus (Just) Being in the Field," but my hope is that you will allow me first to develop some parallels between fieldworkers and artists.

CHAPTER TWO
FIELDWORK AS ART?

If it is true that the main task of art is the assertion of the authority of intuition to counterbalance the discursive method, it might appear at first sight that the artist is a natural opponent of the scientist.

—E. L. Feinberg
Art in the Science Dominated World, p. 147

I would not go so far as to say that fieldwork is an "art"; but like an art there are basic rules of the form within which the artist-anthropologist is working. The research anthropologist in the field must know, respect, and play with these rules. Beyond that, fieldwork is a creative endeavor, with some anthropologists more creative than others, and this is true in any discipline.

—Charles Wagley
"Learning Fieldwork: Guatemala," p. 16

As I began planning this book, I discovered that I needed to think about everything the title *The Art of Fieldwork* might imply and how to place the emphasis among various aspects that I identified. Did I intend to delve into philosophical issues defining art or arguing whether art is a consequence of creative urges or the need to dominate? Did I want to get into a discussion of art at all—what it is, what it does, how it is achieved—or was art only a metaphor to prompt a different way to look at qualitative inquiry? Was the emphasis to be on what we already do that reflects the artistic element in our work or on inspiring fieldworkers to new heights of artistic achievement? I was dismayed to discover more ambiguity in my self-imposed task than I had anticipated.

Consider how we customarily approach the work of the scientist and the work of the artist. We neither expect nor need to know much about the former—the work stands apart, aloof, and we assess it the same way: coolly, objectively. By contrast, a first question related to a work of art is often, What can you tell me about the artist? That seems a relevant question to ask of the fieldworker as well. Recall how quickly I put myself in the scene in this writing—by the sixth paragraph of the opening chapter. Perhaps that was too soon, too self-absorbed on my part. Yet I felt it important for you to know something about who is presenting all this. I guess if I thought of myself as a scientist, that wouldn't matter. My sense is that it does matter. A lot!

Keep in mind that my purpose is to examine fieldwork processes, not to create some noteworthy breakthrough in the philosophy of science. I was not altogether certain how sharp a distinction is needed between art and science. In looking at fieldwork analogs for the science-versus-art contrast, I considered examining the root word "graph," which comes from the Greek *graphos,* meaning something drawn or written. In a broad sense, then, "graph" refers to a kind of picture. One might contrast the artistic touch of the ethnographer, who composes a picture reflecting the lifeway of some group, with the scientific result produced by the photographer, who renders what the (camera) eye "sees" as a result of variation in reflected light.

Yet the distinction is too slick. True, the photographer records, the ethnographer renders, but art and science are superbly melded in the best efforts of both. The work of amateur photographers who lack an artistic eye is paraded constantly before us, point-and-shoot cameras having crystallized the placement of subjects at dull dead center by dictating that readings of both light and distance be taken there. Dead-center photographs are about as interesting as the work of ethnographers or other qualitatively oriented researchers whose accounts lack balance, swinging between the extremes of an overdose of or outright disdain for empirical data. Further, with darkroom and computer magic, the photographer can superimpose, add, or subtract elements, change shapes and sizes, and do any number of wondrous tricks; there is no guarantee that a photograph depicts a real-world event.

In *Transforming Qualitative Data: Description, Analysis, and Interpretation* (HFW 1994b), I broached this question by suggesting that qualitatively oriented researchers make a distinction between analysis and interpretation. I intended to set the two dimensions apart and to treat them separately. Although I probably built a better case for the one with which I feel the closest sympathy (interpretation), I had no intention of casting my allegiance totally with one at the cost of the other.

Analysis, as portrayed in that writing, seems to fall within the parameters of the scientist at work, leading to "findings" not ordinarily contested, even in fieldwork, where it sometimes seems that everything can be contested. As others point out, there is a "there" out there, and it can be counted or measured and reported within limits of accuracy generally acceptable to all. That gives to analysis a certain undeniability, to be matched only by the plausibility with which we assess interpretive effort. The artistic potential may be more obvious in matters of interpretation, but questions of what gets analyzed and how the analysis is to be conducted can also be viewed as artistic choices.

It is tempting to drag creativity into the discussion, as Charles Wagley does in an epigraph to this chapter in which he states boldly, "Fieldwork is a creative endeavor." This can lead to a subtle implication that creativity is what distinguishes the artist from the scientist. Such an argument risks losing the ear of anyone who identifies closely with science and who sees creativity as essential to the progress of that work. Similarly, imagination and intuition are not easily surrendered as belonging solely to artistic endeavor. Although there is an implied playfulness in both terms, one that I do not ordinarily associate with my stereotype of the scientist at work, one can wonder where science would be without them. As the philosopher of mathematics Imre Lakatos has noted (1978:99), "The direction of science is determined primarily by human creative imagination and not by the universe of facts which surrounds us."

No, art and science are not so easily separated; there is opportunity aplenty for good science in the work of the competent artist, good art in the work of the competent scientist. Temperament or style might be drawn into the argument, but the exceptions challenge rather than prove the rule. Surely there are high-strung, temperamental scientists, just as there are staid artists for whom the tantrum is not a correlate of talent.

Perhaps it makes sense to inventory the kinds of artistic endeavor that come easily to mind and to assess whether or how they offer a useful analogy for looking at the fieldworker as artist. Let me examine that possibility.

A Fieldworker Is (Most) Like A . . .

How far to press any analogy? For every type of art form and artist, an analogy can be drawn to fieldwork, highlighting some aspects and obscuring others. For example, we can compare the fieldworker with either the potter who works with clay or the carver whose medium is wood or stone.

Fieldworker and potter alike are intent on shaping and molding some object out of formless raw material. I found the work of a potter expressed beautifully by a poet:

When Mud Woman Begins
Electricity
> down my arm
> through this clay
> forming into
> spirit shapes
> > of men
> > > women
> > > and children
> > > I have seen
> > > somewhere before.

—Nora Naranjo-Morse

This vision of the potter represents the artist's task as building up from previously collected material, fashioning something dependent on the artist's skill, whether intended as original or replica.

Compare this vision with that of the artist—or fieldworker—who perceives the task as one of revealing something already present but hidden. I think particularly of the (perhaps romanticized) Eskimo carver whom I heard anthropologist Edmund Carpenter describe years ago:

> As the carver holds the unworked ivory lightly in his hand, turning it this way and that, he whispers, "Who are you? Who hides there?" And then: "Ah, Seal."

He rarely sets out, at least consciously, to carve, say, a seal, but picks up the ivory, examines it to find its hidden form and, if that is not immediately apparent, carves aimlessly until he sees it, humming or chanting as he works. Then he brings it out: Seal, hidden, emerges. It was always there: he didn't create it; he released it; he helped it step forth. [1971(1961):163]

This is not unlike a story attributed to Michelangelo. When asked to describe how he carved the magnificent *David*, his explanation was, "I took a block of stone and chipped away everything that was not David." His famous set of statues, the *Prisoners of Stone*, suggests something of the same. Once he had freed the figures, Michelangelo did not return to "complete" the works. His task was finished, in spite of the fact that the statues were not.

This second type of artist—like some other fieldworkers—views and engages in a task perceived differently from that of the potter. This artist does not attempt to fashion something anew but to reveal something already there so that the viewer may see it as well. Yet I think anthropologist Carpenter overstates the case with his phrase "carves aimlessly." Although there are moments in fieldwork when each of us no doubt worries about working aimlessly, moments of thoughtful reflection about how next to proceed also mark another striking similarity between artist and fieldworker.

I like these two contrasting analogies. Not only are they powerful and dramatic in themselves, but they also illustrate dramatically different ways through which fieldworkers may approach a new assignment: to shape and mold something that has never been or to uncover and thus reveal what was there all along.

It is hardly surprising that provocative analogies can be drawn between fieldworkers and artists when we realize how connected with life fieldwork can (should?) be and how all-encompassing the term *fieldwork* is. Although I did not supply a crisp definition of fieldwork, keep in mind that I use it here to refer not to all on-site research but to on-site research involving a long-term relationship and direct personal involvement. (See also Agar 1996:120, who characterizes ethnographic relationships as "long-term and diffuse.")

Let me turn the tables to ask, When I use the terms *fieldwork* or *fieldworker*, what image comes to your mind? In whatever mental picture you create, do you include yourself? Alone, or with a team of researchers? Or is your imagined fieldworker drawn from some well-known photograph, such as that of Gregory Bateson and Margaret Mead on the jacket of *Fieldnotes* (Sanjek 1990) or Steve Tyler on the jacket of *Writing Culture* (Clifford and Marcus 1986)? While you may imagine someone sitting on the veranda of a tropical hut or walking briskly down the corridor of the local hospital, or another reader imagines interviewing Sherpas in Nepal or assembly-line workers in Detroit, I had in mind a thirty-three-year-old doctoral student standing before his classroom of Kwakiutl Indian children on an island along the coast of British Columbia in the fall of 1962. Today's fieldworkers may turn up anywhere.

When I prompt with the term *artist,* what vision pops into your head this time? My immediate impression is both literal and a caricature: the painter standing before an easel, brush in one hand, palette in the other, wearing the essential paint-spattered smock and dark beret. No reason my painter cannot be outdoors, capturing on paper or canvas—or even in a notebook of quick sketches—some natural scene or group activity, thus strengthening my analogy between an engagement with the fine arts and the fine art of fieldwork.

My dictionary leads me on a merry chase this time as I try to tease out all-inclusive categories to describe everything artists can do or be. If "painter" or "sculptor" occur most frequently as examples, I am reminded that we have categories and subcategories for fine arts and applied arts, for plastic arts and graphic arts, for commercial art, performing arts, and now performance art, which fuses such artistic media as dance, drama, film, music, painting, and video, and derives in part from the 1960s invention of the performance "happening." Whether we are thinking of the artist as recluse painter or public performer, there is also an expectation of advanced skill so that whenever boundaries blur between art and craft—as for example, in the graphic arts involved in engraving, etching, woodcuts, or lithography— the individual who exhibits exceptional skill may be recognized as an artist. Of course, that includes the con artist as well—the trickster "adept at lying, cajoling, or glib self-serving talk," as my dictionary summarizes it.

Artists and Artisans and "All That Is Required"

A distinction is sometimes made between the artist engaged in one of the fine arts and the artisan engaged in a craft or applied art. In practice, however, artisans can win accolades for achieving high art in their craft.

A crisp distinction between art and craft would serve well here, but the differences remain blurred. And perhaps that is for the best. To attend adequately to the art of fieldwork, it is necessary to consider how it is viewed as both craft and art.

I do not mean to diminish the craft aspect of fieldwork. No disservice is done by using that label. Note such works as Kimball and Partridge's fieldwork dialogue presented under the title *The Craft of Community Study* (1979), or Epstein's fieldwork manual, *The Craft of Social Anthropology* (1967). Nevertheless, I point out how, in fulfilling and exceeding craft dimensions, those who perform well are often recognized, and emulated, as artists.

Perhaps the resolution of the tension between fieldwork as art and fieldwork as science—a unifying purpose in which all parties recognize a common objective—lies in efforts to refine fieldwork as craft. I was surprised and pleased to find two strong proponents of systematic fieldwork and ethnoscience methodology arguing on behalf of craft as that part of the whole enterprise that can be taught:

> We have to separate the craft of ethnography from the art. The craft can be taught. Art can be taught—up to a point—and practice is an important dimension of becoming a good artist. But great art is ultimately dependent on the talent of the artist. [Werner and Schoepfle 1987b:16]

In their very next sentence, however, these authors explain what they had set out to do in preparing their two volumes on systematic fieldwork (1987a, 1987b), which set a course quite different from the one I pursue here:

> For many applications of ethnography a master craftsman-ethnographer is all that is required. These volumes address the problem of becoming such a master craftsman. [P. 16]

I admire and respect the work of master craftsmen. (With today's gender-sensitive language, I will refer henceforth to "master craftspeople," or a "master craftsperson." However, I will use the term "craftsmanship," rather than the cumbersome "craftspersonship.") Whether I am having my automobile repaired, new lenses ground for my eyeglasses, or my income taxes prepared, skilled craftspeople are the ones I seek out. But I want to encourage, and to some extent inveigle, committed fieldworkers to think beyond and to reach beyond skill—to regard themselves not only as craftspeople, but as artists as well. If, as Werner and Schoepfle suggest, the artistic side can be taught only up to a point, then we need to consider how that dimension can be nurtured, coaxed, teased out, fanned—whatever it is that one individual can do to encourage another to do by way of providing experience, advice, ideas, illustrations, anecdotes, resources, or, sometimes, simply great expectations.

The point is to encourage fieldworkers to regard the fieldwork enterprise not merely as a craft, in the sense that Kimball and Partridge, Werner and Schoepfle, and others use that term, but as an approach to research in human groups that involves more than technical skill, more than a time-consuming way to conduct thick surveys. Surveys are fine when the objective is to know how everybody does or thinks about something: frequencies, distributions, average or "typical" behavior. Fieldwork ought to inform us about how—and to some extent why—*somebody* does it, someone whose way of thinking about things and doing things promises in some significant way to help us understand similarities and differences between their ways and our own.

E. L. Feinberg, quoted in an epigraph for this chapter, suggests that the main task of art is "the assertion of the authority of intuition" (1987:147), with intuition understood to include both sensory and intellectual elements (p. 21). What can be done, or done more, to encourage fieldworkers to exercise the authority of their intuition and thus to capture their artistic insight rather than subjugate it to a determined objectivity?

One way to provide such encouragement is to remind fieldworkers of the many ways in which their forebears exercised intuition, regardless of whether they called attention to it. Another is to ensure that artistic sensitivity and endeavor in fieldwork and reporting are today recognized and applauded rather than discouraged or trivialized. We have to take it upon ourselves self-consciously and publicly to commend qualitative researchers for artistic as well as scientific accomplishments. That is an attitude and activity in which everyone interested in qualitative inquiry has a role to play. If we really want to see fieldwork carried out and written up more artfully, the first step is to give adequate recognition to what is already being done and encouragement to anyone willing to venture (risk?) doing even more. As readers, reviewers, critics, or users of qualitative research, our efforts can have an immediate effect.

Among colleagues or students, a slight push in the right direction may be all that is needed, with a well-timed question as to whether one might be more daring with an interpretation or with the way a research problem has been framed. Perhaps fieldworkers need only to feel less cowed by demands for rigorous science that may in fact be neither as demanding nor as rigorous, nor even as prevalent, as is generally assumed. We can make it all right for others to think about and practice fieldwork as an art when we ourselves demonstrate that it can be done and ensure that others are rewarded for the doing.

The potential each of us has individually to influence and bring out the best in another may get lost in the chapters that follow, so I close this chapter with a vignette as a reminder of that potential. This account was related by an eighty-three-year-old woman recalling how she learned to quilt. The story originally appeared in *The Quilters: Women and Domestic Art,* by Patricia Cooper and Norma Bradley Allen (1989[1977]:52) and was the basis for a Broadway play, "The Quilters." It came to my attention while reading Howard Becker's *Art Worlds,* to which I turn in the following chapter:

> Mama was a beautiful quilter. She done the best work in the county. Everybody knew it. She never let nobody else touch her quilts. . . .
>
> I always longed to work with her and I can tell you how plain I recall the day she said, "Sarah, you come quilt with me now if you want to."
>
> I was too short to sit in a chair and reach it, so I got my needle and thread and stood beside her. I put that needle through and pulled it back up again, then down, and my stitches were about three inches long.
>
> Papa come in about that time, he stepped back and said, "Florence, that child is flat ruinin' your quilt."
>
> Mama said, "She's doin' no kind of a thing. She's quiltin' her first quilt."
>
> He said, "Well, you're jest goin' to have to rip it all out tonight."
>
> Mama smiled at me and said, "Them stitches is going to be in that quilt when it wears out."
>
> All the time they was talkin' my stitches was gettin' shorter.

That may be all it takes if you are putting together your first fieldwork account and you have the support of a discriminating audience—most likely committee members willing and able to offer the help you need and patient enough to let you develop your account within an appropriate framework without stifling you in the process. That kind of support is reflected in an appreciation my colleague Duncan Waite found in the words of Shelley Mishoe, who acknowledged the help she received from members of her qualitative dissertation committee. She expressed her thanks for "teaching me to trust my instincts, value my experience, and go with what I know."

If you have done, or are planning to do, fieldwork, you are already engaged in a potentially artistic as well as scientific endeavor. You need a capacity for careful observing and reporting, but you need as well to trust your instincts, value your experience, and have a clear sense both of what you know and what you do not know. You also need an audience of others standing by—not all that big an audience, but an audience, nonetheless—with help and encouragement and patience as you find your way into an activity that cannot achieve its full potential through the exercise of technical skill alone.

These chapters—necessarily more impersonal but intended to provide help and encouragement nevertheless—may serve in the interim until you find your own supportive audience, but find it you must. There are always people around to take on the role that Papa so readily assumed with Sarah's first efforts at quilting, critics determined to uphold standards and make sure that your work conforms. Systematic approaches to fieldwork demonstrate such conformity through adherence to established procedures, but that is not to suggest that artists—or fieldworkers—are ever completely free to do their own thing. A look at some of those "others" and the collective influence they wield over the doing of art is the focus of the next chapter.

CHAPTER THREE
HOW ART WORKS

All artistic work, like all human activity, involves the joint activity of a number, often a large number, of people.

—Howard S. Becker
Art Worlds, p. 1

No matter how much care an ethnographer devotes to his or her project, its success depends on more than individual effort. It is tied to outside social forces including an anthropological community that accepts the project as meaningful and international relationships that make fieldwork possible.

—Barbara Tedlock
"From Participant Observation
to the Observation of Participation," p. 78

In the chapters to follow, you may find me writing about fieldworkers as though each were the center of the universe, a free agent who delves into the social life and social contexts of everyone else, unencumbered by social contexts of his or her own. Although hardly the complete story, such a perspective serves well enough for reviewing how fieldworkers go about their tasks, for considering the artistic dimensions of the tasks, and for inventorying some of the professional problems and personal satisfactions of these endeavors.

In this writing, I will relate what I have observed and experienced firsthand, as well as learned from others, and I will offer whatever insight or advice I can, the old hand passing on his own version of a tradition. I must leave it to you to distinguish between the art of fieldwork and "Harry's version of fieldwork" if at times I seem to confuse the two. Before getting to the basics, however, I want to take a step back, to examine the social milieu in which fieldwork is conducted by drawing upon the social milieu of art worlds for perspective.

In a paper written some years ago (HFW 1994a), I examined several of the extraneous forces that influence the doing and reporting of fieldwork. In that writing, I drew upon the passing of time for my perspective, identifying influences past, present, and future.

- The past exerts its influence through the accumulated lore and literature of the various traditions in which we work. In pointing a way, it often points *the* way for the studies we undertake.

- The present exerts its influence not only by the nature of the particular assignment and setting but through the resources (duration of the study, energy, funding) available for getting the work completed. There is never enough time to realize the infinite potential of fieldwork. By constantly threatening to run out on us, time forces us to recognize the limits of what we can accomplish. In that important sense, our works are never completed. Rather, as Clifford Geertz suggests (citing Paul Valéry), instead of finishing our studies, we abandon them (Geertz 1983:6).

- Future influences take into account the options we have for reporting our work. Our various audiences, both professional and public, hold rather rigid expectations about how, where, and what we report.

In this chapter I want to return to an examination of these external—and in some ways seemingly irrelevant—constraints, drawing upon a social-interactionist perspective. Maintaining a focus on art, I draw an analogy between the art of fieldwork and other creative endeavors in which the term *artist* is more customarily heard. To draw these parallels, and for a general outline in the discussion that follows, I rely heavily on sociologist Howard S. Becker's *Art Worlds*, published in 1982.

A personal note is in order. Both in person and through his writing, Howard Becker often came to my rescue in helping me find a perspective or procedure for working through data or thinking about how to write up research. (For examples of that advice, see Becker 1986 or Burgess 1995, an edited compilation of Becker's writings.) He was also one of the earliest researchers to conduct fieldwork in schools, beginning with his 1951 dissertation study of the role and career problems of Chicago teachers (Becker 1980), following what is known as the Chicago school or Chicago tradition of hands-on sociological studies.

For several decades, Becker has been a source of wise counsel for qualitatively oriented researchers, particularly in the fields of education and sociology. By the time I caught up with him in person in the mid-1960s, his interests had taken him into other arenas. One of those was a sociological inquiry into the world of art, prompted in part by the combination of his sustained interest in photography and his experiences as an accomplished jazz musician. I did not follow Becker in his pursuit of art worlds at the time. Not until this writing did it occur to me that his excursion into the aesthetic realm might provide valuable insight for my own examination into the art of fieldwork. But indeed it has!

In Becker's view, the social systems of art *worlds*—comprising many more people than only artists themselves—are the real producers of art works. As he explains, "I have made art worlds my central concern, treating them as the producers of art works, looking at their careers, workings, and results, rather than at those of individual artists" (Becker 1982:351).

Becker describes his approach to art as "conventionally sociological." Here he examines the art worlds of everyday experience with high culture, rather than the cross-cultural perspective that might lead an anthropologist into comparative studies. His influence should be apparent throughout this chapter as I borrow from his text about other art worlds to lend perspective on the art of fieldwork.

I found striking parallels. I could not help wonder why Becker had not turned a mirror back on himself to examine the artistry in his own professional career as a field-oriented sociologist. He does make occasional reference to writers as artists, although I doubt that he was thinking of himself as one. I had to remind myself that this preoccupation with finding parallels between fieldwork and art is my own. Any inquiry must have boundaries. Becker's examination of artists at work was not intended to embrace his own artistry as an astute observer of, and writer about, the social scene.

Defining Art and Artists

Taking the role of the conventional sociologist—to whatever extent that is possible for such an unconventional one—Becker describes his intent in *Art Worlds* to approach art by focusing on "the social organization of people who work at art and of the audience which responds to it" (p. 352). That is not to suggest a simple two-way arrow between individual artist and receptive patron, however. The audiences are multiple and complex. An artist never works entirely alone. As Becker explains,

> Whatever the artist, defined as the person who performs the core activity without which the work would not be art, does not do must be done by someone else. The artist thus works in the center of a network of cooperating people, all of whose work is essential to the final outcome. [Pp. 24–25]

This perspective that Becker brings to his discussion is the one I borrow here in drawing an analogy to the social organization that supports the conduct of fieldwork. Obviously that network must include fieldworkers themselves. Perhaps less obviously, it also includes a wider circle of individuals whose efforts and interactions are essential to the final outcome. It also includes the varied audiences that fieldworkers hope to reach and other audiences that, like it or not, will reach them.

A moment's reflection reveals how extensive are the strands that link, and in important ways bind, seemingly lone, independent researchers in the field or at their desks to larger and more embracing social systems. We all must contend with the literature of the past as well as the fads and fancies of the day. We contend as well with the critiques of reviewers, the interests of publishers or funding agencies, the influence of colleagues who either do or do not cite our works or assign them as texts, and the potential outcry from unseen masses ready to remind us when, on the one hand, we overstep our bounds or, on the other hand, we avoid issues to which we ought to be giving attention.

The point of Becker's inquiry is to show how these multiple contexts define an art world. Artists do not and cannot control that world, nor are they its gatekeepers. Nor could there ever be enough room at the top for everyone who aspires to be recognized as an artist to be awarded that recognition. Creativity or genius that we applaud in the abstract gives way before a powerful insistence upon conformity in practice. Our recognized artists themselves must be aware of how hard to push, and their pushing is reassessed with the unveiling of virtually every new art work, performance, or public showing in the perpetual swing between extremes, here too little, there too much. ("That's not art!" exclaims a character strolling through a gallery exhibition in Jesse Green's novel *O Beautiful.* "That's someone skipping therapy." I have read or listened to fieldwork accounts that prompted a similar response in me.)

Becker takes the paintings hung on motel walls to represent a broad category he refers to as "canonical art."

> Imagine, for any particular organized art world, a canonical art work, a work done exactly as the conventions current in that world dictate. A canonical art work would be one for whose doing all the materials, instruments, and facilities have been prepared, a work for whose doing every cooperating person—performers, providers of supplies, support personnel of all kinds, and especially audiences—has been trained. Since everyone involved would know exactly what to do, such a work could be created with a minimum of difficulty. . . . Such a work might bore everyone involved. By definition, it would contain nothing novel, unique, or attention getting, nothing that violated anyone's expectations. It would create no tension and arouse no emotion. The paintings on motel walls are just such canonical works. [P. 228]

One hears phrases similar to "motel art" bandied about: airport art, bank art, tourist art. Although Becker does use "hack" as a descriptor, I do not think he means to denigrate such art as much as to suggest that although it is acceptably competent and conforming, it is also just what one would expect. More charitably we sometimes label it "decorator art," acknowledging the work of those who produce art that makes no pretense to being great.

Becker proposes the term *integrated professional* to describe the people who produce such art. We can draw parallels between the integrated professional artist and what we might describe as the integrated professional fieldworker whose work can be characterized as competent and acceptable, conforming but uninspired.

> Imagine, too, a canonical artist, fully prepared to produce, and fully capable of producing, the canonical art work. Such an artist would be fully integrated into the existing art world. He would cause no trouble for anyone who had to cooperate with him, and his work would find large and responsible audiences. Call such artists integrated professionals.
>
> Integrated professionals have the technical abilities, social skills, and conceptual apparatus necessary to make it easy to make art. Because they know, understand, and habitually use the conventions on which their world runs, they fit easily into all its standard activities. [Pp. 228–29]

Integrated professionals—artists and fieldworkers alike—turn out conventional studies. In art worlds, Becker notes, both the works and the professionals who produce or participate with them are treated as interchangeable (p. 231). Whatever their distinctive differences or unique abilities, they can more or less be substituted for one another.

To our wider audiences, fieldworkers probably exhibit that same interchangeable quality. Nuance we may cherish within a particular orientation or discipline is shrugged off as too minor to be of concern; witness, for example, the cavalier disregard sometimes exhibited by qualitative researchers for distinguishing ethnography from related, but nonetheless distinguishable, allies. Conversely, differences cherished across disciplines may be quickly rationalized away when a hasty call goes out to recruit researchers ready and willing to accept an assignment. I once received a telephone call from an official in Washington, D.C., inviting my participation in a funded project that sought my perspective as a sociologist. When I pointed out that any contribution I might make would be from an anthropological perspective rather than a sociological one, the project officer replied, "That's just fine, too." My name was on the approved list of those to be contacted. A disciplinary affiliation I had endeavored to establish for the previous twenty years was of virtually no consequence. (I accepted the assignment anyway. As the old saying goes, I ain't cheap, but I can be had.)

A central question Becker addresses, of relevance here, is how some activities get defined as art, and others do not. I turn next to his insight on that issue, which leads as well to examining the nexus between art and craft.

Art versus Craft as a Public Decision

When does an activity become defined as art? The judgment is not left for artists to make among themselves. "Whenever an art world exists," Becker writes, "it defines the boundaries of acceptable art, recognizing those who produce the work it can assimilate as artists entitled to full membership, and denying membership and its benefits to those whose work it cannot assimilate" (p. 226). That is the tough reality of art worlds. It is also the experience of those who have produced great art without being recognized in their own time as great artists.

Being able to claim one's work as art offers advantages that some seek self-consciously and others modestly eschew. Household or folk art that sometimes become a cottage industry—cooking and baking, needlework, basketry—or hobbies and recreational activities pursued seriously, such as social and folk dancing, flower arranging, and choral singing, are examples of activities for which it seems of little consequence among those who engage in them how they are perceived by others (p. 37). Naive artists enjoy a similar independence, often having no connection with any art world, typically working alone (pp. 258–59).

Becker points out that art worlds "frequently incorporate at a later date works they originally rejected, so that the distinction must lie not in the work but in the ability of an art world to accept it and its maker" (p. 227). He notes that most contemporary high arts started out as some form of craft (p. 298), reminding us by way of illustration that the making of paintings was once thought of as no more than skilled work (i.e., craft) that became redefined during the Renaissance as something special (p. 17). We are told that Michelangelo himself "had great difficulty as a boy in finding time for the work he loved, such was the antipathy of his father and other elders in the family to his 'wasting' his time on matters considered base" in his own household (Nisbet 1976:11).

Drawing a line between arts and crafts is, therefore, a function of art worlds. When a distinction is made, it is done in recognition that "making art requires technical skills that might be seen as craft skills" (p. 272). However, Becker notes—and here you may detect his influence on my definition of art offered earlier—artists contribute something more beyond craft skill, "something due to their creative abilities and gifts that gives each object or performance a unique and expressive character"

(p. 272). In some cases, skilled personnel who support the work of the artist may be recognized as craftspeople who do craft, while other activities may be called by either title.

> The histories of various art forms include typical sequences of change in which what has been commonly understood and defined by practitioners and public as a craft becomes redefined as an art or, conversely, an art becomes redefined as a craft. In the first case, participants in an art world borrow from or take over a craft world; in the second, a mature art world begins to exhibit some of the characteristic features of craft worlds. [P. 272]

In the previous chapter, I raised the question of knowing where to draw the line that distinguishes fieldwork as craft from fieldwork as art. Following Werner and Schoepfle (1987b), I relegated to craft those aspects of fieldwork procedures and techniques that can be taught. That leaves to art whatever it is beyond those teachable elements that allows some fieldworkers to carry out and report their inquiries in a fashion clearly exceeding the guild average. We, too, sometimes discover provocative and superbly executed studies that failed to draw attention or acclaim in their day. Gregory Bateson's *Naven* (1958), for example, was rediscovered twenty-two years after its original publication; Paul C. P. Siu's *The Chinese Laundryman* (1987) was unpublished and deemed unmarketable until after his death (see Sanjek 1990:408).

I continue to search for terms to describe that special something that sets art apart from craft. Social scientists have long had a fascination with the term *innovation*, but their attention has been directed toward issues of social or technological change rather than to purely artistic invention (for early examples, see Barnett 1953; Spicer 1952). *Creativity* might seem an obvious choice, except that some attributes associated with creativity are not ones we relish in association with fieldwork, particularly the suggestion that, unlike researchers in any other field, those of us who do fieldwork create our own data. As Ottenberg notes, "Historical scholars working with archives do not usually employ materials that they themselves have written!" (1990:152). Similarly, there is an ever-present caution not to become too creative in the retelling and, especially, in the interpretation of one's fieldwork.

Perhaps the term *genius* serves here, used in the broad sense of "extraordinary natural capacity." Yet genius in reference to extraordinarily high intelligence may not signal any special advantage. Fieldwork can easily disarm anyone gifted with what intelligence tests measure but lacking in common sense. One kind of common sense in fieldwork, for example, is the art of knowing how to catch on without catching on too quickly and thus appearing too smart, a know-it-all.

Becker offers an alternative to problems of trying to distinguish between art and craft by looking instead at a category combining them, the "artist-craftsman." Cumbersome as it is, that label seems well suited for fieldworkers who, like artist-craftspeople recognized in other lines, sometimes demonstrate extraordinary natural capacity, yet neither are nor desire to be recognized as artists.

Art worlds customarily look for something unique and expressive in performance or product that sets the artist apart, while craft pride customarily derives from a consistency of both product and quality. Thinking of fieldwork as the work of artist-craftspeople allows us to keep our claims modest in terms of outcomes (qualitative inquiry is relieved of the responsibility to demonstrate its capacity to achieve great art), while at the same time acknowledging that some fieldworkers, and the accounts their work generates, clearly stand apart from and above the rest. There are better and poorer accounts. As Becker states the case,

> Crafts ordinarily divide along the line between ordinary craftsmen trying to do decent work and make a living and artist-craftsmen with more ambitious goals and ideologies. Ordinary craftsmen usually respect artist-craftsmen and see them as the source of innovation and original ideas. [P. 276]

The "Minor Art World" of Fieldworkers

Becker makes a useful distinction that examines the development of certain "minor arts" and "minor art worlds." These labels pertain to crafts in which artist-craftspeople are recognized and rewarded for superior achievement based on criteria like beauty that differ from criteria ordinarily employed (usefulness, for example) to judge a competent level of craft skill.

The recognition that minor arts and minor art worlds coexist with major arts and major art worlds invites another perspective on the art of fieldwork. Fieldwork, too, can be pursued as a sort of minor art, one in which highly accomplished individuals are recognized and generously applauded, although their work does not presume to be great. That would preclude us from having to claim that there have been—or ever will be—great fieldworkers, comparable to great painters, great sculptors, or great composers. Malinowski probably comes closest; one can search far to find higher praise than this from Margaret Mead, who once wrote, "I am convinced all over again that Malinowski was perhaps the most thorough field worker God ever made" (quoted in Sanjek 1990:217–18). However, that same thoroughness, redefined as "haphazard" documentation, is also a major criticism leveled at both Mead's and Malinowski's work.

Becker's description of the apparatus of art worlds invites further comparisons. What do fieldworkers have by way of analogy to the shows, prizes, sales to collectors, and teaching positions associated with both the major and minor art worlds?

> Artist-craftsmen develop a kind of art world around their activities, a "minor art" world. The world contains much of the apparatus of full-fledged major arts: shows, prizes, sales to collectors, teaching positions, and the rest. Not all craft worlds develop such an artistic, beauty-oriented segment (plumbing has not). But where an art segment develops, it usually coexists peacefully with the more purely utilitarian craft segment. [P. 278]

Shows. With the exception of fieldworkers who report through visual media—photographic exhibits, film—and thus actually have something to exhibit that can be seen by viewer or critic (and increasingly by participants-turned-critics, as Allan Burns points out [1993]), we cannot display our results in any form comparable to the gallery or art show. Individually, our output is too small. A fieldwork-based monograph produced every few years would represent a prolific output, yet the cost of renting a tuxedo to go look at four or five books on a table hardly seems worth it. Conversely, the collective outpouring from all the fieldwork reported from even one year would be far too great to assemble or display, especially if one were to try to include, in addition to published books and monographs, all the papers presented in seminars or read at regional and national meetings, plus all the reports submitted to funding agencies.

We do not have the equivalent of art shows, but that does not mean we lack critics ready to pick us off, one at a time, in the constant outpouring of published and electronic reviews. We also "vote with our feet" in attending the volunteered sessions or invited addresses of author-researchers deemed to be at the cutting edge of our various disciplines or momentarily able to capture the public spotlight. "Academics attending seminars have impeccably subtle ways of assessing colleagues' opinions before deciding whether to respond to the presentation of a visiting speaker with praise, contempt, or silence," observes anthropologist Sally Price in a chapter titled "The Mystique of Connoisseurship" (1989). We are expected to know who is current, who is passé. Should we display a momentary lapse in our powers to discriminate, the person sitting next to us may quickly bring us up to date. "Good grief, she's still pumping the same stuff from a chapter she published years ago," mumbled the stranger sitting next to me when I appeared too enthusiastic in my applause for a speaker at a national meeting.

Prizes. As professionals we are, of course, above such things as prizes: We take no firsts, covet no ribbons. But there are other ways, subtle and not so subtle, to reward fieldworkers and acknowledge their works. Acceptance by a publisher or professional journal—especially a refereed journal—is not the least among such rewards. Some organizations regularly announce committee-based selections of outstanding new studies. Workshop organizers and presenters promote professional lives and works by the mere mention of particular studies or by identifying researchers whose work, or promise, should not be overlooked. Many organizations make official recognition of exemplary dissertation studies or the work of scholars early in their careers. Most long institutions have named awards to bestow on researchers making a particularly noteworthy contribution or in recognition of distinguished careers in teaching, service, and, especially, published works. An example is the Society for Applied Anthropology's annual Malinowski Award, which does double duty by recognizing the achievements of a contemporary social scientist while keeping Malinowski's name before us as that of a scholar/fieldworker worthy of emulation. The Solon T. Kimball Award recognizes excellence in public and applied anthropology. The George and Louise Spindler Award is given by the Council on Anthropology and Education, the American Educational Research Association gives annual recognition to the best qualitative dissertation, the American Educational Studies Association has its Critic's Choice Awards, and so on.

Sales. We have nothing comparable to those well-publicized sales to collectors that occasionally bring fame (usually without the accompanying fortune, to be discussed below) to producing artists. Nevertheless, there is a discernible market in qualitative research, and its gatekeepers play key roles in determining what gets printed in the journals and what gets published commercially. At least two acquisitions editors of my acquaintance, the late David Boynton of Holt, Rinehart and Winston and Mitch Allen, who now publishes under his own imprimatur, AltaMira Press, have played major roles as gatekeepers in deciding what is to be published and as enthusiastic advocates for authors fortunate enough to be tapped. These two editors, and their counterparts in other publishing houses favorably inclined toward qualitative works (such as Falmer Press; Harcourt, Brace; Sage; Teachers College Press), have also worked in concert with a number of formal or informal academic advisers and consultants who exert an influence on the selection and development of materials for publication.

Under the direction of Neil Rowe, Waveland Press carved a new niche in the qualitative market by reissuing studies that originally appeared during the heyday of case study publishing in the 1960s and 1970s. With typically thin markets, more and more monograph-length studies were going out of print as harsh realities of increased costs, coupled with a sudden preoccupation with corporate profit making, turned venerated old publishing houses into corporate footballs. Able to bypass the expensive outlay for initial publication, Waveland was able not only to revive promising titles but to set some of them on the road to becoming minor classics.

The original intent in developing the case study format was to keep costs low so that instructors could assign several monograph-length studies in lieu of having students purchase a single, traditional text. The quality of the monographs in these series was high. Attention was given to writing style, and manuscript length was carefully monitored. (See, for example, such early entries as Solon Kimball's Anthropology and Education Series, the Spindler-edited Case Studies in Cultural Anthropology as well as the Case Studies in Education and Culture, the Kiste–Ogan Social

Change Series in Anthropology, as well as series published by several university presses.)

Except in a few cases—Napoleon Chagnon's successful study *Yanomamö: The Fierce People*, first published in 1968, undoubtedly topping the list—demand never quite met expectations. Meeting the potential of the case study approach requires a sophisticated level of teaching that is neither easily achieved nor easily adapted to the lecture hall. Furthermore, the unanticipated recycling of used copies by university bookstores cut deeply into the anticipated market costs for new ones, dampening publisher enthusiasm and driving up unit costs. Nevertheless, as Spindler himself was quick to remind me, forty-five years after its inception the original Case Studies in Cultural Anthropology Series was "alive and well," with many titles in print and new cases still being added.

More recently still, Mitch Allen has found a way to reissue out-of-print books by photocopying them, thus avoiding the expense of resetting type and allowing for printing on demand without carrying a huge inventory. Three of my own oldies-but-goodies have been reissued this way in 2003: *A Kwakiutl Village and School*, originally published in 1967; *The Man in the Principal's Office: An Ethnography*, originally published in 1973; and *Teachers versus Technocrats: An Educational Innovation in Anthropological Perspective*, originally published in 1977.

Publishers are not bashful about informing their purchasing publics of text adoptions (sometimes listing all the institutions that have adopted a particular work) or boasting of how many printings their more successful texts have undergone. Beyond the boundaries of cultural anthropology, where ethnographies continue to hold their own, the market for texts dealing with issues of method far outstrips that for descriptive accounts. As a consequence, some of us who do not think of ourselves as methodologists find that our publication lists suggest otherwise. We are free to write what we want, of course, but there is a certain satisfaction in the assurance that what one is writing has some chance of being published and read.

A visit to the book exhibit at the national meeting of professional associations provides a good indicator of what publishers in each field believe is being used, particularly in lecture hall adoptions. Publishers try simultaneously to read their markets and to cultivate them. Like their artist counterparts, fieldworkers do not and cannot control the publishing world. Nor do we instruct publishers about the market. Right or wrong, publishers instruct us. And like any art dealer, when a publisher tells you, "Nobody's buying that stuff anymore," rest assured the publisher is not interested in what you are doing. Quite up to you if you want to keep trying to promote it, and perhaps you should. Not all academics are concerned with being in fashion. Just maintain your perspective and recognize your problem for what it is.

Teaching positions. Interesting that Becker includes mention of teaching positions as part of the apparatus of the arts. In doing so, he draws attention to the impact of teaching as an occupation for practitioners as well as a means of selectively recruiting new members. Not at all incidentally, teaching helps maintain a solid corps of enthusiastic followers more likely to exert their influence as consumers of the works of others than through what they produce themselves. For art worlds, Becker refers to these enthusiastic neophytes as "trainees":

> People study the arts seriously and semiseriously, taking courses, practicing difficult disciplines, devoting large amounts of time and other resources, often making substantial sacrifices and requiring them of their families and friends as well. Few of them ever become full-time professional artists. No art has sufficient resources to support economically or give sympathetic attention to all or any substantial proportion of those trainees in the way customary in the art worlds for which they are being trained. [P. 52]

The effect of costs incurred against potential income generated is important in the selection of art worlds, particularly among those dependent on self-support:

> Artists who lack substantial financial resources cannot do work which requires costly materials, equipment, personnel or space. Media like poetry and photography, requiring relatively small investments, thus attract many practitioners. [P. 95]

Clearly the gatekeeping function mentioned earlier is at work here. Many hear, or believe they hear, the call; few are chosen. Still, the status of beginner, hobbyist, or amateur offers a protective aegis. Beginners often escape the harsh judgments directed at the serious devotee. There is tolerance, a certain spirit of encouragement, shown toward promising first works. That protective aegis extends to proto-ethnographers as well. The ethnographic endeavor has been joined by individuals making the most modest of claims, especially those who substitute experience and intuition in lieu of formal credentials. The oft-alluded-to accounts of travelers, missionaries, and explorers are a case in point. Such authors are better off letting others make their claims rather than presuming to encroach on the sacred ground of the professional.

I have urged the same restraint on qualitative researchers who sometimes appear too eagerly to have embraced an ethnographic method they may not fully understand or to have appropriated a label their work may not warrant (HFW 1987). When in doubt as to whether one has produced genuine ethnography, my advice is to select a more cautious label (for example, "case study") so that the work is not faulted simply on the basis of an ill-chosen descriptor. Should a work prove subsequently to warrant the label "ethnography," let others confer it.

I do not skip lightly over the role of training in preparing fieldworkers, except to note that we would never refer to our graduate students as "trainees." Pursuit of a graduate degree with the intent of making social research a career focus—which today virtually requires the doctorate if one seeks a university position—must be among the more expensive career routes in terms of time commitment and tuition costs, especially given current occupational uncertainty. If one is unable to locate a source of funding, there are additional travel and living expenses to anticipate in meeting the requisite stint of fieldwork.

As with those who pursue careers in art, researcher ranks also lack sufficient resources to lend more than partial support to any substantial proportion of the trainees who enroll in such courses. Yet the research requirements for advanced degrees in many fields now allow, and sometimes require, a brief excursion into qualitative research. Students who pursue an extended field study may discover that they have lengthened their graduate program by a year or more, thereby increasing the chance of never completing it at all. For students in those social sciences where fieldwork can become an integral part of the career, such a risk is a calculated one. For students in professional schools, the extra time may only prolong student status while involving them deeply in acquiring research skills they will probably never use again.

That does not mean the effort is necessarily wasted. To the contrary, the experience may prove one of the highlights of one's graduate studies and possibly of one's professional life, a point I will take up later. Nevertheless, Becker's observation is germane: There are many more "trainees" in qualitative research, too, all devoting large amounts of time and making substantial sacrifices, than will ever have opportunity to conduct further field research as professionals. Today the disparity seems to be growing between the number of people holding higher degrees and the number of people with such degrees who find suitable employment.

The relationship between teacher and taught invites further comparisons between the training of artists and the training of fieldworkers. With the strong bias toward research that characterizes graduate study, students can be batched in large numbers through introductory courses in both quantitative and qualitative approaches. Beyond such basic courses, however, opportunities for further study are constrained by the limited size of most graduate faculties, the limited time of faculty members, and the limited faculty experience in qualitative work. Students sometimes develop a formal or informal mentoring relationship with faculty, but over the years I have talked with numerous doctoral students well into a descriptive study who felt ill prepared and quite vulnerable in working entirely on their own. They do not speak lightly of the sink-or-swim position in which they find themselves. There are limited opportunities for graduate research assistantships, but even in those cases, fieldwork does not lend itself to apprenticeship in a way that an apprentice actually sees the master at work. Wary faculty may also attempt to redefine the professor–student relationship as a seemingly collegial one ("You really know as much about that as I do") to keep students from becoming overly dependent and thus a further drain on their limited time for their own work.

By comparison, training in the art world is set up on a model of close, almost intimate supervision. Not all trainees gain access to that intimacy, but even in institutions given to huge lecture classes, studio courses tend to be small, providing hands-on instruction and individual tutoring. Master craftspeople and artists take on *apprentices* and *pupils*, terms seldom heard in reference to the learning of fieldwork. Neither are our various schools, periods, or distinguishable styles named after the masters, past or present. There is no Michael Agar or Clifford Geertz school of fieldwork. We might look askance upon anyone committed too wholeheartedly to one field scholar, wondering if perhaps a young colleague mistakenly—or too enthusiastically—apprenticed rather than sought to gain intellectual independence.

The Patron Effect

Many years ago, anthropologist Alfred G. Smith proposed a contrast between two major and distinctly different audiences to whom his colleagues address their studies, audiences whom he labeled "peers" and "patrons" (Smith 1964). He illustrated the differences between the two audiences by providing a series of paired statements contrasting the research-oriented reports written for peers (other anthropologists, in this case) with more popularly focused accounts addressed either to the public as patrons at large or to some subset of it, such as introductory texts written for class adoptions or papers addressed to professionals in other fields (e.g., educators, public health specialists, sociologists). Briefly summarized, the contrasts he posed included the following, with the peer objective listed first:

- Regarding other cultures for their own sake versus offering cultural alternatives for the patron's way of life

- Analyzing the constants and variables between cultures versus emphasizing what is unique about each

- Presenting a maximum amount of data versus assuming that patrons prefer a high ratio of explanation to information

- Linking past to present, providing explanations in terms of causes, versus presenting patrons with "value-oriented formulations and goal-directed explanations," involving evaluative criteria for judging how to make things better, thus anticipating how the future informs the present

- Emphasizing a uniquely anthropological approach to cultural analysis versus blending disciplinary perspectives, especially including psychology and sociology

- Offering technical analyses and discrete conclusions warranted by scientific evidence concerning subsistence patterns, kinship

> systems, or material culture versus presenting patrons with broad, aesthetically satisfying interpretations

Smith wrote not so much to pose the peer/patron contrast itself as to examine the impact of Ruth Benedict's still widely read anthropological classic *Patterns of Culture* (1934) and what he described as Benedict's "Dionysian innovation." Smith proposed his peer/patron distinction as a way of explaining why Benedict's book continued to enjoy a wide readership outside anthropology, yet found constantly diminishing support within it.

I found the peer/patron distinction provocative and useful, particularly in trying to understand the nature of the dialogue in anthropology and education. As with any interdisciplinary endeavor, the audience for that dialogue is mixed. Anthropologists working in formal educational settings who persist in doing their own thing have often missed the mark in efforts to reach their educator audiences; anthropologically oriented educational researchers fail to pass muster among their anthropology colleagues when they write for a patron audience of professional educators. The peer/patron distinction has also helped me read the literature and listen to the dialogue in other disciplines (psychology is a prime example) in which my patience and interest are quickly lost in peer-oriented discussions but can sometimes be rekindled in more pops-oriented presentations addressed to patron audiences unimpressed with collegial in-talk.

In delving into art worlds, the patron notion takes on a different connotation, one more closely related to the concept of patronage. Although we do not recognize or refer to patrons as influences on fieldwork, we most certainly have our equivalents. A patronage system, Becker points out, makes an immediate connection between what the patron wants and what the artist does. "Patrons pay, and they dictate—not every note or brush stroke, but the broad outlines and the matters that concern them. They choose artists who provide what they want" (p. 103). That places patrons in a powerful position vis-à-vis the artists they patronize. In turn, Becker observes,

> The ability to pick the best artists and commission the best work shows the nobility of spirit and character the powerful and wealthy think they possess, so that being a good patron supports the claim to high rank. [P. 100]

The education of the powerful and wealthy thereby becomes an important influence on what they will pay the artist to produce. In turn, their tastes stand to influence the tastes of others. When they succeed at that, they enhance their claims to status and thus gain further recognition as patrons of the arts. Sometimes power and wealth foster an independence of spirit; when they do, patrons are in a position to indulge their personal tastes, oblivious of the acclaim of others:

> Stubborn patrons, sure of their own judgment, often ignore public criticism, and have supported much innovative and unpopular work. In any event, politically, financially, and socially powerful patrons often control opportunities to exhibit or to have performed the work they commission. [P. 100]

The expectations are clear, even when not necessarily every artist's dream, for as Becker points out, "the artist with a patron need only please that patron" (p. 100). The cost may seem high to the artist who feels constrained by a patron's fancy, but the artist with a patron has the comfort of knowing that there is a client. Whether commissioned on a piece-by-piece basis or through continuing sponsorship, such art is virtually guaranteed a market with time and expenses negotiated in advance—to the agreement, if not always the total satisfaction, of both producer and patron.

We do not have patrons to support field-based research, but we have our equivalent in the funding agencies, both private and public, that support our work. It is more than a little disconcerting to recognize similarities between the sources of funding for fieldwork and those "politically, financially, and socially powerful patrons" who exert their influence in art worlds.

Funding agencies announce what they are interested in, sometimes with broad goals and loosely administered grants, more often with narrowly defined objectives and tightly monitored contracts. Researchers reply, sometimes by presenting their credentials, more often by submitting formal proposals. Whatever the case, they open their skills to the bidding of those in control of the purse strings. Paradoxically, the more determined you are to carve out a role as an independent researcher, the more likely you are to find yourself conducting your work at the bidding of powerful others. In order to be truly independent, you would have to join the unenviable ranks of struggling artists everywhere who attempt to support themselves through their work. Researchers who wish to maintain their independence usually support themselves through teaching, sandwiching research interests between full-time duties and short periods of unpaid leave or accumulating paid leave through the institution of the academic sabbatical.

A seemingly ideal arrangement would be to garner funding that allows one to devote full time to research of one's own choosing. There are funds that allow such freedom to a few fortunate recipients (for example, the five-year carte blanche "genius" grants of the MacArthur Foundation), but most unrestricted grants are for small amounts and limited time: summer research grants awarded by universities to their own faculties or competitive grants like the Fulbright scholarships that support work overseas for periods of up to one year. Most funding comes with strings attached; one is not really free at all. The funding agency, rather than the researcher, dictates what is to be studied, in what fashion, for how long.

The successful grant-getting researcher is also likely to be drawn into a never-ending cycle in which the ability to continue a line of work is contingent on further funding, so that scrambling for grants becomes part of the work cycle. Time must be borrowed from present projects to seek out new announcements (the request for application [RFA] or request for proposal [RFP]) and to prepare and submit bid-like proposals on future work. Just as artistic success can link one to a particular style or medium, success in grant writing can doom one to writing similar grants forever. Satisfactory prior performance provides a strong basis for renewed funding, but it tends to lock one into following essentially the same line of inquiry in project after project.

For years the so-called research universities have been recruiting some researchers on a self-sustaining basis, offering promotion in rank without the corresponding security of indefinite tenure. The position disappears anytime the researcher is no longer able to garner funds adequate to support continuing work. Although that does not create cohorts of starving researchers, it does create cohorts of anxious ones whose uncertain futures are linked to game playing in the politics of grant getting. Like their struggling-artist counterparts, these soft money researchers nervously anticipate a future in which they may be able neither to please their former patrons nor to find new ones.

The patron–researcher relationship is not restricted to those who conduct fieldwork. It prevails throughout the research world, within academia and among for-profit and not-for-profit agencies and independents alike. For qualitatively oriented researchers, the relationship poses a double-edged sword. Relatively speaking, fieldwork is difficult to monitor yet inexpensive to fund. Seasoned bureaucrats know that the time and money required to oversee modest little projects are about the same as for costly large ones. From a funding agency's point of view, big, expensive projects are preferable. In addition, fieldwork is not likely to produce the kind of dramatic results that reflect well on a sponsoring agency.

If patronage seems an unfortunate way to fund research (or art), the absence of such support is even worse! These days we also see more waffling among earlier supporters of qualitative inquiry. Some agencies seem to run hot and cold in their enthusiasm, at one moment insisting that every proposal include a qualitative or ethnographic "component" (frequently unspecified), at the next, funding only tightly designed experimental studies that produce hard data rather than the sort generated by participant observation and open-ended interviews.

In days when funding went to academic institutions, rather than to named individuals in them, the oscillating between qualitative and quantitative orientations was less critical; one could pull together teams of colleagues with requisite skills. Today's qualitatively oriented researchers must be more nimble footed, able to conduct their work in quantitative or survey mode, if that is the order of the day, and able to contribute a qualitative study, if that is allowed or required. As noted, the trend has been for fieldworkers to add some rapid techniques to their fieldwork repertoire. It is not only art patrons who "choose artists who provide what they want" (Becker 1982:103); our patrons, too, call the shots.

Observing Conventions

Thus far I may seem to have indicted every source of restraint in the art world, and by analogy every source of restraint on the lone fieldworker, except the restraint that artists impose upon themselves through too-well-internalized traditions or conventions. I must correct that impression, for in practice the consequences of these dynamics are known to and tacitly accepted by everyone involved. As Becker observes (p. 29), "People who cooperate to produce a work of art usually do not decide things afresh. Instead, they rely on earlier agreements now become customary, agreements that have become part of the conventional way of doing things in that art."

I underscore this important point: Contemporary art worlds, both in Becker's sense and in the way I employ the phrase here, consist of all the people whose activities are necessary to the production of works that the world defines as art. Thus, works of art "are not the products of individual makers, 'artists' who possess a rare and special gift. They are, rather, joint products of all the people who cooperate via an art world's characteristic conventions to bring works like that into existence" (p. 35).

Although a particular convention may be revised for a particular work, the fact remains that, in general, artistic conventions cover all the decisions that must be observed with respect to works produced. Becker inventories several of them.

- Conventions dictate the materials to be used, as when musicians agree to base their music on the notes contained in a set of modes or on the diatonic, pentatonic, or chromatic scales, with their associated harmonies.

- Conventions dictate the abstractions to be used to convey particular ideas or experiences, as when painters use the laws of perspective to convey the illusion of three dimensions or photographers use black, white, and shades of gray to convey the interplay of light and mass.

- Conventions dictate the form in which materials and abstractions will be combined, as in music's sonata form or poetry's sonnet.

- Conventions suggest the appropriate dimensions of a work, such as the proper length of a performance or the proper size and shape of a painting or sculpture.

- Conventions regulate the relations between artists and audience, specifying the rights and obligations of both. [P. 29, paraphrased]

Recognition of such conventions operating in art worlds prompts an examination of comparable conventions that impose upon both performance

46

and product in fieldwork. Such conventions become especially apparent in the reporting phase, when others must be involved in order to realize the final product. Our materials prepared for publication, for example, include an adequate descriptive account presented in standard written English, with computer-produced copy appearing on one side only of letter-size (size A4 outside the United States), sixteen-pound or better, white paper, ordinarily accompanied by a computer disk containing files that match the printed text exactly. The precise specifications here, as with conventions pertaining to form, may vary slightly from one occasion to the next, but any researcher knows roughly what they entail without ever having to give them a thought. And that, of course, is precisely how conventions exert their influence: We don't think about them because there is no need to. We simply observe them.

The fieldwork equivalent for conventions of abstraction includes showing proper deference to our forebears as well as giving attention to theories and concepts currently in vogue. It is better still, of course, to catch sight of the next wave. This task of staying ahead of the curve becomes more formidable every year, for today's fieldwork scholars, as Van Maanen has pointed out, "must now know not only their Marx, Weber, and Durkheim but also be familiar with the works of Gramsci, Bakhtin, Habermas, and Rorty and au courant with the fashionable French such as Bourdieu, Derrida, and Foucault" (1995:27n). Alas, another decade. Who is fashionable now?

Conventions for the form in which material and abstractions are combined have been drilled into us since kindergarten: Keep your work neat, provide ample margins, and give evidence of the niceties you have picked up along the way regarding the placement of footnotes or endnotes, reference style, distinctions between first-, second-, and third-order headings, and a logical exposition and flow of the account from a well-constructed problem statement to a well-thought-out and warranted conclusion.

Similarly, you should give evidence of having internalized the dimensions appropriate for the kind of account you are preparing. In academic writing, for example, you need a sense of how long a sentence should be to lend an element of erudition; short, readable sentences can raise suspicion that you yourself seem not to grasp the complexity of the issues you address. You need a similar feel for paragraphing and for stringing paragraphs into coherent subunits and units.

One of the finer sensibilities in this regard is that of bringing the length and proportions of a journal article into proper alignment or recognizing when a piece of writing simply must be of monograph length (and substance) to achieve your intended purposes. Casually discussing the topic of article length with my anthropology colleague Phil Young, we found ourselves in easy agreement that fieldwork reported as ethnography must be of monograph length; anything shorter than that (e.g., article, chapter in an edited volume) may be ethnographic in orientation, but it cannot properly be ethnography. We doubted that any ethnographer would disagree with us—although of course one well might—and yet we realized that neither of us had ever heard the question posed. Right or wrong, we just knew. Similarly, Allan Burns tells me that among ethnographic filmmakers, convention holds that to be genuinely ethnographic a film's length has to exceed forty minutes.

We also recognized that there is no authority to which we can turn to confirm our convictions. Technically length is, or ought to be, as irrelevant as time spent in the field for defining a proper ethnography. There are unstated, yet generally acknowledged, standards about such things, which are the very kind of tacit understandings that fieldworkers search out in other settings but take largely for granted in their own.

Finally, we can find parallels in conventions that regulate relations between the producers of fieldwork accounts and the consumers of them—their reciprocal rights and obligations. For example, we can withstand, expect, and sometimes even relish a degree of thoughtful criticism from those who read our accounts carefully. But we brook no nonsense from anyone who exercises the role of critic without meeting a prior obligation to be well informed.

Similarly, the producer of an account does not expect it to be plagiarized or even to be duplicated (in the literal sense) without credit. The technological ease of duplicating material—the making of exact copies—today raises thorny issues that confound another unresolved one: Should artists be entitled to a proprietary interest in their works after being compensated for them initially? If an art work gains in value after it leaves the artist's hands, should the artist receive additional compensation, or does appreciation in its tangible form belong only to a patron or dealer?

Philosophically the question is of particular interest when we hear the astronomical prices paid to the resellers of art treasures, but anyone who has ever bought a secondhand book has similarly deprived its author of benefit from that resale. The pleasure of finding my own accounts for sale in secondhand bookstores carries with it the ambivalence of realizing that the shopkeeper will take more profit from each resale than I originally received as royalty. Becker's point—one I seem not to heed in this case—is that secondhand booksellers are part of my authorly world. Both literally and figuratively, the shelf life of my publications is entirely in their hands.

Audiences expect artistic works not only to be original but also to be worthy of time and money, which they invest largely on faith or reputation. Whether paying for a book, ball game, or ballet, the consumer pays up front. Only afterward—usually too late to do anything about it—can audience members know for sure whether they have had their money's worth or have simply been had. Truth in advertising is important to consumers and audiences; audiences do not like to be deceived. A study advertised as being fieldwork-based must be just that; a study claiming to be ethnographic will be judged on that claim. Admittedly, we live in a world of media hype; we do not necessarily feel cheated if we purchase an account destined to become a classic that fails to meet such expectations. But stand clear of an audience led to believe it was going to be privy to a spectacular but has just been presented with a spectacular flop.

The Limits of Convention

Knowing the conventions must not be confused with observing them to a T. To do that is to risk losing one's audience after all, paradoxically for being perceived as too conventional. Here might be another way to distinguish the craftsperson from the artist. The former is recognized for consistently achieving the same standard time after time, while we allow, and even expect, the artist occasionally to strive for something unique and expressive. Conventions place a multitude of constraints on the artist, yet successful artists sometimes find ways to tweak convention's nose—just the right amount, at just the right time:

Though standardized, conventions are seldom rigid and unchanging. They do not specify an inviolate set of rules everyone must refer to in settling questions of what to do. Even where the directions seem quite specific, they leave much to be resolved by reference to customary modes of interpretation on the one hand and by negotiation on the other. [P. 31]

Becker cautions that artists tempted to free themselves from the constraints of the art world "lose or forego all the advantages the integrated professional more or less automatically enjoys" (p. 236). Remember, too, that

> the conventional way of doing things in any art utilizes an existing cooperative network, which rewards those who manipulate the existing conventions appropriately in light of the associated aesthetic. [P. 306]

These seem strange words of caution where one might instead expect an exhortation for artists to free themselves from their cultural trappings, strike out on their own, and let the world beat a path to their doorstep. Bear in mind that Becker is describing the system as he believes it actually works, taking a cool analytical look instead of making an impassioned plea for creativity. In his assessment, the fate of most artistic mavericks shows what happens to those who ignore the "crucial importance of organizational development to artistic change" (p. 300). Becker elaborates that theme.

> Artistic mavericks show what happens to innovators who fail to develop an adequate organizational support system. They can make art, but they do not attract audiences or disciples, and found no schools or traditions. . . . The history of art deals with innovators and innovations that won organizational victories, succeeding in creating around themselves the apparatus of an art world, mobilizing enough people to cooperate in regular ways that sustained and furthered their idea. Only changes that succeed in capturing existing cooperative networks or developing new ones survive. [Pp. 300–1]

Becker goes so far as to suggest that artists can "predict accurately" the likely responses of others, that they more or less create the effect they want, because the artistic process itself is so conventionalized (p. 203). Some artists are unusually canny in their powers of prediction. Others are simply more daring:

The limitations of conventional practice are not total. You can always do things differently if you are prepared to pay the price in increased effort or decreased circulation of your work. [P. 33]

I am not so easily convinced that artists are endowed with the power of prediction; in fact, that may be an important criterion that distinguishes successful (that is, recognized) artists from the rest. Becker hedges his position, suggesting not that recognized artists always predict accurately but that they "guess wrong less often than non-artists do" about the effects they will create in others (p. 203). I do think he is correct that, right or wrong, artists engage in prediction in the choices they make throughout their careers. Anyone who has temporarily set an idea on the back burner or selected the less innovative, but more likely to succeed, of two alternatives for conducting or writing up a study may recognize a comparable element of prediction in choices confronting the fieldworker. Becker proposes that we might track how artists make choices intended to enhance their reputations:

It would be interesting to compare, for a variety of artists during different periods, the work they made and threw away, the work they made and kept but did not feel it safe, politic, or wise to show to anyone else (each choice reflecting the social constraints they operated under), and the work they actually displayed to the public as characteristic, the work they were willing to let decide their reputations and professional fates. [P. 207]

For some artists—and some fieldworkers—there is another dimension to this issue: deliberately setting out to produce something unconventional or intentionally taking a risk that puts personal reputation in jeopardy on behalf of some supposedly higher purpose. In fieldwork, this might occur when our characteristic in-depth study reveals circumstances in which the researcher feels that some group is being oppressed, that some individuals are at risk in ways they themselves do not recognize, or that public trust has been betrayed. Qualitatively oriented researchers have long been noted for a tendency to link their approach with sociopolitical causes and to pursue openly ideological inquiries.

Similarly, an established artist might make a foray into new territory in order to pave the way for talented but unrecognized younger artists, stepping aside to let others have the spotlight. We might simply note that not all prima donnas are *prima donnas*. Art worlds are peopled by individuals, not a few of whom take delight in being different, free of convention rather than constrained by it. Such individuals face what Becker calls the "interesting and difficult dilemma" of being creative as well as reflective, innovative as well as repetitive and routine.

> To produce unique works of art that will be interesting to audiences, artists must unlearn a little of the conventionally right way of doing things they have learned. Totally conventional pieces bore everyone and bring the artist few rewards. So artists, to be successful in producing art, must violate standards more or less deeply internalized. [P. 204]

Unlearning may account for some artistic behavior, occasions when an artist deliberately goes against convention in striving for ways to be interesting. Still, Becker may attribute too much uniformity to participants in art worlds, giving too much credit to the ability of cultures to replicate themselves and too little attention to the fact that no two individuals ever get exactly the same message or make sense in exactly the same way. Whatever accounts for it, there is variation aplenty in all cultural systems, variation that is at once a source of internal tension in dealing with nonconformists and an impetus for change. Things may not change much, but neither do they remain exactly the same, regardless of how much effort is devoted to trying to keep them so.

Artistic License Reconsidered

Among the dictionary definitions of license are ideas of intentional, exceptional, even excessive deviation from rule, convention, or fact, often for the sake of literary or artistic effect, for example, poetic license. I have followed Howard Becker's exploration of *Art Worlds* to draw comparisons between the real world of the recognized artist and the realities of the world of the fieldworker. Unlike subsequent chapters intended to underscore the creative, expansive side of fieldwork—as well as to point to some of the hazards and traps that await the unwary—in this chapter I have looked for parallels in the ways both artist and fieldworker move within complex, highly conventionalized, and rather restraining social networks.

If in some ways fieldworkers are engaged in an art form that allows them to indulge their artistic genius, they also are constrained by tacit rules—unspoken traditions imposed by myriad social forces, past, present, and future. As native artists and craftspeople alike often explain to inquiring fieldworkers, of course they do not have to follow the same patterns time and time again, of course they are free to think up a new design. They regard themselves as free to do as they wish. But they wouldn't consider actually exercising that freedom, not for a moment!

Fieldworkers are not so very different in the ways they regard their own options. Of course they are (relatively) free to conduct their work any way they want. Of course they are (relatively) free to present their work any way they want. But for the most part, they don't consider doing so, not for a moment. The traditions are firmly in place. If we do not observe them, how will others know that we ourselves recognize and understand them? Better perhaps to exhibit only a modicum of creativity. And if not just now, perhaps after the award of tenure or the success of a first and admittedly "somewhat more conventional" study. Timing is critical.

Taking stock of the expectations and conventions under which we operate, the artist-craftsperson does seem an appropriate analog for the fieldworker who, in the long run, must demonstrate that standards of rigorous scholarship have been observed, rather than have a work recognized only for demonstrating a certain artistic flair. Genius has been described as one percent inspiration and 99 percent perspiration. Fieldworkers can be guided by a similar ratio. There does need to be a spark. Just be wary that allowing as much as even 1 percent for inspiration might prove a bit high.

PART II
THE FIELDWORK PART OF FIELDWORK

I have a general idea about their life and some acquaintance with their language, and if I can only somehow "document" all this, I'll have valuable material.

—Bronislaw Malinowski,
A Diary in the Strict Sense of the Term, p. 167

Fieldwork is correctly regarded as a time for gathering data, but it is not the only way of or time for doing so, it is not the only label that points to field-based research, and it is not restricted only to data-gathering. Thus, the term *fieldwork* has a broad meaning and a narrow one. For the title and scope of this book, I take the broadest of meanings: Fieldwork includes everything one does from the outset to the completion of a field-based study. But in these chapters of part II, fieldwork is examined in its narrower sense, limited to that part of the research process when the fieldworker is actually in the field.

Sociologists sometimes express a preference for the term *field study* (see, for example, Zelditch 1962) and leave the term *fieldwork* for their anthropological colleagues. But fieldwork never did belong exclusively to anthropology, and today the term is sometimes used so broadly as to be synonymous with qualitative research in general, as in "taking a fieldwork approach." Anthropologists might have preferred to be more protective of their special term *ethnography*, but in some circles even that term is used so widely as to be synonymous with the other two.

However, titling this book *The Art of Ethnography* might have suggested that I was writing only for anthropologists. Although I address fieldworkers more generally, it is worthwhile to keep in mind that for the activities described in part II, how an anthropologist goes about fieldwork differs little, if at all, from how any other qualitative researcher goes about it. The critical differences that distinguish these orientations are in the mindwork that accompanies fieldwork, to be discussed in part III.

Today's researchers have been reared in an era when everyone has become more methodologically self-conscious—researchers in applied fields like education seem almost totally preoccupied with method—so it is not surprising that what was often referred to as "ethnographic research" in the past has become today's "ethnographic method." That fact is reflected in a course I used to teach with a title already chosen for me: "Field Methods in Cultural Anthropology." I was surprised to find myself teaching a cultural anthropology course with "methods" in its title. Younger colleagues, on the other hand, were uneasy when I proposed changing the title to "Ethnographic Research," concerned that students would not recognize that the focus of the class was on methods nonetheless.

Part II deals specifically with the art of the fieldwork part of fieldwork. I begin the discussion (chapter 4) by making a contrast between fieldwork and just being in the field. Then I examine fieldwork in terms of what I call its "basic arts" (chapter 5) and its "darker arts" (chapter 6). The latter chapter is devoted to examining some disconcerting aspects of looking so closely into the lives of others.

CHAPTER FOUR
FIELDWORK VERSUS (JUST) BEING IN THE FIELD

How ethnographic. In Morocco only several days and already I was set up in a hotel, an obvious remnant of colonialism, was having my coffee in a garden, and had little to do but start "my" fieldwork. Actually, it was not exactly clear to me what that meant, except that I supposed I would wander around Sefrou a bit. After all, now that I was in the field, everything was fieldwork.

—Paul Rabinow
Reflections on Fieldwork in Morocco, p. 11

Throughout this book I make an important distinction between doing fieldwork and being in the field. I have added the word "just" to help mark the distinction. Fieldwork does, of course, require one to be there, but Rabinow's observation "Now that I was in the field, everything was fieldwork" to the contrary, simply being in the field is not enough to make "everything" fieldwork.

For example, we might be reluctant to accept the idea of a telephone pollster calling coast to coast as fieldwork. But what about a survey researcher canvassing door to door? A mailed questionnaire may be sent from afar, but what about a face-to-face interview when someone promises to take only a moment of your time? Newscasters touting live, on-the-spot coverage invariably include interviews held at the site of real or invented media events in the field. By their very presence, can they be said to be doing fieldwork? And what about the individual who accepts an assignment away from the home office or local campus to learn what it is like to live abroad or what it is like at either end of the corporate ladder? Need one go far afield to do genuine fieldwork? Conversely, does any research conducted far afield qualify as fieldwork?

On five occasions in my professional lifetime I have spent the better part of an academic year living in another country. On only three of those occasions did I conduct fieldwork. I have also conducted fieldwork under circumstances where I traveled to my field site by automobile, almost without exception returning home every evening. One of those occasions was overseas, three were research inquiries conducted while I was in residence on my home campus, and all were within a twenty-five-mile radius of where I resided. My last major study was conducted literally in my own backyard. Yet I consider them all to be bona fide examples of fieldwork. So, wherein lies the distinction between doing fieldwork and just being there?

To me, the essence of fieldwork is revealed by intent rather than by location. To repeat the working definition offered earlier, fieldwork is a form of inquiry in which one is immersed personally in the ongoing social activities of some individual or group for the purposes of research. Fieldwork is characterized by personal involvement to achieve a level of understanding that will be shared with others. There may be discomfort and hardship aplenty connected with the experience, ranging from the distractions of diarrhea or lost luggage to the despair of personal failure or lost hope, but the extent of one's suffering and sacrifice are not factored into judgments about the worth of the fieldwork as fieldwork. What does count is what others stand to learn as a consequence of the fieldworker's investigative effort through the subsequent recounting of it. Fieldwork in its narrow sense must become part of something more, something that catapults it beyond the range of personal experience, beyond simply being there.

I take a firm position that there is no such thing as unreported research. No one can claim to have done all the fieldwork who has not also written it up. Therefore, fieldwork is validated only through the requisite reporting that results from it. Fieldwork that does not get written is partial and incomplete; by itself, it amounts to no more than what may have been anything from an intellectually rich to a psychologically devastating personal experience.

Taking the position that the information shared from the experience is what validates fieldwork activity, I do not intend to dwell in any great length on what kind of image a fieldworker should try to create, how to be a gracious guest in a strange place, or how to avoid giving offense by pointing, gesturing, refusing food or drink, and the like. The travel guides can coach you as to how and how not to place your head, hands, and feet in one place or the next. I concern myself primarily with what's inside your head—and heart.

By the time we get to part III, we can leave the rest of your body out of it and focus exclusively on what is going on in your mind. I leave it to you to keep your mind in touch with your heart. Although I do press for more candor in fieldwork reporting, I will make only brief mention of the role of emotion, at least until I come to the examination of some of my own studies in chapter 11. Emotion is an aspect of fieldwork that has begun to receive special attention (see, for example, Coffey, 1999; Ellis 1991; Kleinman and Copp 1993), as we have come to regard it as a potential ally in our work rather than a sign of weakness in the worker. Here is where art can embrace as a treasured source of energy and insight what the more systematic approaches manage too often and too well to exclude.

That's what I mean by fieldwork; it may not be what you mean by it. You may have had something not quite so all-consuming in mind. For example, you might have been wondering about adding some unstructured interviewing to a field-research project originally designed to gather information through a mailed questionnaire. Or you may have encouraged your field assistants to record their own impressions as well as to record respondent comments, even when their comments are not related directly to the questions on the printed form.

Let me propose a critical distinction between doing fieldwork, a process that assumes a degree of wholehearted commitment, and simply borrowing a fieldwork technique or two to enhance or complement an essentially quantitative or survey approach. Admittedly this is a matter of degree, as well as of personal judgment and professional association. An anthropologist able to study in a group setting only intermittently or for an embarrassingly short period may nonetheless refer to the research— even if it consists mostly of what Rabinow calls "wandering about"—as fieldwork. A quantitatively oriented researcher who spends an unusual amount of time doing essentially the same thing before initiating more systematic inquiry might insist, rather indignantly, that the research—the real research, that is—didn't begin until some hard data were collected.

In the sense I use the term, fieldworkers are researchers who make the commitment that full-time—or at least longtime—on-site presence demands. As quoted in the epigraph, Rabinow was not wrong to observe, "Now that I was in the field, everything was fieldwork," but it was his intent, not his presence, that made it so. There were others (rather few, it seems) in that Moroccan hotel, but they were not in the field, and they were not doing fieldwork.

At the same time, I have not meant to kindle interest in fieldwork only to suddenly turn the tables and define it in such a way that few can meet such rigorous criteria of time and commitment. I do not mean to discourage the efforts of any quantitatively oriented researcher contemplating how to add qualitative dimensions to an inquiry, whether through observation, interviewing, or just wandering about. Nor do I disparage the work of researchers who may employ these techniques but whose research pursuits neither demand nor allow the level of involvement ordinarily associated with fieldwork. It is not necessary to commit to fieldwork to want to be perceived as a sympathetic and humane researcher, someone interested not only in collecting information but also in the people from whom one is collecting it. For the fieldworker, however, achieving some depth of human understanding provides the rationale for the whole endeavor. I use the label "fieldwork" for research involving the intimate, long-term acquaintance necessary to gain that understanding.

Data-Gathering as Technique

When I began to write anthropological texts, I followed the conventions of my training. I "gathered data," and once the "data" were arranged in neat piles, I "wrote them up." In one case I reduced Songhay insults to a series of neat logical formulas.

—Paul Stoller
In Sorcery's Shadow: A Memoir of
Apprenticeship among the Songhay of Niger, p. 227

Field workers have started accumulating case material in somewhat the same fashion as the social scientist in modern communities, the influence of whose methods is perceptible in the newer techniques.

—Audrey Richards
"The Development of Field Work
Methods in Social Anthropology," p. 305

"If I can only somehow 'document' all this," Malinowski mused as he wrote in his personal diary, "I'll have valuable material." That is certainly the crux of it—deciding first how to record and then how to convey to others what the fieldworker has observed and experienced firsthand.

Early anthropological fieldworkers were especially interested in the classification and distribution of peoples. The kinds of data they sought lent themselves to categorical statements so that groups could be compared. (Radcliffe-Brown went so far as to insist that anthropology was in effect "comparative sociology.") Those early fieldworkers were unabashed data gatherers. What set them apart from an earlier generation of armchair anthropologists was that they set out to collect their own data rather than preoccupy themselves with data gathered and reported rather more haphazardly by others.

Understandably enough, the practice of and pressure for gathering hard data, thus to be assured of having something to report, persists today. The problem with such a focus is, as it has always been, that simply gathering data can become an all-consuming, mindless, and endless task. The first casualty of fieldwork experience can be experience itself. I have seen this happen even with students pursuing modest fieldwork exercises, when some slick technique turns a study around by offering (and delivering) neat numbers that leave the people, and more creative original purposes, behind. Anthropologist Audrey Richards, quoted immediately above, noted this tendency of fieldworkers to start working "in the same fashion as the social scientist in modern communities." She was writing in 1939!

There will never be an end to the kinds of data-specific techniques to be developed, and computer capabilities make it possible to handle previously unthinkable quantities of data. We have entered a data-obsessed era, and fieldwork practice has been affected accordingly. I peruse professional journals and newsletters apprehensively, aware that today's fieldworkers-in-the-making are being introduced to a far broader range of field-oriented techniques in courses taught by others than they ever were in my courses.

For more than a quarter of a century, I taught such courses, sometimes with a broad qualitative approach, more often with an anthropological emphasis on ethnographic research. At one time my course was designed primarily for doctoral students in education and related professional schools; more recently, it was taught as ethnographic research in a department of anthropology. I was always satisfied that the course was solid. Students experienced field-based research firsthand. They did not simply read about fieldwork or talk about it, they did it—at least to the extent possible within the time constraints of an eleven-week term. Yet I cannot help wondering whether my students received too soft a version of field-work, a version gained largely on my own in the days before texts and courses on anthropological methods or qualitative research had become the vogue.

As I had suspected (and feared), the list of procedures and techniques that today's students are expected to know—at least when cultural anthropologists convene to set standards for what others should teach and others' students should know—is formidable. For example, below is a sampler from one of the first lists heralding this new era of what "a professional ethnographer, of any theoretical persuasion, specializing in any geographical area, ought to master" (Plattner 1989:30) and, thus, ought to have been taught in a comprehensive training program. Such a list, rigorous as it may be, is but one among a number of forces urging—and in a sense, pressuring—all of us to become more data-oriented in thinking about, pursuing, or teaching fieldwork.

- Structured direct observation of events: time allocation analysis, interaction analysis

- Observation and recording of the physical environment, to include how to read (and preferably how to draw) topographical and other maps, and, as needed, skills in remote sensing, soil analysis, biomass transects, and so forth

- Still photography, video recording

- Approaching informants, maintaining an interview situation, and disengaging from an interview in a manner that leaves open the possibility for further interviewing

- Designing and pretesting interview schedules to include semi-structured interviews on both broad and narrow topics (e.g., child rearing for the former, a specific ritual for the latter), an open-ended life history/life cycle interview, an ethnogenealogical interview, a structured interview

- Systematic interview techniques to determine the limits of a domain of study (e.g., free listing); informant judgments of the similarity among items in a domain (e.g., triad tests, free pile sort, successive pile sort, paired comparison); belief frames and componential analysis; consensus analysis; cultural-model research; analysis of decision making

- Data recording, coding, and retrieval skills, perhaps through a database-management system

- Finding and using published and archival sources

- Specific training in the use of the Human Relations Area Files

- Thematic analysis of textual materials

- Use of microcomputers for word processing and data manipulation

- Translating and back-translating of interview schedules and interview protocols

- Developing a research design for the quantitative testing of a hypothesis

- Designing a data codebook; coding and entering data into computer files

- Statistical processing of data and interpretation of statistical results (e.g., level of measurement, central tendency, dispersion, regression, significance levels)

- Using common multivariate methods such as factor analysis, cluster analysis, and multidimensional scaling

- Reading and interpreting graphs, plots, charts, and tables

- Understanding basic sampling theory and common sampling procedures

- Exploratory data analysis to produce and interpret stem and leaf plots, scatter plots, bar charts, cross tabulations

My own microcomputer rests opposite me at my desk. I use the word "rests" advisedly, for if microcomputers pick up any vibes at all, mine surely suspects that I will never tap into all its capabilities, even to present or display information. It will never have an opportunity to show me what it can do to list data, lay out frequencies, or produce spreadsheets or contingency tables. But it can—and does—taunt me with all that might be, were I more computer literate. I inadvertently clicked on "Grammar" while working on the earlier edition of this manuscript, and my computer had the audacity to question my high percentage of passive constructions and lengthy sentences, habits my personally chosen reviewers have never had the heart—or nerve—to mention. Meanwhile, the manual accompanying my once-new laser printer exhibited an audacity of its own, contradicting the style requirements of my professional journals by admonishing me about underlining, referring to such practice as a throwback to the typewriter that would henceforth make my work look unprofessional!

Simply by sitting opposite me, the computer taunts me with a voracious appetite that makes me feel I am wasting not only its potential capabilities but its capacity as well. If nothing else, at least shouldn't I try to fill it up with data? Its kind of data, of course—which are not necessarily my kind of data. The answers to my best questions do not lie in the accumulation of data. See the extended discussion by Flyvbjerg (2001), on this topic, but note that John Seidel, author of the computer program "The Ethnograph," identified the problem early on.

> My concern is that, because computer technology allows us to deal with large volumes of data, we will be lured into analytic practices and conceptual problems more conducive to breadth analysis rather than

depth analysis. We will start trading off resolution for scope. [1992: 112]

Breadth as a trade-off for depth points to the problem that concerns me: Fieldwork continues its relentless march toward becoming a data-driven activity. And that is why I make the distinction between fieldwork and just being in the field. Neither activity achieves a higher purpose or confers more dignity than the other, but fieldwork demands a different mental set and achieves a different goal, one that is qualitatively different from a quantitatively driven study. You can have either, and you can have both. But they are not the same.

Not only do journals and my computer, and now paperless e-journals as well, remind me of this preoccupation with data; the mail, the telephone, and the vexing research issues posed by students and colleagues serve as constant reminders of the tilt toward more systematic, thus presumably more scientific, aspects of our work. Colleagues representing other disciplines also gently goad me with the reminder that their data and mine differ. Theirs, they insist, are "real," at least in the sense of being external to themselves. They argue that as a fieldworker I make up most of what I call data.

The telephone rings or e-mail arrives from near and far with authors or publishers seeking advice or critical review about how far to go in allowing qualitative inroads into territory once the exclusive domain of the psychometricians. My impression is that today finds many closet quantifiers having to hold a brief for qualitative/descriptive approaches that they do not personally find sufficiently rigorous. Their resolution is a ceaseless effort to shore up qualitative research procedures by perpetuating the same criteria for assessing them that have for years been standard in the dialogue of traditional quantitative researchers—criteria such as objectivity, reliability, validity—an issue to be taken up in chapter 7.

E-mail boasts its own network of qualitative researchers in a dialogue of immediacy once reserved for the hard sciences. I receive announcements and flyers advertising workshops and summer institutes not only available to my students but offering to upgrade me! As someone who taught fieldwork, I am nevertheless encouraged to enroll myself as a student. At the very moment I was originally drafting this chapter, an announcement appeared on my screen about another of the highly regarded

National Science Foundation–sponsored Summer Institutes on Research Methods in Cultural Anthropology. The workshop experience promised to upgrade my skills in areas not all that different from the minimal skills listed above that I should be teaching my students:

- Structured interviewing techniques: free listing, pile sorts, ratings, and rankings

- Use of computer software: questionnaire construction, data analysis, and text management

- Direct-observation data: coding behavior, time allocation

- Social-network analysis: map structure, detect cliques, measure centrality, autocorrelation

- Detecting and visualizing relationships among variables: measures of similarity and distance, multidimensional scaling, cluster analysis, correspondence analysis, and log-linear modeling

With the passing of another decade, we see more concern for what one does with data collected and with (and for!) the people from whom it is collected (e.g., the 2004 NSF Training Opportunity announcement). In addition to collecting, coding, storing, and "cleaning" data, doing preliminary data analysis and write-up in the field, and achieving inter-rater reliability across sites, we find such topics addressed as explaining human–subject protection protocols, learning to deal with logistical and ethical problems in the field, and giving back and explaining research findings to the community.

A bit of content analysis suggests the shifting emphasis in the offering of such workshops in recent years. Everything familiar to an old-fashioned ethnographer like me is getting tightened up, with the focus shifting toward neat data—the kind that can be plugged into a computer program—rather than to neat (i.e., intriguing) problems that only a fieldwork approach can address. Key-informant interviewing, for example, has disappeared as a topic, as has open-ended interviewing. Structured interviewing has become structured interviewing techniques. More tellingly, interviewing itself has shifted toward questionnaire construction guided by a computer software program. Principles of direct observation yield to the collection of direct-observation data. And whole new analysis-oriented facets have emerged focusing on social-network analysis and visualizing relationships among variables.

An aspect I initially found so delightful in the work of many field-oriented researchers, one that made it refreshingly different from the experimental and social psychology of the day, was the absence of those mysterious qualities called "variables." I never have figured out the logic of calling the variable you manipulate "independent" and the variables you leave alone as "dependent," and I have never met a variable I liked. I share Michael Agar's preference for what he has called the "holistic perspective," the belief that "an isolated observation cannot be understood unless you understand its relationships to other aspects of the situation in which it occurred" (1996:125). "From a holistic point of view," Agar continues, "the very idea of a variable is enough to make one skeptical" (p. 126).

I repeat that the purpose of this writing is not to rail against efforts to make fieldwork more scientific. Nor will I inventory excesses that sometimes seem intended to displace fieldwork rather than render it more effective, or to make fieldwork not only more efficient but virtually researcherproof, safe from the foibles of fieldworkers themselves. But in drawing attention to the art of fieldwork and contrasting fieldwork with data-gathering, I hope that fieldwork's unique contribution to seeking human understanding can be preserved and strengthened, even as the disciplines that have fostered it seek self-consciously to become more scientific and, in the process, to look more and more like each other.

Who Are Today's Fieldworkers?

A dramatic shift has been occurring that now finds many cultural anthropologists acting more like traditional social scientists—the very trend Audrey Richards detected more than sixty-five years ago—at the same time that researchers from allied fields are drawn toward ethnographic approaches. Anthropological research has never been limited to fieldwork, although fieldwork has always been, and remains, the sine qua non for cultural anthropologists. Efforts to make all of anthropology more scientific have caught fieldwork in their sweep. The benefit is the positive influence this has on the data fieldworkers gather; the downside is that data-gathering is being mistaken for fieldwork.

Fieldworkers of any persuasion ought to feel free to develop the artistic potential in their work at a time when many anthropologists are endeavoring to establish themselves more broadly as social scientists. Russ Bernard, himself a major force on behalf of a more rigorous anthropology, sums it up thus:

> In the past, cultural anthropologists were more concerned with description than with explanation and prediction. . . . Many anthropologists today, however, are interested in research questions that demand explanation and prediction, questions like: Why are women in nearly all industrial societies, socialist and capitalist alike, paid less than men for the same work? Why is medical care so hard to get in some societies that produce plenty of it? [1994a:176]

These are among the kinds of issues addressed by today's social scientists, and anthropologists have a contribution to make from their holistic, comparative, cross-cultural perspective. But it is crucial to realize that while individual researchers can bring such a perspective to their inquiries, problems of such magnitude are not well suited to fieldwork approaches. Only by carefully rephrasing a question to ask, What, if any, contribution toward understanding this issue might be made through fieldwork? is there any possibility of a match between research question and research strategy when the issues addressed are so sweeping.

There is little question that the social sciences will turn more and more to systematic approaches to address such issues in meeting increasing demands for explanation and prediction. That should afford ample opportunity for those who find their identities as scientists, but it is all the more reason to recognize fieldwork as a different form of inquiry attracting an ever-expanding network of qualitatively oriented researchers. The latter are less concerned with data per se and more concerned with an approach that offers insight into the human experience through the fieldworker's own firsthand experience.

Fieldwork as Intimate, Long-Term Acquaintance

It is by intimate, long-term acquaintance with culture groups that one gains insight.

—Robert Redfield
In Rubinstein, ed., *Fieldwork*, p. 126

Fieldwork takes time. Does that make time a critical attribute of fieldwork? According to ethnographic tradition, the answer is yes.

In our hurry-up world, that tradition has been buffeted by time itself and has been steadily eroding. Two years (or longer) in the field was once the standard, perhaps related to the success of Malinowski's inadvertently long fieldwork among the Trobrianders. (He had to sit out World War I because of his Polish ancestry.) Today the ideal has been shortened to half that time at best. Realities of academic life make even twelve months a standard that few ethnographers can afford (often literally) to meet. Old-fashioned fieldwork of any sort is almost out of the question for privately funded agencies that do not have the luxury of making "contributions to knowledge." Against the pressure to reduce the expectation of at least a year in the field is the compelling argument that anyone contemplating fieldwork should be present at least through a complete cycle of activity. For most of the peoples among whom earlier anthropologists worked, that cycle was related to the annual growing seasons. The ideal of twelve months—the minimum now having become the maximum, as it often does—remains well entrenched.

That does not mean a twelve-month minimum is always observed, but fieldworkers whose stay must be brief usually go to some length to explain their circumstances and to shore up doubts raised by their shorter tenure. One way to do this is to pay close attention to identifying and observing through whatever constitutes a cycle of activity and to recognize that short, recurring cycles may be nested in larger ones. In micro- as well as macro-studies, fieldworkers often link brief visits that extend over a long period so that the brevity of the time one is actually in the field is mitigated by the effect of long-term acquaintance. Anthropologist Simon Ottenberg's review of his own fieldwork among the Igbo (formerly the Ibo) of southeastern Nigeria provides an example:

> I spent 15 months in 1952–53 in a group of villages called Afikpo, another like period in 1959–60 at Afikpo and nearby Abakaliki Town, and brief visits to Afikpo in the summer of 1967, the winter of 1988, and in March and October 1992. [1994:91]

Ottenberg notes a paradox: "What is curious about my Igbo project is that the field research aspect has not been that extensive, but the writing has been." He goes on to explain, "Thus, long-term research has a somewhat different meaning for me than for others who have spent more time in the field" (p. 92). I suspect that many fieldworkers would admit to giving a "somewhat different meaning" in accounting for the time actually spent on site. And anyway, what could ever be enough?

However it is reckoned, Ottenberg's total time in the field is extensive. Numerous others honor the same tradition. William Crocker, for example, whose fieldwork among the Canela was reported in 1994, accumulated a total of more than five years, with eleven trips that dated back to 1957. And Wade Pendleton reports that from 1967 to 2001 he spent a total of nine years at his research site in Namibia (in Kemper and Royce 2002:36).

Interestingly, however, is Ottenberg's claim that his is long-term research is based on the length of time he has been writing. It might have been equally appropriate, although a bit unusual, for him to have staked his claim on the basis of how long he had been thinking about the Igbo. If at first blush such a claim seems a bit strained, we might turn the tables to realize how seldom we are treated to studies that even mention the extent of deep and profound thought in reflecting on the fieldwork experience. Perhaps you already recognize some advantage in taking the broad view that fieldwork is far more than only time spent in the field.

The question remains: By itself, can time guarantee the breadth, depth, or accuracy of one's information? I think not. Mere presence guarantees rather little, and most assuredly there have been fieldworkers and research problems that required less time to get the job done. Margaret Mead, for one, was neither bashful nor apologetic about the short duration of her fieldwork experiences. She was quick to note that she considered herself a quick study who could accomplish a great deal in a relatively short period. But what might Redfield have meant by intimate long-term acquaintance?

How Intimate Is Intimate?

Many years ago I got to thinking about the crossover point in fieldwork when I felt I knew enough about even one individual—let alone an entire people, like the Kwakiutl—in sufficient depth that I could write with confidence because I knew what I was talking about. I decided upon three admittedly arbitrary criteria that could serve as indicators of the adequacy of my personal knowledge about another individual's life. Although strange in the telling, they continue to caution me, at least as a reminder of how little any of us customarily knows about others, except for possibly the most intimate of our personal rather than our professional associates.

My first criterion asks, What do I know of this person's sleeping arrangements? Optimally, this means sleeping in both a figurative and a literal sense. Figuratively, who are and who have been the person's sleeping partners? Have there been offspring resulting from any of these unions? As for sleeping in the literal sense, where does this person sleep and whom does he or she "sleep by" (see Shweder 1996:30)? What constitutes bed and bedding, how many others share it, how many others sleep in the same area but not the same bed, and where do others sleep who share the same quarters? For example, do children have a room, or rooms, of their own? What accommodation is made for guests?

I must admit surprise in discovering how my own assumption that middle-class Americans necessarily sleep in beds has had something of a jarring. I was asked to stand in for a prospective out-of-town investor interested in the purchase of a large old house near my campus that had been remodeled to accommodate a number of profit-making rental units for students. Master key in hand, an obliging manager insisted that we inspect every apartment, following the courtesy of only the briefest knock on each door. I was relieved that with what seemed his incredible invasion of tenant privacy, only one resident was at home on Sunday afternoon. But my shock at the rudeness of the approach was matched by my surprise at finding only one bed in some fifteen apartment units. Everyone appeared to sleep on mattresses or air mattresses on the floor, and almost as many used sleeping bags as used bedding. Nothing could have better underscored for me the transient nature of student life and the cramped conditions under which many students live—and how out of touch I am with their lifestyle. The experience reminded me how much we assume, yet how little we may know, about how others live, including others whom we perceive as being just like us.

My second criterion asks, What do I know about how this person's laundry gets collected, washed, dried, and put away? Although the topic does not, at first blush (a blush that might be literal as well as figurative), seem as intimate as knowledge about sleeping arrangements or sexual partners, laundry is not only an intimate item but is also revealing of personal relationships and/or the division of labor within a household.

I first became aware of the social significance of laundry while reading Oscar Lewis's *La Vida*. As I recall, an older woman was "keeping" a younger man, and one of the things she did for him was to look after his laundry. To her, that meant taking care to have clean underwear folded and tucked away in a drawer each day, ready for the following morning. As a single young adult, I found the idea of having someone else look after my underwear surprisingly intimate. As a child, my laundering needs had been attended to by my mother, assisted at various times by a maid or cleaning lady. After I began living away from home (summer jobs, other employment, the military, returning to graduate school), laundry was my own responsibility—at least whenever I was living too far away to save up and bring it home on intermittent visits.

Those who do their own laundry also reveal something of their lifestyle. When and where does the laundry get washed? And does the amount of laundry washed at one time provide an indirect measure of personal wealth? Ever notice a not-quite-dry white shirt on a young waiter or busboy in a Third World country and realize it is probably the only formal shirt he owns? Even closer to home, I could not resist commending a student I encountered on the campus one brisk autumn morning for what I interpreted initially as robustness. He was clad only in a T-shirt and what appeared to be gym shorts. He shook his head to the contrary. "Laundry day," he offered by way of explanation. I nodded in acknowledgment and revised my too-hasty interpretation. On whatever day he suddenly finds himself without clean clothes to wear, every possible item of clothing is taken immediately to a coin-operated washing machine at the local launderette.

Anyone who has resided where laundry is ordinarily delegated to others has probably had to give undue attention to getting the laundry done. The task requires the cooperation of another human, rather than simply the convenience and availability of a machine. During my first field experience, living and teaching as a bachelor on a Canadian Indian reserve, I washed (in an electric wringer-type machine powered by the school generator) and hung out my laundry. That I did my own laundry amused the adults and baffled the children. "Where's your mom?" the children asked whenever they caught me hanging out the washing to (perhaps) dry in the damp coastal climate, reminding me that certain tasks were properly the responsibility of a wife or mother. It was perfectly all right for males to help with the washing, even to do the washing when someone was indisposed. It was not all right, or at least not customary, for an adult male to live alone and thus to attend to such things for himself. To the consternation of her male siblings, one of the older girls in my classroom offered to do my washing for me to save me from what she felt must surely be ineptness coupled with embarrassment.

On subsequent occasions when I have lived overseas for extended periods, finding a way to get the laundry done made it necessary to have at least a part-time housekeeper. Although cooking and cleaning posed no serious problem, the very thought of having to wash laundry in cold water in a plastic tub on a concrete floor posed an insurmountable obstacle. Yet on my most recent assignment overseas, a young American male teaching in a rural area in southern Thailand explained that local Muslim women wouldn't even consider washing underwear for him.

Laundry is but one of many possible indicators of the level of a researcher's intimate knowledge. How anyone's laundry gets done is itself curiously personal, something a researcher might learn about with no intention of reporting. I mention it as a reminder that our knowledge of everything or everybody else (and of ourselves as well) is invariably partial and incomplete. Part of the art of fieldwork lies in being attentive to and able to acquire ordinary, everyday information, rather than letting our assumptions fill in the gaps or using a questionnaire that is as likely to elicit socially correct responses as honest ones. A related art is communicating to a reader what it is that we do know and with what degree of certainty rather than trying to create the impression of knowing everything. We must also be able to communicate the extent to which such details are of professional interest, not because we necessarily intend to report them but because having such detail at our command helps to ensure that what we do report is both accurate and properly contextualized. Accustomed as we are to the role of researcher, it is also difficult to realize how foreign that idea is in many groups. My Kwakiutl pupils helped me appreciate that point with their customary response to almost every direct question I posed: "What do *you* want to know for?"

To compensate for the seemingly mechanical nature of my first two criteria for gauging intimate knowledge, my third criterion tests a quite different domain. As researcher, I ponder, How much do I know about any of my informants' grandmothers? I have no particular set of questions in mind about grandparents, only the general issue of a researcher's familiarity with family members who, living or not, may be presumed to have had an influence on an informant's life. Grandparents play important roles in that regard. Older ones exert an influence that a researcher is unlikely to have observed firsthand but might reasonably be expected to know about as a consequence of extended life history interviewing or being privy to occasions for family reminiscing.

I have described three criteria that serve as a personal litmus test and reminder of how little any researcher is likely to know about those among whom we work or study. They are not a guideline for conducting research, even for the sort of person-centered fieldwork that most interests me. They are only a means for reflecting on the depth of my knowledge. None of the three is relevant in problem-focused studies in which it is more important to represent multiple views of a given problem or how it might be addressed. Yet a phrase like Redfield's "intimate, long-term acquaintance" is not to be shrugged off lightly.

My criteria address the question of what one might expect to know as a consequence of long-term fieldwork. Every fieldworker needs guidelines for assessing the adequacy of his or her expanding knowledge base. Even as a child, I became aware of how much better I felt I knew my playmates or school chums whenever I had the opportunity to meet their parents, to visit their homes, or, especially, to meet their grandparents. (Come to think of it, that may have been the earliest hint that someday I might find my métier in the study of cultural acquisition.)

Some fieldworkers assess the adequacy of their accumulating knowledge by their ability to shop local markets and prepare local foods. The ability to make appropriate jokes, especially in a different language, provides another measure. Redfield's student Sol Tax took the challenge of negotiating the construction of a new house for his mentor as the opportunity "to test and expand his practical knowledge of Guatemalan culture" in the village where the two of them were conducting research (Rubinstein 1991:199).

In fieldwork we grapple constantly, both within ourselves and with our more objectifying colleagues, about how much we know and whether we ever know anything with certainty. On the basis of intimate, long-term acquaintance, however, we should be satisfied that even our conjecturing is informed, regardless of whether we necessarily are able to produce evidence that might prove us right. While our critics may express concern about the paucity of our hard data, we find solace in knowing that we know more than we feel we need to tell. Part of the art of fieldwork is learning to live with such tension. And part is finding ways to distinguish what we can present as fact from what we can only surmise on the basis of extensive firsthand experience.

Performance First, Then Script

In exploring analogies between fieldwork and art, fieldwork itself might be viewed as a performing art. In drawing that analogy, we find a paradox. In fieldwork, performance comes first, script comes later. The two may be totally unrelated.

Fieldwork—how one acts while in the field—is not a performance that everyone gives well. Those who do give it well are unlikely to be applauded, for the audiences to one's performance in the field ordinarily remain unimpressed unless the fieldwork goes badly or interferes with performances of their own. The audience that would be interested—one's critics or colleagues in research at the time, one's students at a later date—are not privy to what is going on. Except for scrutiny by a tiny set of technical readers who must grant conditional approval—a funding agency, a dissertation committee, an institutional review board, a governing body with authority to grant or deny access—the public announcement of the performance follows rather than precedes it, in that section typically titled "Method" or "How I Proceeded with This Study."

One important rationale for, and benefit of, conducting extended rather than short-term fieldwork is that those in the study cannot maintain a pretense or pose forever. Sooner or later things get back to normal, and the fieldworker will be able to observe the everyday life of real people, not an individual or group putting on an act to win favorable review.

Time works the same for the fieldworker as well. One can play at being Mr. or Ms. Goody-Goody just so long. The real you will show through soon enough, even without the additional hazards of social or physical isolation, bureaucratic misunderstanding, or external factors over which you have no control. Fieldworkers may feel especially vulnerable to being "put upon." They want access to the knowledge those in the setting have. For the information they seek, how much should they give in return?

A further analogy with performance is with an actor's lot—waiting in the wings, or waiting for one's cue to go on. Since the days of Franz Boas, experienced ethnographers have bemoaned time spent waiting for events to take place or for informants who show up late or not at all. As one of my students noted in frustration in a written field report, "Anyone was never around during the interviews." Waiting is sometimes described as the primary activity in long-term fieldwork, waiting reckoned in weeks and months rather than hours or days. One might characterize fieldwork as an inquiry process in which the researcher's task is to distill time, his or her own endless waiting magically evaporating in the final account so that the reader jumps from one action moment to the next with a terse phrase such as "From 10 days to 2 weeks later . . ." or "Not until they become adults . . ." or "In the Winter Ceremonial, by contrast. . ."

I do not mean to make either a virtue or an art out of waiting, but time and timing are a genuine cost of fieldwork. Living as we do in a society predicated on the notion that time is money, I cannot escape a feeling that much of the effort ostensibly devoted to making fieldwork more scientific is really directed at making it more expedient, less time-consuming, and thus less costly.

Is efficiency itself relevant here, or is this a problem created by confusing fieldwork with techniques of data collection? Time is what most modes of inquiry either compress or overlook. Perhaps individuals drawn to fieldwork have an intuitive regard for the important workings of time in the present, just as historians have great respect for the important workings of time in the past. To hurry through is to miss the point of what both fieldwork and life itself are about.

Can anyone clearly demonstrate that efficient fieldwork is better than inefficient fieldwork? One way fieldwork might be allied more closely with art or science is with the calculated, intentional efficiency we associate with scientific activity. Fieldworkers, by contrast, often get caught in situations where they have no alternative but to tough it out and allow time to run its course. We cannot hurry the lives of those about us, only our own. Compare this with the determination of data-oriented researchers to get the data-collection phase over and done with in order to get on with the real work of analysis that lies ahead.

After the script is completed, the major performer in the fieldwork drama—the fieldworker—may appear to disappear from sight and site alike, as was the custom when accounts were rendered in the third person and left literally to tell themselves. Today's fieldworkers are encouraged to put themselves into their scripts, but we do not expect them to burden us with their hardships or regale us with self-reports of how splendidly they conducted themselves.

And thus their performance goes unremarked. We have only the account as rendered by the fieldworker for making our judgment as to the nature of the performance itself. That underscores the importance of what comes out of the experience rather than what one puts into it.

First things first, however. Part II continues with two chapters directly concerned with the art of in-the-field fieldwork. There is a definite work cast to this part of the discussion, a sort of all-this-will-be-worth-it approach. A review of some of the personal rewards and satisfactions of fieldwork is reserved for a later section.

CHAPTER FIVE
FIELDWORK: THE BASIC ARTS

There may be kinds of information that are in fact vital to the task of anthropological analysis but that are fairly consistently excluded from our field notes—in other words that we have conventional criteria for identifying observations as data that are inappropriate for the kinds of hypotheses and theories we wish to develop in our analysis. The frequent assertion that anthropology is an art as well as a science might depend precisely on the unsystematic or unreflecting way in which we accumulate part of our basic data.

—Fredrik Barth
preface to *The Social Organization of the Marri Baluch*, p. x

This chapter is as close as I come to presenting a fieldwork manual. It brings me perilously close to dwelling on the techniques and strategies of fieldwork as craft. However, I focus on the less systematic aspects of the experience rather than on data-gathering per se. Behind every strategy or technique employed in fieldwork there needs to be sound human judgment—an artistic decision guided in large measure by what passes as ordinary courtesy and common sense. I have made "Courtesy and Common Sense" my first subheading, to highlight some pervasive elements in fieldwork before dealing with topics more customarily addressed in such discussions. Under the unconventional subtitles "Being There," "Getting Nosy," and "Looking over Others' Shoulders," I review fieldwork's major dimensions: participant observation, interviewing, and archival research.

Courtesy and Common Sense

On first thought, participant observation would seem to be the obvious choice as a starting place for discussing the basic arts involved in fieldwork.

On second thought, focusing on participant observation hopelessly confuses whatever is unique to fieldwork with the display of everyday courtesy and common sense.

A fieldworker can easily offend through inappropriate behavior, comment, or question. Fieldworkers are not clairvoyant, and they, too, are subject to making social errors. Thoughtful explaining to get out of a tight or embarrassing predicament that one shouldn't have gotten into in the first place is certainly not an art limited to researchers. Nor are those who do fieldwork necessarily gifted in the handling of human relations. I have heard colleagues reportedly successful at fieldwork ask rhetorically, "Can you imagine me doing participant observation?" and a voice inside me whispers, "Well, frankly, now that you mention it . . ."

Presumably the human-relations aspect of fieldwork is enhanced for those to whom such qualities as empathy, sympathy, or everyday courtesy and patience, come naturally. I see no evidence that such qualities can be taught or that they are particularly abundant among the practitioners of certain disciplines to the exclusion of others. For example, the consequence of anthropology's supposed humanizing message seems not, in my experience, to be any more or less evident in the everyday behavior of anthropologists than of ordinary folk. If it were, then to be a member of an anthropology department would be the envy of members of every other department on the campus.

The idea of participant observation, which James Clifford characterizes as a predicament transformed into a method (1988:93), can raise a straightforward question: How does one go about being artful when assuming so obvious a role? I recall a senior colleague in the 1960s who flat-out rejected any proposal he was asked to review that explained, or attempted to explain away, the question of method with the simplistic response "participant observation." Michael Moerman, writing in the heyday of postmodernism, has observed that participant observation, "once anthropology's secret shame," had subsequently become "the fashionable focus of its self-absorption" (1988:68).

Nevertheless, participant observation will surely continue to occupy the preeminent role Russ Bernard ascribed to it, not only as the foundation of fieldwork but as the foundation of cultural anthropology (1994b:136). It is all-encompassing as a method, yet it is not really a method at all. Rather, as Bernard explains, it is a strategy that facilitates data collection in the field. And it is a strategy that covers all kinds of data collection, quantitative as well as qualitative, for as he notes, "All participant observation is fieldwork, but not all fieldwork is participant observation" (p. 137). Administering a structured interview, for example, or observing patrons in a market may require fieldwork, but they do not require participant observation.

Employing participant observation as a strategy in qualitative research requires common sense. It needs to be examined in terms of what brings fieldworkers into a setting in the first place and whether they are well situated to observe what they hope to observe. This is where many qualitative researchers get off on the wrong foot, hoping that simply being there will enable them to observe or experience what they are interested in observing and experiencing. A first question to ask is, Can whatever I want to study be seen by a participant observer at all? And, if so, am I well positioned to see what I hope to see? These questions need to be followed by another: What are my own capabilities for participating and observing in this situation? Many descriptive studies pursued through participant observation have elected a time-consuming approach with only an outside chance that the researcher proposing them will ever have the opportunity to see whatever purportedly is to be observed.

I remember talking with a student years ago who had heard of an Alaskan village where television was about to be introduced. Intrigued with the possibilities of ethnographic inquiry and the tradition of village studies, the student asked whether I thought ethnography would work as the appropriate research strategy for a study of the impact of television on village life and, if so, how I would approach it.

My personal reaction was, Why bother? The broad sweep of a community study did not seem warranted with such a narrowly focused question. With a well-funded project one might assign an ethnographer to every family, or, lacking such generous resources, one might assign a lone researcher to any household willing to have a longtime observer. In either case, the purest observer would not want to influence the results and therefore would be hesitant to describe the study as one about TV's impact. Yet a live-in observer in a village household might prove far more entertaining than TV fare, the researcher's presence creating the very kind of distraction that dedicated participant observers try to avoid. It looked to me like a low-yield investment of researcher time to catch a few possible comments and to record some TV watching. Even then, at the end of the year, how would anyone actually assess impact? The proposed project seemed to illustrate what Fredrik Barth has described as a tendency to confound process and change (1994b:76).

Granted the village had been without TV before, but was the occasion for introducing it all that interesting? It was not the inefficiency of the research strategy that bothered me so much as the mismatch between the magnitude of the problem and the resources that would be assigned to study it. A year devoted to a study of village life in modern Alaska (or anywhere) ought to be a provocative experience and rich source of data. A commitment of that sort seemed to warrant a more imaginative scope of work than tracking TV viewing and attempting to assess—or guess—its impact. I gently asked whether the student could think of any other ways to get relevant information if the social impact of TV was the burning issue.

Another example illustrates the complex crossover (or heavy residue) from tightly designed quantitative studies to the creative use of qualitative ones. This time, sampling was the bugaboo. A student in a seminar I was presenting overseas was interested in studying what she called "discovery learning." In my suggestion that participants engage in some modest field research during the seminar, she saw an opportunity to try her skills at classroom observation. But she had become distraught over a major obstacle she foresaw, and she made a special appointment to discuss it with me. "I have always understood that any school or classroom in which I do observations must be selected by random sampling," she explained. "What if the school and teacher I happen to draw isn't using discovery learning?" Her faith in sampling procedures was as profound as her misunderstanding of when to apply them. Common sense should have guided her to a setting where she was likely to find the phenomenon of interest; questions of frequency and distribution were beyond the scope of her proposed inquiry.

I was intrigued that the student felt so rigidly bound to sampling procedures in spite of the fact that hers was to be an exploratory study. It signaled that my explanations about qualitative research were not powerful enough to dispel her previously held beliefs about how research is supposed to be conducted. There was room for some teaching here, but there was also a challenge for me to try to learn what I could about the beliefs associated with research from my seminar participant. Might that be where the real art is in all inquiry: recognizing what might be learned as situations present themselves? If so, then, as anthropologist Mariam Slater once caricatured it (1976:130), whether or not you eat soup with a chicken head floating in it is rather incidental to the business at hand. What counts in fieldwork is what is going on in your mind.

Even to describe participant observation as a strategy may be going too far, except to prompt researchers to seek an opportune vantage point for seeing what they want to observe. The element of strategy turns on two complementary questions that need to be reviewed over and over:

- Am I making good use of this opportunity to learn what I set out to learn?

- Does what I have set out to learn, or to learn about, make good use of the opportunity presenting itself?

What is going on in the researcher's mind is critical to all this. If nothing is going on, not much is likely to come out of the experience except experience itself, with a possible residue of "empathy, a rapport high, and headnotes," in Roger Sanjek's terms (1990:238). This is not unlike actors whom we criticize for simply mouthing words rather than getting into their roles. (I address this issue more fully in part III.) It may seem strange here to separate mind from body, but the distinction helps to underscore the difference between what others observe us doing as we go about fieldwork—how we get around and conduct ourselves—from what is going on in our heads as we do it.

The way researchers move their bodies around does not make art out of fieldwork. Nevertheless, one can offer suggestions as to how to move about with sufficient grace to be received graciously by those with whom we hope to interact. I can identify at least four areas of social behavior that seem especially important for the successful and satisfactory conduct of fieldwork—its performance aspects, if you will. Alone or collectively they are no more than the demonstration of everyday courtesy and common sense:

1. *Gaining entrée and maintaining rapport.* These two terms, joined so often as to have become a single and often trite phrase in fieldworker accounts, mask a great deal of the angst associated with fieldwork, especially among those who have never done it and who worry that they may not be successful in achieving its personal dimensions. I remember a young graduate student in anthropology who returned from a difficult (not impossible, just difficult) year of fieldwork in the Canadian Far North. He was anxious to communicate to his fellow students not only how terribly important this aspect of fieldwork was but also that these were critical aspects for the duration of fieldwork, not just a pair of tasks to be attended to first thing on arrival.

   Maintaining rapport presents a continuing challenge through the presence of an intrusive and inquiring observer forever wanting to know more and understand better. The long-term nature of fieldwork and the likelihood of both physical and emotional/intellectual isolation exacerbate interpersonal tensions. Fieldwork can be its own worst enemy; I know because I've been there. No one was stealing my mail during the year of my induction into fieldwork as village teacher. There simply were times when there was no mail to bring or only unimportant mail when important mail hadn't been sent. A couple of families were regularly relieving the school of a few gallons of fuel oil; I needed to maintain perspective more than I needed to maintain rapport, for I had not been sent to the village as an agent of the government with a primary responsibility for safeguarding the school's fuel supply.

2. *Reciprocity.* There is an art to gift giving. There is something of an art to gift receiving. These arts are by no means unique to the conduct of fieldwork, but fieldwork entails a subtle kind of exchange, one that often involves gifting across cultural boundaries where exchange rates may be ambiguous or one wonders what to offer in exchange for intangibles such as hos-

pitality or a shared life history. For example, whether, and how much, to pay key informants always presents problems. Grant-rich investigators are concerned that they may offer too much; resource-poor graduate students are concerned that any payment at all is a further drain on already overtaxed resources. Employing local field assistants or choosing a dwelling to rent or a family with whom to reside invariably puts researchers at risk of siding with factions or otherwise being accused of being partial, parsimonious, or extravagant—and perhaps all of these at once.

Conventional wisdom cautions fieldworkers to remain as neutral as possible, especially when new to a site, but even that option is not always open in the field. Conversely, one must learn how to manage being put upon by those who recognize the fieldworker's inherent vulnerability to requests when success depends on being able to make requests of others. If as fieldworker I am unsure what I may need from you by way of help or information at some future time, I have to be cautious in turning down requests you make of me at present. I dare not fully reveal how vulnerable I feel, lest you impose unduly. Such decisions are not made easily. Along with extending the depth of one's understanding, long-term commitment extends both the depth and the duration of one's vulnerability.

One-shot interviewers or pollsters have it easy. At most, they may be hit up for a cigarette or a ride to town. They don't stay around long enough for requests to start escalating, as they inevitably do over time. Questions such as whether to pay a standard rate for interviewee time ought already to have been worked out as a matter of project policy. Requests for food, money, medical assistance, or a job can put a resident fieldworker in an awkward bind; damned if you do, damned if you don't. In the abstract, a firm policy seems advisable ("Sorry, I just don't loan money—to anyone"), but in the world of diplomacy, everything remains negotiable, and fieldwork unquestionably requires the art of diplomacy. One seeks knowledge in the professional role of researcher but prays for wisdom in the personal roles that make it possible.

3. *A tolerance for ambiguity.* Another admonition that becomes trite in the saying, but essential in the doing, is to remain as adaptable as possible, to exhibit a tolerance for ambiguity. In terms of priorities, perhaps this point deserves first mention, yet one can hardly claim that all fieldworkers exhibit it or that only fieldworkers need it.

There is no way anyone can prepare another person for all the vagaries of fieldwork, any more than one can train or prepare another for the vagaries of life. Of course, there is no way one can pass on to another the quality of tolerance, either; merely mouthing it does not make it so. But there have been times in my own fieldwork (and life) when, with nothing more than the cliché to sustain me, I have managed to eke out just a bit more patience than I thought I could muster. Someday the admonition to develop a tolerance for ambiguity may be helpful in your own work (and life). Simply suppressing a too-hasty comment or reaction is a good step in this direction.

Fieldworkers would hardly go wrong to take tolerance for ambiguity as their professional mantra if it is not by nature a personal one. I have seen it treated exactly that way in a summer workshop designed to help prepare teachers for assignments in the Alaskan bush. I was not able to think of any other phrase that might someday prove more helpful. The workshop instructor used the expression so often that participants groaned every time he repeated it, and they presented him with a special T-shirt with that slogan on it. By the following winter, I assume that his message took on more significance as daylight hours and patience shortened, and the realities of bush living began to take their toll.

I have heard the phrase "life shock" in reference to a related problem. Those of us who make our entry into the real world via protected mainstream lives and respectable academic routes—the usual pool from which fieldworkers are recruited—are not necessarily well versed in the harsher realities associated with life itself. During the years we spend in the library studying about life, most folks are actually knocking about in it. We may never have witnessed anyone dying, the sort of thing genteel folk do in hospitals, out of sight. We are even less likely to have witnessed a birth, especially in my day. The ragged and deformed may also have remained out of sight. All those statistics we read—poverty, illness, accidents, violence, abuse—may suddenly materialize for a fieldworker whose most traumatic experience to date has been a ticket for speeding.

The ambiguity comes in the meaning of human life, which proves not to be so universally revered as we have been schooled to believe. "How many children do you have?" you inquire of your Ndebele informant in southern Africa. "Six, maybe five," he responds, leaving you to wonder if he really does not know how many children he has. But that is exactly why he has answered with such calculated ambiguity. When he last saw his children, there were six. In the interim, something may have happened to one of them, even if they all were okay this morning. One does not want to provoke fate by taking anything for granted.

Not even natural disasters—fires, floods, earthquakes— shake us from our Western belief, or faith, that we are essentially in control. Our language comforts us: fireproof, earthquakeproof. Foolproof! Fieldwork can sorely test the belief that we exert such control. A tolerance for ambiguity is an essential element in the art of participant observation.

4. *Personal determination coupled with faith in oneself.* Self-doubt must be held in check as you go about your business of conducting research, even when you are not sure what that entails. In part this means being able to maintain balance in the face of what anthropologists have termed *culture shock.* Michael Agar describes culture shock this way:

> The shock comes from the sudden immersion in the lifeways of a group different from yourself. Suddenly you do not know the rules anymore. You do not know how to interpret the stream of motions and noises that surround you. You have no idea what is expected of you. Many of the assumptions that form the bedrock of your existence are mercilessly ripped out from under you. [1996:100]

And that's only half of it, because whatever shocks you probably was not what you originally set out to understand. The complexity of your task grows before your eyes; you want to understand more and more as you realize you understand less and less. At such times you cannot help wondering if any fieldworker before you has confronted anything quite like this!

Rest easy—no one about to undertake fieldwork can ever anticipate exactly what will be encountered or exactly what is to result from the experience. If we could, there would be no point in doing research this way, for our studies are constructed in the doing. Even hard-nosed experimentalists recognize, as Ludwik Fleck observed seventy years ago, that if a research experiment were well defined, it should be altogether unnecessary to perform it (1979[1935]:86). The more that is known about a topic, the less likely a qualitative broadside of the kind that results from fieldwork is well suited to explore it further. There is a becoming level of uncertainty in this work, and you must be prepared for the unsettling experience of constantly having to reset your course.

Should you feel so baffled by what confronts you that the only recourse you see is to record everything, you will realize that certain "everythings" take precedence over others. What do you see and hear that strikes you as important? How might you direct the attention of a newcomer to this setting? How can you best distill its essence for a reader who will only be able to see through your eyes or hear through your ears? Description is the starting point, square one. You need never be at a loss as long as you remember you can always go back to description when you feel overwhelmed.

Being There

Used in its broadest sense, participant observation is so all-encompassing that it can refer to virtually everything that qualitative researchers do in pursuing naturalistic inquiry, that cultural anthropologists do in pursuing ethnography, that sociologists do in pursuing a field study, and so forth.

Here I use participant observation in a somewhat narrower sense that makes it the complement to interviewing rather than inclusive of it. That still leaves it to cover any field activity not specifically related to some form of interviewing. Its essence is captured, although oversimplified, in the phrase "being there." In a chapter with that title, Clifford Geertz offers a lighthearted image of the proper role of the fieldworker:

> What a proper ethnographer ought properly to be doing is going out to places, coming back with information about how people live there, and making that information available to the professional community in a practical form. [1988:1]

Somewhere between "going out to places" and "coming back with information," every fieldworker has to achieve a workable balance between participating and observing. There is always a question of whether those two processes constitute discrete functions or are hopelessly intertwined in the very act of anyone being anywhere, but it is comforting to have our own special label for what we do to reassure ourselves that our being there is different from anyone else's. That self-conscious role is what we examine when we discuss participant observation—how we can realize the potential not simply of being there, but of being so agonizingly self-conscious about it.

How to participate effectively, how to observe effectively (especially that), how to keep the one from interfering with the other, and how to get others to act naturally while we try to appear nonchalant about our own presence—those are the confusions and challenges of the participant dimensions of the participant observer role. They, in turn, are confounded by the perennial problems of the process of observation. Those include what to look at, what to look for, and the never-ending tension between taking a closer look at something versus taking a broader look at everything.

Many sources are devoted to the topic of field observations and participant observation (e.g., Adler and Adler 1994, Bernard 2000, DeWalt and DeWalt 2002, Jorgensen 1989). In a paper titled "Confessions of a 'Trained' Observer" (HFW 1994a), I have joined these efforts to demystify that which cannot necessarily be explained. My purpose was to help neophyte fieldworkers recognize what the problems are, rather than to offer simplistic solutions for resolving them. Each of us addresses the problems in specific ways in specific cases; there are more-or-less appropriate adaptations, not definitive answers. But no old-timer is going to forsake an opportunity to offer a bit of advice. My suggestions here underscore the dilemmas and inventory the options that confront the participant observer.

Doing Better Participant Observation: Using Participant Observation Better

- *Focus your observations.* You may tell others you are just observing, and doing so may satisfy their curiosity, but do not believe for a minute that there is any such thing as just observing. A lens can have a focus and a periphery, but it must be pointed somewhere; it cannot see everywhere at once. Kenneth Burke's aphorism reminds us, "A way of seeing is also a way of not seeing" (1935:70). Our marvelous human eye has its scotoma, its blind spot; the analogy to fieldwork has been duly noted (see, for example, Crapanzano 1980:ix).

  When you are not sure what you should be attending to, turn attention back on yourself to see what is it you are attending to and try to discern how and why your attention has been drawn as it has. What are you observing and noting; of that, what are you putting in your notes, at what level of detail; and at what level are you tracking your personal reactions to what you are experiencing? Kleinman and Copp (1993) suggest that note taking is not complete until you go back over your notes to make notes on notes. The point is to ensure that you are coupling your analysis to your observations (rather than putting that task off until later) and to help you remain attentive to your own processes as a human observer. Don't worry about all that you are not getting; focus on what you are getting. Observe yourself observing.

- *Constantly review what you are looking for and whether you are seeing it (and if not, whether you are ever likely to see it).* You may need to refocus your attention to what is actually going on, and discard some overconceptualized ideas you brought into the field (such as "watching" decision making or "observing" discrimination). Begin by looking for recurring patterns or underlying themes in behavior or action. That should include patterns of things not happening as well as things that are happening. The latter kind of observations are most likely to be made comparatively: "Back home this would be a major source of stress, but here no one seems concerned." You will probably catch yourself becoming prematurely evaluative, particularly when righteous indignation tells you what people should be doing but are not. In case you don't recognize it, that's culture at work. But it's your culture, not theirs! Tracking your own "shoulds" and "oughts" may provide valuable insight into your processes as an observer.

Another kind of comparative question that can help focus your observations is to reflect on what a fieldworker of another persuasion within your discipline, or schooled in a different discipline entirely, might find of interest in a setting. Take the economist's concern for the allocation of scarce resources, for example. Questions addressing the distribution of resources can prompt fresh insight for a fieldworker who may not have thought about what is in short supply in a seemingly affluent community (for instance, time) or what seems to be in abundance (perhaps time, once more) in a community stretched for material resources.

In opportunities for fieldwork, watch also for recurring themes in your own evolving career that lend focus and continuity to it. A common thread running through my own work is a focus on cultural acquisition. In any setting where I am an observer, I find myself asking, What do people (individually, collectively) have to know in order to do what they are doing here? And how do they seem to be transmitting or acquiring that information, especially in any absence of didactic instruction?

• *Be prepared to discover that observation itself is a mysterious process.* At the least, it is something we do off and on, and mostly off. No one can remain acutely attentive for long. We compensate for that by averaging out our observations, reporting at a seemingly constant level of detail that implies we are keener at this than we are. A realistic approach for the fieldworker is to recognize and capitalize on the fact that our observations—or, more accurately, our ability to focus on them—are something comparable to a pulse: Short bursts of attention are followed by periods of inattention or wandering.

Capitalize on the bursts. Be especially observant about capturing little vignettes or short (but complete) conversational exchanges in careful detail. For example, you could never capture all the conversation you hear, and you would neither want nor ever need to. But what conversation you do record needs to be recorded in sufficient detail that you can report it verbatim. Beginners often gloss their observational efforts in a way that leaves them with no reportable data. Every statement they record is paraphrased in their own words, rather than in segments of conversation as actually spoken. A guideline I suggest is this: What you do record, record in sufficient detail that, should the need arise, you can report it directly from your notes. I am not suggesting that you actually report that way—field notes don't usually make for great reading—but I urge you to make a record of pertinent information at that level of detail. Otherwise, why bother?

- *Assess your participation, your observations, and the information you are recording in terms of what you will need to report rather than the type of data you feel you ought to gather.* (For more on this idea of remaining goal-oriented, see chapter 9.) Keep asking yourself how you intend to use whatever data you are recording and whether you are recording it in a usable format.

- *Reflect on your note taking and subsequent writing practices as a critical part of your fieldwork work.* There is a balance to be struck with writing up field notes. For some observers, note taking is one (and perhaps the only) activity in which they feel they are really doing research. They may be tempted to overwrite because of the satisfaction note-making brings. I worry about them less than I worry about those who resent the time they must devote to writing and who procrastinate, thus making the task increasingly formidable. If you are one of the latter, I suggest you try to discover how short you can make entries that nonetheless satisfy you for their adequacy, and then find a way to maintain that level of note-making as part of your daily routine (e.g., finishing up yesterday's notes while having your second cup of morning coffee).

However you approach it, you must make note-making sufficiently doable that you will always do it, rather than ever put it off. It may prove to be a chore, but it need not become a dreaded one if you follow the simple rule of keeping your entries up to date. There isn't much sense to going out and getting more information if you haven't digested what you took in last time. (For more on field notes, see Bernard 2000; Emerson, Fretz, and Shaw 1995; Sanjek 1990.)

Recognize that regardless of how much you write, most of what you observe will remain what Simon Ottenberg calls "headnotes" (1990:144–46). But some observations will make it into written jottings, whether simple or elaborate, and those jottings will prove invaluable. Your elaborated note-making also provides a critical bridge between what you are experiencing and how you are translating what you observe into a form you can communicate to others. Make a practice of including in your notes not only standard entries about day, date, and time, accompanied by a simple coding system for keeping track of entries, but also reflections on and about yourself—your mood, personal reactions, even random thoughts. These may later help you recapture detail not committed to paper but not lost, either.

Note taking is not the only kind of writing for you to consider at this stage. There is something temporary about any kind of notes that effectively says the real writing will come later. What is to prevent you from doing some of that real writing as fieldwork proceeds? Instead of putting everything in an abbreviated note form, take time to draft expanded pieces written in rich detail in such a way that they might later be incorporated into your final account. Disabuse yourself of the idea that as long as you are doing fieldwork, note taking is the only kind of writing you should do.

The key to participant observation as a fieldwork strategy is to take seriously the challenge it poses to participate more and to play the role of the aloof observer less. Do not think of yourself as someone who needs to wear a white lab coat and carry a clipboard in order to learn how humans go about their everyday lives. If you find you are comfortable only when distant and aloof, why insist on describing yourself as a participant observer? Perhaps a more formal approach will get you the data you want with less personal discomfort. If so, you can turn your focus to activities that get you data. Semistructured interviewing offers a good compromise. If that doesn't do it, turn to more structured forms of interviewing (to be discussed next) that lead to questionnaires and surveys. Consider the possibility that you may not have a natural affinity for fieldwork, especially if you begin to feel that it is getting in your way rather than helping you make your way. Genuine fieldwork entails more than data-gathering.

While I was preparing the original manuscript for this book I had the good fortune to correspond with Peter and Ellen Demerath, who were conducting fieldwork in Papua New Guinea. At the time they were more dramatically situated than any other beginning fieldworkers I knew, and I was anxious to solicit their thoughts on the essence of fieldwork while they were actually immersed in it. Peter's response gives a sense of the fieldworker's participation as performance, as making oneself believable.

> When I think of the "art" in fieldwork, and ways in which the artist rather than the scientist is called for, I think primarily of how much of what we are trying to do here is to present, or compose, both personas and projects that are appealing and attractive (or at least comprehensible) enough, so that people will talk with us and ultimately participate in our research. In this sense, perhaps much of the art of fieldwork lies in effective public relations.
>
> We find that we do many things—housework, pumping water, chewing betelnut, playing soccer and volleyball, chatting, greeting, poling a canoe, eating sea turtle stew after having just seen the animal slowly and painfully butchered—with an eye on how these things are perceived by the people here. We hope they will regard us and our actions as attractive (or non-threatening) to the extent that they will regard us as fellow human beings. It seems to us that the anthropologist must constantly attend to the "composition" of this public persona, and perhaps this is one

of the areas where the art of fieldwork is visible. [Peter Demerath, personal communication, February 1995; see also Demerath 2001]

Peter and Ellen did not go halfway around the world to chat, play volleyball, or pump water, and ordinarily they would have had no opportunity at all to pole canoes or eat sea turtle stew. They were doing what intuition and common sense guided them to do as "fellow human beings," participating in the activities of others in the hope that those others would participate in their research. Their strategy addresses the concerns reviewed at the beginning of the chapter: gaining entrée and maintaining rapport, reciprocity, a tolerance for ambiguity, and personal determination, coupled with faith in themselves. There are no guarantees. But any experienced fieldworker will recognize that this is what genuine participant observation entails.

Getting Nosy

A ready topic for debate among experienced fieldworkers is whether interviewing or participant observation is the key dimension in the work. Which is more important? Which logically should precede the other when you are initiating a new inquiry? Again, the best answer seems to be, It depends. Interviewing, to be presented here as a complement to participant observation, includes a broad spectrum of activities, but it is easier to define. Participant observation is the residual category that includes anything that is not some kind of interviewing.

I emphasize a distinction between the two in recognition of the profound difference in what fieldworkers do when engaging in participant observation (used in the sense of experiencing) and interviewing. It is the difference between passively accepting whatever comes along—information that is virtually handed to us—and aggressively seeking information by getting nosy.

In the simple act of asking, the fieldworker makes a 180-degree shift from observer to interlocutor, intruding into the scene by imposing onto the agenda what he or she wants to know. That does not mean questioning is a sinister business, but there is a quantum difference between taking what happens to come along and taking charge of the agenda. The difference might be likened to the contrast between being served a hosted meal or ordering from an à la carte menu. In the first case, one takes what is offered; in the second, one states one's preferences.

There are artful ways to conduct interviews, artful ways to ask questions, artful ways to make informants more comfortable when using a tape recorder, and artful ways to check the accuracy of informant responses. Decisions about how much to record from informal conversations, how much to transcribe from formally recorded ones, or how long to conduct interviews in the course of an inquiry all require judgment calls. One needs to develop a sixth sense about which data may ultimately prove most useful, with the long-range objective of accumulating less data rather than more. I will highlight a few points deserving of special mention, but I offer no magic formula for helping a poor interviewer become a better one. We all can improve our interview style by attending as carefully to our own words recorded in transcribed interviews as we attend to the words of our interviewees.

Longtime fieldwork allows a researcher to develop a keen sense of what, when, and under what circumstances it is appropriate to ask a question and when it is better to remain quiet. That requires distinguishing between what you wish to know and how to go about making your interests known. Sometimes it means holding questions for later; sometimes it means holding questions forever; as often, it means recognizing the moment to raise a question because circumstances open a window of opportunity on a normally taboo, sensitive, or seemingly irrelevant issue.

I recognize a cultural norm that guides my own behavior in this regard, one that makes all fieldwork a dilemma for me and rears its head on every occasion when I want to interrupt with a question, even in ordinary conversation: Do not intrude. In *Halfway Home*, novelist Paul Monette describes the reluctance to intrude as "the first WASP commandment." This is why the most thorough and inquisitive of researchers might be aghast at the suggestion that they ought to seek the same level of intimate information about their own colleagues or students at home that they feel professionally obliged to achieve in the field. Anthropologist Fred Gearing reveals the uneasiness he felt from the first moments of his introduction to fieldwork:

> During the next several days I sought out certain Indians, and we talked. Our conversations were typically low-keyed, filled with long

silences. I never quite felt that I was intruding, but was never fully confident that I was not. [1970:9]

Asking does more than merely intrude, however—at least when it goes beyond exchanging pleasantries of the day. Even exchanging pleasantries can lead to unexpected awkwardness, as when a friendly Thai asks, "Where are you going?" in the custom of a people for whom this, rather than our innocuous "How are you?" is the proper greeting in passing. Our questions as fieldworkers become increasingly intrusive as we seek to understand what is going on. Too easily we may put informants on the defensive by insisting or implying that they should be able to explain not only what is going on but why. In framing our questions we also tip our hand in ways that subtly influence the future course of our work. Although we routinely insist that we are interested in everything about the lives of our informants, our questions belie our claim by revealing that certain "everythings" are of far greater consequence than others.

Years ago, while writing a methodological preface to their pioneering study of male sexual behavior, which turned out to be a spectacular chapter on interviewing in general, Alfred Kinsey and his colleagues pointed out that although their questions were on sensitive topics, the very act of questioning can make any topic sensitive (Kinsey, Pomeroy, and Martin 1948:chapter 2). Through interviewing, we risk turning any topic on which we have expressed interest into a sensitive one, inadvertently alerting informants to issues of special concern to us. As well, local issues of purely academic concern may be fraught with political or economic overtones for respondents. We cannot naively assume, for example, that informants are delighted to be asked about the value of their personal possessions, the size of their livestock herds, or the amount they pay in taxes (Christensen 1993).

Let me offer an illustration of the difficulties in obtaining sensitive information. I was invited to comment on a redrafted proposal for researching condom use in AIDS prevention among minority populations. Indicative of the influence qualitative approaches now exert—even among agencies that insist on final reports with totally quantifiable results—researchers applying for a grant had been directed to augment their essentially quantitative approach by including semistructured interviews among their data-gathering strategies. I pointed out that the way the interview schedule had been designed required researchers to introduce the topic of condoms early in the interviews. As a consequence, interviewers were likely to lead respondents to give answers along socially acceptable lines that did not necessarily square with actual behavior.

An underlying question is one of the most difficult in nondirective interview strategies: how to learn what you want to know without framing questions in a way that you, rather than your informants, introduce and pursue certain topics? How can the context remain theirs rather than your own? In this case, with one-time interviews, some possibilities presented themselves. Interviewers might, for example, have asked respondents to identify (free list) all the safe-sex practices they could think of, returning to those of special interest to project personnel later in the interview, perhaps prompting with other practices not mentioned. Or they might have provided a comprehensive list of their own, burying items of special concern to the researchers, as, for example, a list that included but did not specifically highlight condom use. In addition, specific questions on the topic might have been introduced near the end of the interview, so that interviewers (and coders) would be able to track when, where, and how the topic was formally introduced.

It has taken years for me to become so bold that I risk the disapproval of dental hygienists by looking them directly in the eye and stating flatly that I do not now and never intend to floss! Why would a minority respondent, answering intimate personal questions about sexual practices, want to disappoint a researcher by claiming to be socially irresponsible about the risk of transmitting a disease as devastating as AIDS? Further, if you tell interviewers what you think they want to hear, maybe they will go away sooner. Interviewing is not all that difficult, but getting people to tell you how they really think about things you are interested in learning or how they think about the things that are important to them is a delicate art. My working resolution to the dilemma of assessing what informants say is to recognize that informants are always telling me *something*. My task is to figure out what that something might be.

What interviewing can do, of course, is introduce efficiency into fieldwork. That efficiency can reach a point in which fieldwork itself—the participating kind that is the focus of this discussion—may be eliminated altogether. If the questions to be asked can be tightened up enough, perhaps the principal investigator need not enter the field at all. Research assistants, even contract pollsters, can get the needed information.

One cannot do participant observation without being there, although, as pointed out in the previous chapter, fieldwork consists of more than just being in the field. One can conduct fieldwork through extensive interviews that do not assume or require residency on the part of the fieldworker.

Most qualitative researchers consider participant observation and interviewing to be complementary, but that does not require drawing on them equally or necessarily drawing on both of them in every study. Fieldworkers invest more heavily in whichever of the two better accommodates their research style and their research question. Some fieldworkers do little or no formal interviewing, maintaining instead a casual, conversational approach in the manner of Gearing's "low-keyed conversations." Michael Agar takes the opposite view on behalf of his ethnographic concern with meanings: "Ethnographic question asking is a special blend of art and science. . . . Ethnography without questions would be impossible" (1996:95). If his statement is too strong to apply to all fieldwork, we must at least recognize that fieldworkers who ask or are allowed no questions are tempted to become their own informants.

I take interviewing to include any situation in which a fieldworker is in a position to, and does, attempt to obtain information on a specific topic through even so casual a comment or inducement as, "What you were telling me the other day was really interesting . . ." or "I didn't have a chance to ask you about this before, but can you tell me a bit more about . . ." To categorize the major types of asking in which fieldworkers engage, I offer the following list. Descriptive titles make the categories seem obvious, yet each is worthy of the scholarly attention it has received in an extensive literature devoted to specific aspects of interviewing:

- Casual or conversational interviewing

- Life history/life cycle interviewing

- Semistructured (i.e., open-ended) interviewing

- Structured interviewing, including formal eliciting techniques
  - Survey
  - Household census, ethnogenealogy
  - Questionnaire (written or oral)

- Projective techniques

- Standardized tests and other measurement techniques

The list could easily be expanded or collapsed, depending on one's purposes. My bias toward ethnographic research shows through with the inclusion of two categories. One is the category for household census and ethnogenealogy, once a mainstay in initiating community studies and still a good starting place when conducting them. Another is the category for projective techniques. That category accommodates the once-fashionable fieldwork practice of collecting Rorschach or Thematic Apperception Test protocols (see, for example, Henry and Spiro 1953), as well as more recent interests in projective interviewing such as the Spindlers' Instrumental Activities Inventory (1965) or Robert Textor's work in ethnographic futures. There has been a longtime practice of asking informants straightforward, but nonetheless projectively intended, questions about the foreseeable future: Ten years from now, what do you think things will be like? Note also the intentional ambiguity of the word "things," leaving the respondent to define what he or she has in mind.

Work in educational settings leads me to include as a separate category the kind of tests associated with schooling, thus the category "standardized tests and other measurement techniques." For the fieldworker, however, such measurement techniques should be regarded as a special type of interview. What makes standardized tests different from other forms of interviewing is that the interviewee supplies an answer already known to the person administering the test. As a general rule, fieldworkers ask questions to find out what informants know and know about, not to test knowledge. The questions we ask, the manner in which we ask them, and what we do with the information are intended to signal our interest in and regard for what people know, not what they do not know.

In spite of experiencing too many years under the tyranny of testing in their own lives, practitioners of the art of fieldwork never, never put down those among whom they study. Fieldworkers attuned to the art of teaching as well as to the art of fieldwork are able to follow that practice in the classroom as well. It is critical to keep in mind that testing is a special kind of interviewing, designed for assessment in terms of normative standards. Although fieldwork cannot help but have evaluative overtones, formal testing arises out of a quite different tradition. One can only hope that fieldworkers make nontraditional use of whatever test data they collect.

One way we show appreciation for what informants tell us is the respect accorded to the information they provide. I felt I had conveyed that idea to two African field assistants assigned to help me conduct a questionnaire survey in my study of the beer gardens of Bulawayo (HFW 1974). As soon as we started interviewing, however, I heard each of them roar with laughter at responses to the questions they posed, in marked contrast to the studied reactions they had displayed during an earlier practice session. Out in the real world—we were conducting our interviews in municipally operated beer gardens—their better judgment had taken over. It was risky to ask anything of total strangers, they explained, and if you wanted to keep respondents talking, you had better make sure they understood how appreciative you were of their responses. They weren't laughing at their respondents, they wanted me to understand, they were laughing with them. And how were my somber interviews going, they inquired tactfully?

The convenience of gathering any type of systematic interview data is always undertaken at the risk of losing rapport, although we can never anticipate exactly what anyone's reaction will be. For every individual too busy to talk, someone else may be reluctant to bring the interview to a close. For someone annoyed with questions too personal, another may insist on volunteering far more, and far more personal, information than that requested. Adherents of particular approaches have their stories to offer as testimonials. Chances are, approaches and questions that make the researcher uncomfortable will have a similar effect on respondents.

I know that fieldworkers have sometimes gone out of their way not to appear too inquisitive, too pushy, too calculating in their approach. They are careful not to appear like teachers giving examinations, journalists tracking down a story, or government agents ready to impose more taxes or exert more control. Most people are uncomfortable with the idea that a file is being kept on them, a universal and growing discomfort as we realize how commonplace this has become in an age of information processing. The experienced fieldworker is not likely to make his or her first appearance at the door with a questionnaire to be answered. The researcher who does show up with a questionnaire is not likely to stick around to learn any more than what is asked on the questionnaire form.

Do I seem to be advocating a fieldwork approach in which slow is beautiful and fast is bad? Frankly, when thinking about what fieldwork can and cannot accomplish, that is my position. Issues surrounding the topic of interviewing help me to clarify it. There are things one can learn quickly by asking direct questions revealing of what one wants to know. There are things one can ask directly without much assurance about the answer. There are things about which we do not ask, guided by our own standards, or about which interviewees do not offer answers, guided by theirs. And there are underlying questions, often the kinds of questions that undergird social research, that can neither be asked nor answered directly: What is your world view? Why do we have schools at all? When everyone seems so dissatisfied, why do you continue to support your form of government?

In a hurry-up world, with technologies that devour information byte by byte, there is increasing pressure to get the facts and get on with it. Fieldworkers are in an excellent position not only to get facts but to put them in context. Nevertheless, fieldwork is a grossly inefficient way simply to gather factual data. When time is of the essence—as it is so often perceived to be—then fieldwork as discussed here is out of the question, even when field-based research for collecting necessary data is essential. Thus, to repeat Bernard's maxim, "All participant observation is fieldwork, but not all fieldwork is participant observation" (1994b:136).

It is only the integrity of the label "fieldwork" that I seek to protect, however. No mandate says that if you can't devote at least a year, you shouldn't bother to go into the field at all. I agree with Bernard when he insists on participant observation in the conduct of all scientific research about cultural groups. He argues that "it is possible to do useful participant observation in just a few days" (1994b:140). A few days do not constitute a participant observation study, but they are days well spent, nonetheless.

Contemporary fieldworkers have responded to the need for speed by incorporating survey-type techniques into their standard repertory, although there is nothing new about having to compress a heavy dose of fieldwork into a short period of time. As with any human activity, there are times when everything seems to be happening at once or when a brief foray is all that time or resources will allow. Robert Redfield was so pleased with a three-day field survey he conducted in 1941 with his then student and field assistant Sol Tax that he titled it "Report of a 3-Day

Survey" and coined the term *rapid guided survey*. Nevertheless, the researchers had a clear idea of the information they sought, for their fieldwork was then in its seventh year (see Rubinstein 1991:297, 304). They also attributed their success at least in part to sheer luck.

Rapid appraisal, or rapid rural appraisal (RRA), became more commonplace in development projects in the Third World during the 1970s and 1980s when "appropriate technology" was the buzzword. RRA itself has been recognized as a form of appropriate technology. Today there are numerous variations on RRA in both name and application, including rapid anthropological assessment, rapid ethnographic assessment, and ethnographic reconnaissance. Practicing anthropologists have their own handbook, *Soundings* (van Willigen and Finan 1991; see also Beebe 1995, 2001; Handwerker 2001), that outlines and illustrates a number of "rapid and reliable" research methods. These procedures can retain something of a fieldwork flavor in what is described (or rationalized?) as an iterative and exploratory team approach. In this approach, the research begins with (but moves rapidly beyond) preliminary observations and semistructured interviews with key informants. These preliminary data are used to guide the construction of appropriate survey or questionnaire instruments with the entire process to be completed in a limited time.

To an old-time and old-fashioned ethnographer like me, words like "ethnography" or "fieldwork" join uneasily with a qualifier like "rapid." Then again, I've never been in a hurry to do things. My motto, "Do less, more thoroughly," may be nothing more than rationalization for my preferred and accustomed pace. Perhaps I envision a fieldwork entirely of my own making, having mistakenly accepted pronouncements about its duration (such as one year at the least, preferably two) as minimum standards when today's fieldworkers regard them as impractical and unnecessary. Bernard now proclaims three months the minimum time "to achieve reasonable intellectualized competence in another culture and be accepted as a participant observer" (Bernard 1994b:151). I agree that any amount of time a researcher can devote to participant observation should prove useful for gaining a sense of context.

But I am concerned whenever participant observation is simultaneously portrayed and faulted as a quickie exercise. Similar efforts have been directed at determining how few informants one really needs in gathering technically reliable information about a cultural domain (e.g., Bernard

1994b:chapter 8; Romney, Weller, and Batchelder 1986). It is hardly surprising that these researchers are strong advocates for the efficiency of formal procedures and structured interview schedules. I hope Bernard has not inadvertently foreshortened the acceptable period for fieldwork for those who will carefully misread his statement to reassure themselves that the three months he says is adequate to establish oneself in the field is all the time one needs to devote to a study.

Although I am not an advocate for finding faster ways to do fieldwork, neither am I committed to making fieldwork more time-consuming simply for its own sake. Time in the field is no guarantee of the quality of the ensuing reports. Nor need efforts to speed things up and find ways to get better data in less time be seen as detracting from efforts to make interviewing a better art as well. With that in mind, I offer some suggestions about interviewing, accompanied by a reminder that this topic has been well served in the vast methods literature, including early statements still brimming with cautions and insights (e.g., Paul 1953; Spradley 1979) and more recent how-to chapters and monographs (e.g., Bernard 2000; Douglas 1985; Gubrium and Holstein 2002; Rubin and Rubin 1995; Seidman 1991). My comments relate especially to semistructured interviewing of the sort that virtually all field researchers employ, whether constructing a rapid survey or embarking on a long-term inquiry.

Doing Better Interviewing: Using Interviews Better

- *Recognize listening as an active and creative role.* I once heard the late educational historian Lawrence Cremin revered for his capacity as a "creative listener," a phrase that lingered in my mind as both an unusual compliment and a wonderful insight into the art of interviewing. Creative listener! Certainly that includes being an attentive listener. It implies even more a listener who is able to play an interactive role, thereby making a more effective speaker out of the person doing most of the talking. An interview ought to be a satisfactory experience for listener and speaker alike.

  I regard myself as a listener, but that is not the same as being a creative listener. I confess that I frequently tire of listening, although surely Cremin must sometimes have experienced that same feeling, especially after assuming the role of college president. There are a few individuals for whom I seem to play the role of creative listener, and there are a few individuals who play that role for me. On either side of such conversations, I find the interaction not only satisfying but intensely stimulating. Creative listening seems a wonderful talent for any fieldworker to strive continuously to develop, especially one who intends to use semistructured interviewing as a major field technique.

- *Talk less, listen more.* If the idea of creative listening seems too elusive, try simply talking less and listening more during any interview. As an easy first step, practice waiting one thousandth of a second longer before intruding on a momentary pause to introduce a comment or new question. Interviewers are reminded to distinguish between a pregnant silence and a dead one. A lengthened pause on the researcher's part may be enough to prompt the interviewee to pick up the conversation again. Our own conversational patterns display a certain inertia. A conversation in motion tends to remain in motion; silence poses a threat. We become our own worst enemy during the interview process by rushing in to fill the pauses. If the researcher does not immediately plug the gap, the interviewee is likely to do it instead, without even realizing why.

- *Make questions short and to the point.* If it is necessary to repeat, do exactly that. Do not expand or elaborate, for in doing so you are likely either to start an answer or to change the question. This is usually done inadvertently, in the spirit of helping both the respondent and the dialogue. If you study interview protocols— and I urge you to examine your own—you are likely to discover that a simple question usually becomes two or three competing and increasingly complex ones through the course of any solicitous prompting that follows.

- *Plan interviews around a few big issues.* Successful interviewers return again and again to develop dimensions of an issue, rather than detailing myriad little questions to ask. For initial interviewing, James Spradley recommended what he termed *Grand*

Tour questions (1979) of the sort, So, tell me something about yourself, or How did you happen to get here? The interviewer might then have several major topics in mind to which attention can be turned repeatedly in minor variation. For example, family and kin might be the central topic in the interviewer's mind, to be translated into more detailed questions about each family member, sometimes with an ambiguous prompt like, Can you tell me anything more about that?

- *As soon as possible after an interview, write it up.* Transcribe the interview, if it was taped, or index its contents (topics discussed and their location on the tape) if you do not intend to make full typescripts of each interview. If it was not taped, flesh out your brief notes while your informant's words remain fresh in your mind. Then study the transcript or listen to the tape to see how you are doing as an interviewer and to immerse yourself in what you are learning from and about your informant (for an excellent example, see VanderStaay 2003). If time allows (as it should), do not proceed with the next interview until the present one has been processed. Always be thinking about how you intend to use the information, both for the immediate purpose of guiding future interviews and for your eventual incorporation of the material into your final account.

- *Anticipate and discuss the level of formality you plan for the interview.* If you intend semistructured interviews to be more formal than earlier conversations, explain any shifting ground rules so your informant understands what may otherwise appear as a personality change that has suddenly come over you. Formal taped sessions can provide opportunity for a different kind of exchange, one in which the person being interviewed is clearly in the know, and the researcher is the person who wants to find out. Michael Agar calls this the "one-down" position, where the fieldworker assumes a subordinate role as learner, as opposed to the "one-up" role assumed by the scientifically oriented hypotheses tester (1996:119).

  Recognize nonetheless that the person with the tape recorder ought to remain in charge. You need to decide whether you can live with that. Perhaps you will have to give way to egalitarian urges to make the exchange more evenly reciprocal. If so, be advised that when you listen to the tape you may discover that you were the one being interviewed.

I have always felt that a formal interview is and ought to be a special, asymmetrical form of conversation, one party seeking information, the other providing it. Work toward achieving that format if it suits your style and purposes. Explain that in your formal interviews you want to record your interviewee's words and explanations even if your informant wants it understood that some comments may be made off the record. Stop the tape recorder any time your interviewee prefers to speak off the record, desires a break, or wishes to discuss the interview process with you. You might also suggest that if your questions prompt similar questions that your informant might like to ask of you, they can be noted for discussion later.

Conversational approaches in tape-recorded interviewing are less efficient. They may not be necessary if your informant understands how you distinguish between ordinary conversation and a formal interview in which you take special care to record an interviewee's exact words. You may have to overcome an urge to be more casual, but both you and your informant need to remember that your association, while friendly, is essentially professional. Someday you will go away, and the interview will go with you.

Make informants aware of the importance of the interviews to your work by your actions as well as your expressions of appreciation. Better to err on the side of being too formal than to create the impression of being too casual. Try to use a tape recorder, if possible. Augment recordings with brief notes, if possible. Conduct the interview in private, if possible. Formalize the occasion by arranging an appointment yourself (rather than through an assistant or secretary), if possible, perhaps even suggesting in advance the major topics you would like to discuss. And leave the tape recorder running after the formal interview ends, if possible, in anticipation that although the interview is finished, your informant may not be.

If such formality seems the very antithesis of the kind of interpersonal exchange you want to foster, then follow your intuition to find a style more suitable. There is no rule against being more interactive, no rule that somewhere in your report you must include the words of your informants. Perhaps you did not want to become the kind of fieldworker who "captures" someone else's words. As integral as formal interviewing is to fieldwork in general, you must always consider the possibility that it is not for you.

- *If you are not under the gun to work through your interview data as rapidly as possible, see how long you can hold off before you develop a questionnaire or a tightly structured interview schedule.* The question of when and how interview schedules are developed reveals a major difference between fieldworkers and survey researchers. The survey researcher typically enters the field with a prepared schedule. Fieldworkers are more likely to administer such an instrument near the conclusion of the field research, when they know the questions that have yet to be asked and have a clearer idea of how best to ask them. The exception might be a household census or similar inventory through which the researcher also introduces the research project, gathers relevant basic demographic data, and looks for knowledgeable informants willing to be interviewed in depth. Even under those circumstances, try to keep the interview open. Ask as few questions as necessary and include an open-ended question or two to invite respondents to express what is on their minds or to provide context for the research topic.

A maxim directed at quantitative researchers (although too seldom heeded) holds in our work as well: Behind every question asked, there ought to be a hypothesis. We don't have to be that sticky about formalizing hypotheses, but data should never be gathered simply for the sake of gathering them or because it is so easy to add another question or two. If it doesn't really matter whether respondents own their own homes, graduated from high school, or have ever been arrested, don't ask. If it does matter, give them the opportunity to explain and include their explanations in the information you record. That's the difference between hit-and-run surveys and the fieldworker who intends to stick around to try to figure out how things fit together.

- *Invite informants to help you become a better researcher.* Agar's notion of the interviewer in the one-down position can be extended to the research process itself. Keep in mind that your interviewees have views about your interview techniques as well as about the scope of your questions. Don't fish for compliments, but direct questions like Do you have any suggestions about these interviews? may prove immediately helpful and lend insight into how the interviewee is feeling as a participant in the research process. A further question can get directly at content: Are there topics we might explore that I haven't asked about? Should you get no response at first, you nonetheless are emphasizing the extent of your interest and effort at thoroughness and your respect for the intelligence of your informant.

- *Search for patterns in responses.* Search not only for what is there but for cut-off points (see Henry 1955:196) in discussion or topics consistently skirted or avoided—on your part as well as on the part of your informants. Don't forget to go back through all of your interviews if you work with an informant over a period of time. I discovered that informants often gave valuable information and clues as to what they felt was important in early interviews, but when everything was new and coming at me so fast, I failed to pick up on such clues the first time around.

In studying interview protocols, I have also found it useful to distinguish between what informants are telling me and what else, if anything, they may be trying to tell me. In one sense, everything an informant tells you can be taken as a fact—a linguistic fact, if no other kind. But informants make choices, sometimes leading us, sometimes leading us astray. Occasionally I have found myself anticipating what they would say next, as a way to assess whether my informant and I were on the same wavelength. I believe it important to be able to quote back to informants, in their own words, topics mentioned or alluded to in earlier conversations. There may also be times when an ambiguous reference to an earlier topic is a more appropriate way to reintroduce it. That approach keeps you from leading the discussion or from phrasing questions in such a way that the only response needed is a yes or no.

- *Do not become so committed to the qualitative dimensions of responses that you fail to count and measure those aspects that need to be counted and measured.* Keep your research purposes clearly in mind in deciding what and how much to analyze. Carefully recorded language, for example, lends itself to rigorous analysis, but the rigor can throw up a smoke screen of carefully conducted, but totally inappropriate, analyses, lending an aura of science but indicative of a poor artistic choice. Behind every decision intended to advance science lies an opportunity for exercising sound human judgment.

Looking over Others' Shoulders

Data-gathering is not limited to information that fieldworkers gather through participant observation and interviewing while actively on site. There are additional, often critical, sources of information, especially, but not limited to, personal documents and other written records. A discussion of this third category, archival research, concludes this review of the basic arts of the fieldwork part of fieldwork.

I used to think there was a degree of art involved in searching out information in a library; today, I am willing to concede that task to science. I watch in dismay as students run enormous computer searches on unfamiliar topics, perhaps hoping that if they can press the right combination of keys at their terminal, information will spew forth like coins from a slot machine. Given the exponential increase in recorded information, we can be thankful that the technologies that helped create problems are also available to help resolve them.

There is still some art to using archives, however. The most obvious art clearly parallels the problem one faces in the field: deciding how wide a swath to cut, how deep to burrow; in short, deciding what counts. "No depth of commitment and sense of responsibility will ever be enough to permit any individual to do what is there to be done," Margaret Mead cautioned fieldworkers years ago (1970:258). Today it is quite thinkable that a fieldworker determined to get a thorough grounding in library research might, in Mead's words, be so "attracted by the inexhaustibility of the task" (p. 258) as never to leave the library at all. As with everything else about fieldwork, one needs to recognize how to focus and when to stop.

Libraries and the general proliferation of information are everybody's problem, but those attracted to fieldwork probably are not going to get stuck in the library. We still hear arguments about whether we should go into the field well informed, having consulted what others have said, or do a library search only after forming our own impressions. I believe the better argument can be made for being well informed, as long as being informed is accompanied by the same healthy skepticism befitting all scholarly research. That is the first of the three suggestions discussed below for making the most artful use of secondary sources.

Making the Best Use of Others' Work

- *Be as skeptical of anything you read as you are of anything you are told.* A lesson we learn too well as schoolchildren, that printed texts are sacred texts, must be cast aside in scholarly pursuit. Most certainly, earlier fieldworkers' reports may no longer be correct, even if they were accurate at one time. Skepticism is absolutely essential in all aspects of fieldwork, including any use of printed sources.

  However, a skeptical stance does not give license to demean all prior efforts. Academics sometimes get carried away in their truth-seeking zeal. It is tempting, especially for younger scholars, to find fault with earlier reports and bring down the elders. I think it far more constructive, and more consistent with a spirit of inquiry, to take the position that earlier researchers did not get it quite right, just as future researchers will probably show that we did not quite get it right, either. If it is any comfort, know that fieldwork's greats continue to take a licking. Hear this passage and reminder from Clifford Geertz:

  > Firth, not Malinowski, is probably our best Malinowskian. Fortes so far eclipses Radcliffe-Brown as to make

us wonder how he could have taken him for his master. Kroeber did what Boas but promised. [1988:20]

A healthy skepticism must always be maintained, even when everything seems to be checking out perfectly, past with present, established landmark studies with our own embryonic inquiries. While Ron Rohner and I were doing fieldwork among the Kwakiutl, Ron discovered an excellent informant in Chief Bill Scow and was sometimes surprised at how consistently Bill's accounts validated the early work of Franz Boas. But one day Ron's question stumped Bill, and Bill explained, "I can't answer that one, Ron. I'll have to look it up." Only then did Ron realize that the old informant and the young anthropologist were using the same references. An earlier descriptive ethnography had now become a prescriptive one!

- *Look far afield for all you might include as the work of others.* Sometimes anthropologists join the "stack rats" to do their work entirely through library scholarship, but fieldworkers are more likely to be sensitive to any suggestion that they never, or hardly ever, go to the library. Whether they spend much time in the library or not, most fieldworkers make use of a vast array of materials in addition to the customary library resources. (See a useful guide for conducting original archival research "with quality and dispatch" in Hill 1993.)

  Personal documents are especially high on the list of non-library sources: correspondence, diaries, travelers' journals, any sort of written accounts that might never find their way into a formal collection but can be invaluable to understanding everyday life or special events. Government records, newspaper accounts, surveyor reports—there is no end to the possible resources to be considered. Similarly, fieldworkers examine and frequently collect artifacts of all sorts in addition to textual documents.

  Fieldworkers need to think creatively about available sources of information that are not ordinarily regarded as data, to avoid falling victim to habits that find us invariably gathering the same limited information in the same limited ways. In my study of a school principal, for example, I was interested in getting some sense of how the principal's professional relationships with other teachers and administrators overlapped with his personal relationships with family and friends (HFW 1973). An opportunity to get some hard data on the topic materialized when his oldest daughter announced her forthcoming wedding. I asked the principal if he would review the wedding list and say something about everyone invited, paying particular attention to invitations extended by the parents rather than the bride herself. I might have obtained similar information by going over the list of people to whom the principal and his wife regularly sent Christmas cards. Personal documents such as these are not likely to end up in the Smithsonian, yet they are a ready source of data about social networks. Wouldn't a list of the telephone numbers frequently dialed or a directory of e-mail correspondents provide similar insight into professional or personal networks?

- *Think about new ways to use data easily at hand.* The previous point emphasized looking at sources of data easily overlooked, so that we do not take too constricted a view of what constitutes data. The complement to that is to be equally creative about using readily available data in unusual ways.

  It may, for example, be easier to document, even to discern, patterns or trends by looking at the frequency or space devoted to certain kinds of events in the local newspaper over a period of years than by relying solely on the impressions of older informants. Margaret Mead was able to give a historical perspective to her interest in child training by comparing the topics discussed in government manuals over several decades. The changing tables of contents in introductory texts in fields like anthropology, psychology, or sociology provide an excellent basis for watching the evolution of those disciplines. Old catalogues or photographs offer evidence of changing fashions in clothing, hairstyles, and the like. That such sources of data exist is hardly a revelation, but it doesn't hurt to remind fieldworkers that participant observation and interviewing are not the only ways to get information. Such extraneous sources also invite researchers to compare what they are being told with sources less susceptible to reinterpretation with a knowing backward look.

This chapter has reviewed some basic issues in fieldwork with the assumption that data-gathering is always guided by sensitivity on the part of the fieldworker. Potential problems are recast as challenges to recognize and reckon with. I turn next to examining some related problems from what might be called the dark side of fieldwork. Given the focus of the book, I refer to them as the "darker arts."

CHAPTER SIX
FIELDWORK: THE DARKER ARTS

It is necessary to be relentless in ferreting out the dark side of fieldwork, for only then can the other side, the rebirth of the anthropologist, be fully comprehended and understood in a rigorous manner.

—John L. Wengle
Ethnographers in the Field, p. 169

Cultural analysis is intrinsically incomplete. And, worse than that, the more deeply it goes the less complete it is. It is a strange science whose most telling assertions are its most tremulously based, in which to get somewhere with the matter at hand is to intensify the suspicion, both your own and that of others, that you are not quite getting it right.

—Clifford Geertz
"Thick Description," in *The Interpretation of Cultures*, p. 29

It took me a long time to discover that the key to acting is honesty. Once you know how to fake that, you've got it made.

—John Leonard
quoted in J. Douglas, *Investigative Social Research*, p. 55

One of the definitions of art reviewed in chapter 1 referred to trickery, cunning, or artificiality in behavior. Among the definitions of artist, we recognize the trickster, clever at deceit, or the con artist, who abuses confidence. The last thing any fieldworker wants to be is a con artist. Yet it is virtually impossible to do and report fieldwork without risking someone's integrity, either theirs or your own. Taking a cue from John Leonard in the epigraph immediately above, what do we have to be prepared to fake in order to succeed at fieldwork? I won't take refuge this time in my customary caveat, It depends. I'll say it straight out: In fieldwork one must be prepared to fake everything.

The dilemma is inherent, given the openness of our approach and the subject matter of our concern—the social behavior of our fellow human beings (and ourselves). We are honest enough when we declare that we cannot state exactly what we are looking for, but we ordinarily have more in mind than we let on, and we are not adverse to discovering—or uncovering—information we did not anticipate. Nor are we able to anticipate how we ourselves will use whatever information we get. In its darkest sense, fieldwork's much-lauded openness to inquiry is also an invitation to moral disaster.

In this chapter I identify some major predicaments. As with a parallel discussion of some major conceptual dilemmas (to follow in chapter 7), one needs to be prepared to meet the moral dilemmas discussed here. A first step is to realize that one is not alone in confronting them. Better, I think, to face them boldly than ignore them in the hope they will go away, because they won't. Should you insist that you have no talent for such things, maybe other, safer approaches to research are more your style.

The categories of darker arts identified here, and the sequence for discussing them, are necessarily arbitrary. I have put them under six major topics and presented them starkly. I offer whatever insight I can for addressing them, but my major concern is to get them on the table so that we acknowledge and talk about them forthrightly. The categories are presented as problems, a set of potential accusations directed at fieldwork that we might prefer to deny: superficiality, obviousness, being self-serving, lack of independence, deception and betrayal, and clandestine observation. The categories may seem to be self-contradictory—for example, if fieldwork can be faulted for being superficial, how can it also be equated with spying? How can it be both obvious and clandestine at the same time? The fact is that, as a human activity, it is suspect on every level. Contradictory or not, we are uncomfortable when certain questions are raised about what we are up to, or when what we are up to raises other uncomfortable questions among those whom we study.

Superficiality

Good actors are not the only performers who learn how to fake it. Field researchers usually try to convey a sense of commitment consistent with in-depth study. That does not guarantee the sense is genuine; it may simply be part of a fieldworker's pose. When it is real, as it usually is, it carries no guarantee that the fieldwork will be completed competently or carried through to the critical step, the completion of a final account. Fieldworkers willing to make research commitments on such a grand scale are also likely to be overcommitted in other aspects of their lives. They too easily extend themselves beyond what can reasonably be accomplished or accomplished within restricted timelines.

There is an early temptation to make too many promises while selling a research project, failing to recognize that overzealous promises may eventually work against one. It is particularly easy to overestimate the time one will spend on site during the fieldwork part of fieldwork. I served as a consultant to one generously funded project during the early 1970s that initially promised to maintain resident fieldworkers on site for as long as five years! That level of sustained research had broad appeal for studying change, but it proved unrealistic. Five years was not enough time to study the long-term effects of planned change, but it was way too long to ask of young researchers setting out on new careers. At the other extreme, one of my doctoral students aborted a deeply held commitment to overseas fieldwork after being on site for less than one week, a decision that resulted in a traumatic career change for him and left an overseas research director forever at odds with me. Commitment to fieldwork is like commitment to marriage. At the time the vows are taken, the words are what everyone wants to hear; their strength and intent must be measured in other ways.

Fieldworkers have an understandable but perhaps unfortunate tendency to represent themselves not only as different from those who do quick-and-dirty studies but somehow as more sensitive and caring humans as well. That tendency can invite comparisons in which they portray themselves as a breed apart, more committed, more deeply interested, more determined to hear the whole story. They want everyone to know they are there to grasp what Malinowski referred to as "the native's point of view" (1922:25), a perspective sometimes referred to as the "emic" view. Ideally, of course, such claims ought to be warranted, but that is not a warrant for making them publicly. Claims about commitment are difficult to substantiate. How can we demonstrate in advance that we can be trusted, that we have only our subjects' interests at heart, that we will conduct our studies in depth, and so forth? Only with the passing of time can we demonstrate that we stick around longer, that if we aren't going to stay forever, at least we intend to stay longer than most. We intend, as some anthropologists put it, to live our way into the community. Sooner or later, however, like all outsiders, we too will leave.

Leave taking is itself something of an unrecognized art. It has been pointed out with sexual liaisons that getting out of bed gracefully requires more art than getting into it. I think there is an apt parallel with getting out of the field, especially after we work energetically to create the image of researchers so deeply interested and committed. My hunch is that fieldwork often gets foreshortened due to "unforseeable circumstances" that are really not so unforeseeable after all.

I advise underplaying the depth of involvement we hope to achieve or the extended period we plan to spend in the field. Those circumstances must speak for themselves, and that can only happen over time. Practical considerations arise in addition to the ethical ones of not making false promises. Fieldworkers are admonished not to leave the field any worse than they found it. Certainly that includes not creating a basis for ill will toward future fieldworkers, based on unfulfilled expectations about the duration of one's stay. And one never knows when it might be necessary or highly advantageous to be able to visit or otherwise contact one's informants after fieldwork ends or to invite members in a researched setting to read and critique preliminary drafts of a developing report. (For more on leaving the field, see Maines, Shaffir, and Turowetz 1980.)

I think our commitment to in-depth study should be treated more like a professional pact than a public boast. Whatever depth we do actually achieve is better left for others to acknowledge. I always hope that my work will give evidence of its depth through the understanding I achieve. To whatever extent I succeed in that, however, I should not be the one to boast of it. I doubt that we ever understand anything all that well, including even ourselves. If we never fully understand ourselves, how well do we understand those among whom we conduct our studies? Our efforts to study in depth are destined always to exceed our accomplishments.

In the last decade, that realization has come to haunt me not only figuratively but literally. My awareness evolved out of an anthropological life history collected in 1981, which became what I refer to as the "Sneaky Kid" account (I discuss this study in chapter 11). As readers familiar with that study know, it addresses personal issues with what I call "heady candor"—the effort to lay bare relevant details and to be as frank about what I do not understand as what I do understand. Such candor has drawn unexpected support from some quarters (certainly not all), but to a large extent it is an artifact of reaching the twilight years of a long career during an era that now seems to encourage us to be who we are. If I seem finally to have achieved some admirable level in reporting, let me note that I have struggled with such issues since beginning fieldwork more than four decades ago.

And just how much do we see and understand? We should be the first to recognize that we never do, never could, and wouldn't even want to get it all. Our boast of working in depth is countered by the realization that we never quite get to the bottom of things, never can inquire fully enough into every relevant aspect of human behavior no matter how carefully we define the limits of a study. We can never get all the possible detail into the figurative canvases we set out to paint, and as Geertz reminds us, we can never escape the suspicion that we are not quite getting right the part we do get. We are also put on the defensive about those aspects of a setting to which we fail to attend, given the inordinate amounts of time we dedicate to the descriptive task: You mean to tell me you spent all that time and yet never heard anyone mention such-and-such? So the question becomes, How and how much do we report of what we have seen and understood? And that, in turn, raises another issue in reporting: Do we ever report all that we do learn? There is another art in fieldwork, the art of discretion. It goes largely undetected except when it is ignored, as I discuss in the final chapter.

Time itself does not guarantee quality fieldwork. Full-time participant observation that includes residing in a strange community and coping successfully with the strangeness can be sufficiently demanding and draining that it sometimes works against data gathering. But for all those fieldworkers able to "get their act together"—and fieldwork success, like successful living itself, is all relative—one is faced with seemingly impossible decisions about what and how much to say about what one has experienced.

How much is enough? I have consoled myself with another of Clifford Geertz's observations, that it is "not necessary to know everything in order to understand something" (1973:20). But a nagging doubt remains that we neither are nor could ever possibly be thorough enough. How do we communicate to our audiences, especially the more skeptical ones, that we have reported what we have seen and understood and that we recognize, as must they, that our knowledge is partial at best? How do we reassure them (and ourselves) that what we have seen and understood is what warrants reporting or that we have quite gotten it right? As Charles Bosk has observed (1979:193), "All field work done by a single fieldworker invites the question, Why should we believe it?" Why, indeed?

My answer is subsumed under the phrase "heady candor," a serious recommendation conveyed in a lighthearted play on the name Eddie Cantor, an old-time vaudeville and radio comedian. Heady candor requires being open and up front about both the research process and the persona of the researcher, in addition to paying the customary attention to what has been researched. If that seems obvious today, keep in mind that until recently fieldworkers were in the habit of disappearing from their accounts altogether, as though they themselves had never exerted a presence.

Today's qualitative researchers are advised to leave a paper trail tracing the route along which they have collected data critical to the final reporting. The same guideline can be used to depict the fieldwork experience itself—its duration, circumstances, and limitations. That seems preferable to trying to establish a minimum number of hours of interviewing, days at the site, or months away from home. I recognize that aspiring fieldworkers would welcome firm pronouncements in this regard, just as survey researchers seek in vain for firm guidelines about the minimum number of respondents or minimum acceptable rates of return. To those questions I retreat once again to my catchall response: It depends.

One of the first students to take my graduate seminar "Ethnographic Research in Education" telephoned the year following completion of his doctoral studies to report excitedly on a research project he had proposed. He reported that he planned to do an ethnographic study of a school superintendent, comparable to the study I was then completing of a school principal, although he did allow that his study would not be conducted on such a grand scale. (My fieldwork extended through twenty-four months, the write-up taking about the same amount of time again, all sandwiched in among other faculty responsibilities.) I offered congratulatory and encouraging remarks before I thought to ask exactly how long he did intend to spend with his apparently willing informant. "All day!" came an enthusiastic response. "From first thing in the morning right through a meeting he has scheduled for that evening." Given the full details of his planned study, I must confess that his enthusiasm was not matched by a comparable enthusiasm of my own. A one-day study proposed as ethnography, and by one of my own former seminar students!

What went racing through my mind was whether to inform him, in no uncertain terms, that a one-day study could never warrant being called an ethnography. I could anticipate his next question, "Then how many days would I have to spend before it would be an ethnography?" Whether or not that is the proper question, it did seem reasonable that if one day were not enough, I must have in mind some minimum number of days that would suffice. Thirty-five years ago, however, educational researchers were not doing descriptive work at all. A full day devoted to documenting the activities of one school superintendent would have been a gigantic leap for research in educational administration. And if a single day of research was too short, had it really been necessary for me to tag along with my principal for two years?

The best answers respond not to questions of how long, measured in time, but to questions of purpose. Tighter conceptualization, cautious labeling, and a careful paper trail still seem good protection against the inevitable charge that certain aspects of our work are superficial. A bit more attention to parameters in this case might have set the idea on a manageable course with a more carefully chosen title, such as "A Day in the Life of a School Superintendent." Although such a study might not receive enthusiastic review from an educational journal today, it would have been groundbreaking at the time. Actually, it would have been well ahead of its time. In those days, survey research provided the basis for virtually all reporting in educational administration except for a few hokey experiments in leadership style that invariably showed a democratic approach to be superior to an authoritarian or laissez-faire one.

I do not recall whether the study was carried out as planned, although it probably was, since the superintendent had already agreed to it. But I have a feeling that my former student who so enthusiastically had proposed the study felt uncomfortable about whether one day spent observing really qualified as ethnographic research. Here is where the art of conceptualization might have helped him to think through what reasonably could be accomplished with the opportunity at hand: a single day of intense observation, an energetic and ambitious observer, and a "subject" willing to have a researcher tag along. Some recognition of recurring cycles might also have helped to contextualize his initial observations and to project a more substantial inquiry sometime in the future.

To anyone who has not actually tried to conduct observations for a sustained period, let me also note that the proposed fifteen-hour stint would have proved impossibly taxing for the observer. Most of us who have tried this kind of shadow study recognize that it is difficult to sustain rapt attention for even a couple of hours of uninterrupted observation. Our powers of observation prove a major contributor to the superficiality we seek so assiduously to overcome. The seeming ease of descriptive research—just following another human around in the course of a typical day—is itself a deception, a darker art.

It is not all that clear exactly what anyone does look at, should look at, or should record to fulfill the role of observer adequately. (More on this in HFW 1994a.) Clearly what one can observe and record for five minutes will be more intense, and more detailed, than what one might observe and record during two consecutive hours. Observation itself, cloaked as it is in mystery, may be the darkest of fieldwork's arts from the point of view of those who conduct it. Yet it leaves us subject to the related accusation of obviousness, the next problem to be reviewed.

Obviousness

The obviousness of our approach is not lost on some. It is easy to turn the tables on fieldwork approaches by suggesting that the obviousness of how we go about our research is matched by the obviousness of our results. The end product of our painstaking efforts at description does no more than recount what everyone already knows.

How does one respond to the charge that we only succeed in making the obvious obvious? One response is to argue that making the obvious

obvious is itself an art. Clyde Kluckhohn captured that idea in the title and message of his well-received introduction to anthropology, *Mirror for Man* (1949), a book still worth reading for anyone willing to overlook the language of the 1940s with its masculine pronouns and references to studying "primitives" or "insignificant" nonliterate peoples. Kluckhohn described the cultural anthropologist as the "silverer" of a mirror: "Anthropology holds up a great mirror to man and lets him look at himself in his infinite variety" (p. 11).

Another approach is to question whether what appears to be obvious is in fact so obvious after all. Kluckhohn raised that question, reminding us about taking our surroundings for granted: "Ordinarily we are unaware of the special lens through which we look at life. It would hardly be fish who discovered the existence of water" (p. 11).

In both these points, however, Kluckhohn was building the case for anthropologists who studied not just others but others dramatically different from themselves:

> The preoccupation with insignificant nonliterate peoples that is an outstanding feature of anthropological work is the key to its significance today. Anthropology grew out of experience with primitives and the tools of the trade are unusual because they were forged in this peculiar workshop. [Pp. 10–11]

Collectively those tools of the trade made up the ethnographer's kit bag. They were intended to help describe the cultures of other groups, initially those "insignificant nonliterate peoples" of Kluckhohn's account but always people whose customs differed sufficiently to provide an explicit cross-cultural and comparative basis for description. Comparison is, of course, implicit in all observation, but questions about the role of strangeness came to be ever more vexing as anthropologists began studying closer to home under such rubrics as urban anthropology or micro-ethnography.

One caveat was that ethnographers whose credentials had been validated through cross-cultural fieldwork were then regarded as qualified to conduct ethnographic research in their own societies, a position that conveniently accommodated the work American anthropologists like Lloyd Warner had been doing for years. As a professional concern, this problem is of anthropology's own making as anthropologists have sought to redefine their turf. Sociologists have never been overly concerned with a cross-cultural perspective, and much of the qualitative research currently being conducted addresses applied problems in the researcher's own professional field. Nevertheless, the question of the comparative basis of our accounts remains, turning today on the issue of whether insiders can do adequate research in groups in which they hold membership or to which they owe allegiance. I think the answer lies in recognizing what an insider perspective can and cannot offer. We temper the position popular in some quarters—that only an insider can get the inside view—by noting that an inside view is not the only view. Furthermore, there is no single inside, or emic, view any more than there can be a single outside, or etic, one.

The fact remains, however, that we may stretch the point, even do ourselves a disservice, by making too much either of what we have to report or how we have come to report it. I have already raised the issue of whether we might be better off to insist that fieldwork is fieldwork, rather than allow others to drive us into a corner insisting that it is research. As to accomplishments, Howard Becker suggests that the work of his colleagues in sociology only gives us "a deeper understanding of what people are already pretty much aware of" (1982:x), while the parallel claim for traditional anthropology might be that its comparative perspective offers a deeper understanding by pointing to what people are already pretty much unaware of. This is often characterized as "making the familiar strange," a phrase either coined or reaffirmed by T. S. Eliot (1950:259; see also Spiro 1990:53) and frequently used in anthropological explanations of what fieldwork is all about. Schlechty and Noblit put another spin on the idea by suggesting that what we are up to is "making the obvious dubious" (1982:290).

As for the newness of qualitative approaches and the claim that today we are witnessing groundbreaking efforts, I think modesty is warranted here as well. What strikes us as new may be nothing more than our own conscious awareness of an approach or a sudden interest in some particular field previously not so receptive (e.g., business, journalism, nursing, music, physical education). Even computer scientists have their quarterly journal *Human–Computer Interaction*.

As a latecomer among the social sciences, anthropology is not the best place to look for origins. Terms like *ethnography* and *fieldwork* have been around for decades. No discipline or century claims observation as its own, a point Kluckhohn underscored with a reminder that the Greek historian Herodotus, who "described at length the physique and customs of the Scythians, Egyptians, and other 'barbarians,'" is "sometimes called the 'father of anthropology' as well as the 'father of history'" (1949:2).

The phrase "participant observation" appears at least as early as the 1920s as used rather casually by E. C. Lindeman (1924:191). I believe Kluckhohn's wife and co-researcher, sociologist Florence Kluckhohn, first wrote formally about participant observation as a fieldwork technique, based on research in a Spanish-American village conducted with her husband and begun in 1936 (F. Kluckhohn 1940). Prior to her legitimating it, the idea may, as James Clifford suggests, have been regarded more as a predicament than a technique (see Clifford 1988:93).

Good (i.e., scientific) observers of social settings in an earlier day were content with observation. They neither identified with nor tried to become part of what they studied. Rather, they tended to write themselves out of the script, as though no outsider had been present at all. Boas, for example, directed his attention to a past "from which one hundred years of Western contact was filtered out" (Sanjek 1990:196). I need not reach back so far for illustration. I felt no hesitation in placing myself in the Kwakiutl village as teacher, but no other "white guys" were introduced unless they were official visitors to the school. It just seemed to make my account more dramatic if I were the only outsider mentioned, although occasionally there were others. Today we do not have to re-create a romantic past.

Another element of obviousness is the very nature of our inquiries. Our intent is to render studies on meaningful topics, presented in depth. Our risk in this regard is a double one: rendering studies that lack depth or conducting studies in depth on topics that do not seem to merit it. And when we do address problems that command respect, we cannot escape the nagging question of generalization: What can you learn from studying only one of something?

The cards are stacked against us on this. I do not think we must all become artful dodgers, but any time the argument against qualitative approaches hinges on the obvious fact that our cases typically examine ordinary circumstances, and only instances at that, we are probably better off agreeing rather than arguing. We ordinarily study the ordinary. We study only instances.

Given our concern for and attention to the individual case, it seems reasonable to inquire as to how attentively we select the cases we study, not only in choosing among sites or informants—matters over which we may be able to exercise little control in the field—but in choosing the problems to which we devote our attention. Qualitative researchers have rightly been cautioned about this issue, although it is not unique to their work alone.

Novices intent on gaining formal approval for their research proposals may inadvertently get the idea that anything goes as long as you can get it approved. More senior faculty, besieged with students competing for the precious little time they have for their own scholarship, may offer little by way of guidance or honest assessment. The publish-or-perish ethos that pervades the university community pushes faculty into the same boat with their students: Find some study that will lead to a publication or two; forget trying to pursue topics of genuine significance. The result, at least in those fields where research proliferates but does not aggregate, is that countless research projects are undertaken that are destined to become little more than practice exercises. Nothing will ever come of them, and no one reads them. That is not dark art, but it does seem a darkly kept secret. It is a dark secret because we ignore it rather than attend to it as a collective problem of scholarship. The cumulative effect of the myriad qualitative studies undertaken can be likened to trying to fill the Grand Canyon with popcorn.

And how does that affect you if you are just setting out to do research? Only in this profoundly disturbing way: The research you undertake is not likely to matter. Obviousness is a major detractor, and the modest scope of our studies raises doubts any time our inquiries suggest that things are not as obvious as they seem. We lack any capacity for, or commitment to, aggregating countless little studies into something bigger, something that can transcend the limits within which fieldwork is carried out.

Lacking such capacity means that if anything is to come of your research effort, it will be entirely up to you to make it happen. To say that your fieldwork is just the beginning is a colossal understatement. You will have to figure out what to do with your research, how to bring it to the attention of others. They need to know why you needed to know about the subject and how your work moves things forward, regardless of whether your efforts have made the obvious obvious or dubious.

Self-Serving

Whom does research best serve? The inescapable conclusion is that it best serves those of us who conduct it. It serves even better those who present it—be it their own work or that of others—in papers and publications dealing with either process or product.

This self-serving aspect is especially evident in graduate programs in professional fields where research is added to careers originally set in another direction. Experienced teachers, for example, go back to school ostensibly to become better at what they are doing (classroom teaching) but actually to obtain a license to do something quite different (e.g., administer a school, pursue scholarship or research at the university level). There is a decided emphasis on research in graduate study; the doctorate is usually touted as a research degree. Candidates for advanced degrees must become students of research to obtain their goal.

The kinds of topics often selected by master's and doctoral students in fields where the degree itself, rather than the achievement of any particular level of competence, is what matters suggest the extent to which the research exercise is blatantly self-serving. Rather than engender a deep commitment to learning new skills or making a significant contribution to theory or practice, research often proves little more than one more hurdle along the route to an advanced degree. This churning of topics and churning out of uninteresting and unimportant studies in fulfillment of a research ritual has always struck me as a great waste of energy and talent. I join with others who wonder whether, at the master's level—and perhaps even at the doctoral level (especially in applied fields like education or public administration, in contrast to a Ph.D. awarded as an academic research degree)—a satisfactory effort at synthesis and critique might be a more appropriate way to demonstrate research acumen.

Paul Bohannan goes so far as to identify the need for a good program of synthesis as the "gravest need in social science" (1995:ix). Such an alternative might prove attractive to students who recognize a need to become highly informed consumers of research but who are unlikely to become producers of it, an alternative demanding tough-minded critique of the sort usually exercised by dissertation committees and reviewers of professional journals. Another alternative might be *demonstration,* the critical application and appraisal of the research of others in a genuine effort to translate theory into practice.

Such an alternative would reduce the pressure for and emphasis on new and original research. The emphasis instead would be on making better use of research already reported. It ought as well to improve research quality and significance. The anticipation of intense scrutiny by one's peers could exert a healthy influence on the quality of reported research, since novice researchers would realize that their efforts were more likely to be read and critiqued than has previously been the case. Attending to synthesis, critique, and theory building also suggests ways to promote efforts at aggregating studies of the sort that fieldwork produces as a way to assess whether we are making headway or only spinning our wheels, and to identify areas of neglect. At present, too many students producing theses and dissertations go through the motions to accomplish no more than research exercises on topics of virtually no consequence, with yesterday's inconsequential experiments and field trials replaced today by quickie descriptive studies endlessly inventorying similarities and differences. Surely there are other ways to demonstrate a capacity for independent scholarship that can harness the energy now spent in the trivial pursuit of meeting program requirements.

For those who do find satisfaction and fulfillment in research, another dark secret is that, for the most part, research continues to be self-serving throughout one's career. If there is a call for art in this aspect of our work, it is the art of self-deception in perceiving ourselves as working in service to humanity. I have no evidence that my research ever helped anyone I thought it might help or intended to help, except for testimonials from a few who graciously insisted that something I reported helped them gain a fresh perspective. Although I have realized only modest royalties from my fieldwork publications (as sponsors of my research, my university kept the original royalties on my two biggest studies and another university kept the royalties on a third), the prime beneficiary in every instance has been myself as I worked my way up the academic ladder.

Altruism and research make strange bedfellows. The dark art is to get others to think that your research is for their good and perhaps to convince yourself of it as well, all the while looking for anything you might do to make this really happen. The call today is for community-based, collaborative, or participatory research (see, for example, Harrison 2001). In an earlier day, we talked of action research involving participants or applied research intended to bring desired results. Best intentions notwithstanding, I think we must concede that the person who stands to gain the most from any research is the researcher.

This does not reflect greed or selfishness as much as the fact that research carries with it a host of potential rewards and payoffs for the researcher that cannot accrue to the researched, even if—on rare occasions—they stand to gain something. It is the researcher whose career benefits, it is the researcher who gets the recognition, and it is the researcher who draws the salary and related perks. Researchers may redistribute some of their material benefits—it is not unknown for fieldworkers to dedicate royalties from a study to a common cause or tribal fund, for example—but the researcher reaps the rewards of research along several dimensions, while the benefit to the subjects of a study is limited because they are not in a league where research itself is likely to gain them anything except possible notoriety.

An assigned orator may someday be moved to state on my behalf, "He dedicated his life to teaching, research, and writing." The implication will be that I gave unstintingly of myself, taking little in return. Collectively my research might be heralded in that brief moment as a "major contribution." Had I not conducted those studies and made that major contribution, however, I do not think the world would be a different place. My place in it would have reflected the difference.

We do what we can to dispel the idea that our work is self-serving. For years we have touted the good we have accomplished (see, for example, van Willigen, Rylko-Bauer, and McElroy 1989), and we continue to expound on the potential that should or might result from whatever new inquiry we propose. It is definitely an advantage in gaining access to a research setting if one can claim that those in the setting will be among the beneficiaries of the research. These days such a claim usually receives close scrutiny.

Scientific research has an aura of respectability about it, tending to be associated in the public mind with outcomes so unquestioningly beneficial that medical practitioners now warn an unwary public against the prevailing bias toward intervention and treatment that such faith has engendered. Social research tends to slip in under the same tent; whatever is being examined is charitably assumed to need examination. The idea of a Golden Fleece Award, which recognizes large sums of federal money spent researching topics of questionable merit, may amuse us but seems not to precipitate any concerted effort to stop the fleecing. The Government Accounting Office is responsible for seeing that contracted research services are performed, but it does not monitor the quality of ideas funded by Congress.

A related assumption is that problems targeted for research will eventually be treated and fixed (for instance, that research on homelessness, abuse, or violence will eventually rid us of those problems). In the public mind, "good" research implies both of these conditions: research on topics of importance that will lead to effective remedial action. "Bad" research suggests something altogether different: research that is poorly designed or poorly executed, not research devoted to inconsequential or unworthy ends.

Expectations regarding the helpfulness of social research vary among the disciplines and professions and the prevailing norms of the day. The prevailing mood of an earlier day demanded less researcher involvement or social consciousness; results were reported as basic research, and practitioners were expected to make the necessary applications. The mood at present favors applied, practical research, typically under the broad umbrella of some politically correct cause.

There have always been well-intentioned projects geared toward directed change. Looking at the field of anthropology, one can see interests generated in the 1940s and 1950s in applied or action anthropology giving way to more theoretical interests in the 1960s and 1970s. Somewhere during the 1980s those applied interests reappeared, and so did applied anthropologists. Today we expect anthropologists proposing fieldwork to be able to assure us not only how they plan to protect their subjects but how (not whether) the research will benefit those being studied. We expect the same of qualitative researchers everywhere. "First, do no harm" as a credo is no longer enough, although the no-harm criterion is not that easily met.

I have mentioned anthropologist Fred Gearing. Because his career spans this era, let me quote from his earliest fieldwork to illustrate a then-current mood that has returned to guide our work today—or at least to guide what we say about our work. Although Gearing's account was not completed until 1970, his fieldwork with the Fox Indians began in 1952, under the guidance of his mentor, Sol Tax. Gearing explains, "I was in the

Fox community to do something called 'action anthropology,' to help while learning and to learn while helping" (1970:26). (In today's cost-conscious research arena, Gearing's definition seems to have had the "L" kicked out of it; applied social research "helps while earning and earns while helping.")

By the time I began fieldwork in 1962, some ten years later than Gearing, it was no longer necessary to underscore the immediate benefits of research. A case study examining why Kwakiutl Indian children did poorly in school might lead to some modification in programs designed to educate them, but I was not duty-bound to promise that it would. At the same time, I hoped it would, and sometimes I wanted to shout over the rooftops of the village (as reservation schools usually were, this one was located on a rise above the village), "I'm doing this for your own good." It was a sustaining thought, if not a completely accurate one.

It is the sustaining thought that assuages us. If a teacher affects eternity, then fieldworkers ought to affect eternity too, although we dare not ask just how. I did not have to search far to find an example of an opposite case in which a rapidly changing sociopolitical scene ultimately rendered a research project ineffective:

> The intervention that was designed, however, was never implemented. While the research was . . . "good" grounded research that focused heavily on the problem from the viewpoint of the affected persons, and was specifically designed to develop an intervention that would be tested and evaluated, the project ended when the final report was submitted. [Eisenberg 1994:36]

I like to believe that somewhere along the line, my studies have helped, but if they did, it had to be through my efforts to help others understand things as they were, not through any effort on my part to improve them. Although my field is anthropology and education, which is generally regarded as an applied field, I do not regard myself as an applied anthropologist. I was pleased to see *A Kwakiutl Village and School* used in teacher training, particularly for teachers planning to teach in the Alaskan bush, but that was not the audience I had in mind either in writing the dissertation or in revising it for publication. Similarly, I was pleased to see educator reception to *The Man in the Principal's Office* (HFW 1973) but was surprised to realize that the monograph served far more widely as a model for research than for insight into the principalship itself (see HFW 1982). None of my other studies seems to have fared any better: They have been too little, too late (e.g., HFW 1977, 1983a), ignored by those I thought might be informed (e.g., 1983b), or simply filed away and forgotten. The original report prompting the Sneaky Kid piece was actually commissioned after the fact: A Congress that had already become history had commissioned a report that was never completed. The file was waiting to be shut as soon as our reports were submitted. ("Your government dollars at work," political satirists like to remind us.)

For all the questions that they do ask, fieldworkers are often faulted for failing to ask those in the research setting how the research or researcher might be of help to them, at least in ways other than securing funds. The criticism seems valid. But it also suggests a way for those who wish to be of service, inviting fieldworkers to take the issue of helping into the field with them, making funding itself a topic for investigation. That might seem preferable to initiating new projects with the question How can we help? already answered, as we frequently do at present.

It is unusual to inquire deeply into the life of nearly anyone—certainly the lives of the kinds of people most often studied by fieldworkers—and not develop a sense of empathy or concern. Not infrequently that concern is joined by rage, even outrage, at the conditions under which so many humans live. As poet Robert Burns reflected, "Man's inhumanity to man makes countless thousands mourn." The very nature of fieldwork finds us often among the downtrodden or oppressed or discovering oppression in social systems generally regarded as benign. We are moved to help people tell their stories, even to tell their stories for them, to let the world know of the (needless?) suffering that takes place.

One cannot help but assume an air of self-righteousness in getting the word out. It is immensely satisfying to uncover wrongdoing and to make pronouncements as to what ought to be done about it. One owes one's informants at least that! Perhaps I have become jaded after attending so many national and international meetings and hearing so many fieldworkers describe the plight of so many peoples for so many years. I admit to having indulged in such efforts myself. But I have begun to regard my efforts as self-serving and self-satisfying as well.

Engaging so wholeheartedly as we do in this rhetoric of reform helps us feel we have addressed critical issues and courageously spoken our piece. We make it appear that if we cannot always make a difference in the case at hand, at least we do not dodge responsibility in bringing underlying issues before a wider audience. It's pretty safe work, perhaps all the more satisfying for its safety, decrying the world's injustices from the safety of a podium to an audience of our (not their) peers in Grand Ballroom A of some major hotel in some major city, a pitcher of ice water comfortingly nearby, heads nodding with compassion at the circumstances we can but briefly outline in nine-hundred-second allotted time slots. It is nice to seem to be at the cutting edge without having to do any cutting and without being noticeably near the edge. "Give 'em hell, Harry," a reviewer once commented in commendation. I felt I had. Nothing changed. I was applauded for my spunk in being so outspoken; I wasn't really expected to do anything about it.

Where we derive satisfaction from believing that we are making the world a better place, we ignore how we make a better place for ourselves in it. We prove to be all too human. There's nothing particularly wrong with that; it's just a bit awkward to have to own up to being our own beneficiaries.

If fieldwork efforts are largely self-serving—and I do not see how they could ever be anything else—should researchers themselves, collectively, have a larger hand in what is to be researched? In some ways, burgeoning interest in qualitative research has probably made a bad situation worse: more individuals going off in more directions under the banner of research than ever before. Qualitative studies tend to be smaller in scope, typically conducted with the principal investigator being the only investigator and with little or no supervision, guidance, or assistance.

Perhaps here is one way research-oriented faculty might exert more influence than they have toward the goal of improving the quality of research even if it does not change its self-serving nature. Too little attention, individual or collective, is devoted to discerning what needs to be researched from all that could be researched. As an unintended consequence of the graduate school experience, when finding any topic to call one's own is enough, too little attention is given to establishing priorities as a collective responsibility of a community of scholars. That dialogue is not likely to come out of research units scrambling for grant money, but it is a dialogue for individuals willing to take on the role of the connoisseur/critic already well established in art worlds.

This suggestion is not intended to interfere with the independence of researchers, which I discuss next. What we might do is join together to become more acute critics of the processes by which problems are identified. We have been remiss in our efforts to educate our own patrons. We patronize them when we might instead be politicizing them.

Research itself is highly political. I doubt that we are ever cognizant of the extent to which our research options are bound up by local and national politics, another aspect that art worlds and fieldwork worlds share. As long as academics are able to sustain the comfortable institution of tenure, those of us blessed with it have an opportunity to perform a valuable service to all qualitative (and quantitative) researchers by functioning individually or collectively as critical reviewers of what is and is not being attended to under the broad rubric of research. That is a question of research agenda.

Lack of Independence

Freedom newly won from the academy with the completion of the dissertation may prove ephemeral, especially for newly minted fieldworkers who discover they like doing this kind of research. The performance element of fieldwork occurs in the field, but the discerning audience is back home among those who practice, sponsor, or constitute the market for this type of inquiry. That audience consists not of those laundry lists of individuals whom we try to inveigle into reading our completed studies—legislators and other policy makers, administrators, civil servants, practitioners, community leaders, chief executive officers, board members, teachers, funding agencies, and on and on—but of a relatively small group of others like ourselves who do similar studies or who tell others how to do them by offering courses or texts. That is not an insignificant audience, but neither is it exactly the one we like to imagine. As publisher Mitch Allen has observed in a telling comment, "The writers of qualitative research are also the buyers of qualitative research. It is a closed system."

You may celebrate feeling free as a bird during the fieldwork stage, but unless you are really going to fly the coop, you will have to work in applied research or return to academia—and thus to academic scrutiny—to maintain an audience for your efforts. That cannot help but exert a heavy, even a deadening, influence on the way you subsequently organize and present your account. You do not buy freedom from academia by becoming competent at qualitative research; if anything, your newly acquired competence may envelop you further in it. Ironically, if you were able to support yourself through part-time employment as a field assistant in a university-based research project, you might find that completing your studies, and thus earning your freedom, has cut your ties to an active research arena rather than secured your place in it. To pursue a professional career that includes opportunity to further pursue qualitative work, you may have to demonstrate some art at getting into—or getting back into—academia in the new role of faculty member. And if you succeed at that, you must master whatever art it takes to remain there. In some professional settings, you may even have to deny your qualitative leanings, at least until your reputation as a competent all-round (read "quantitative") researcher is firmly established.

Of course, there is some opportunity for employment in which research plays an important, but not exclusive, role. Usually this involves working under university auspices or conducting fieldwork for private contractors or agencies underwriting specific projects. Unless you are able to write your own ticket by securing funds for a project entirely of your design—a distinction implied in differentiating grants from contract research—you will undoubtedly find yourself subjected to as great or greater restraints than exist in academic research. In part this is simple economics as you take time out from research to do the things necessary to support it—report writing, grant writing, lecturing, and so forth. I have heard independent scholar-researchers lament that they devote as much as one third of their time to garnering financial support, in order to devote another third of their time to field research, leaving the final third for organizing and reporting. Paradoxically, then, the more one enjoys research and wants to devote major time to it, the more likely it is that others will call the shots as to what gets studied.

For the most part, the research that gets attended to is research on topics that attract money and status, political factors beyond the control of researchers themselves. As pointed out in chapter 3, although the constraints are not entirely economic, whoever controls the purse strings has a major voice in determining what is to be researched. In the real world, researchers are a powerless lot; within their own world, it is the administrators of research who wield what little power there is.

If they wish to make research a central activity in their careers, researchers must follow the money around to make (force?) a fit between their interests and the funded problems of the day. In the protective language of grantsmanship, this is called "responding" to proposals, but those responses are as conditioned as the salivating of Pavlov's dogs. Grant and proposal writing are now taught as skill areas in the social sciences. Dollars received through research grants and awards provide a convenient bottom line by which some academic departments assess the relative value of new faculty.

I am not sure what advice prospective fieldworkers can glean from these dour observations other than to realize that the opportunities in qualitative research are likely to be narrow or adjunct to a career focused elsewhere (such as teaching) rather than devoted exclusively to research itself. That would seem to call for making the most of whatever opportunities come your way if you find that fieldwork-oriented research proves satisfying.

One additional art you may have to develop, at least in the early part of a research career, is the art of extricating yourself from pressure toward joint authorship from what probably began as independent research while you were in the field. This is not a problem in genuine team research, but not all research touted as team research proves to be quite so collegial. Although I tend to think of fieldwork as a solitary enterprise because I work essentially as a loner and thus think that is how all fieldwork is best accomplished, there is a long tradition in ethnographic work, especially in community study, for research to be conducted and reported by two-person teams. Among anthropologists these have usually been husband–wife teams. In allied disciplines, the teams seem to get bigger, usually involving a principal investigator and several field assistants.

It has usually been decided in advance whether field assistants will have any responsibility for (or opportunity to participate in) the final reporting. I recommend that assistants be given the opportunity to report their own fieldwork separately, under their own names, in addition to whatever they are expected to contribute to the data pool or to drafting a collective report. It is important to make expectations clear from the beginning, especially if fieldworkers are not going to retain full access to their own data.

A different situation arises when independently conducted fieldwork presented in dissertation form goes on to reappear in joint publications coauthored by professor and student. There may have been justification for this practice in ongoing quantitative research projects in which graduate students took responsibility for tiny segments of a large project and thus became co-investigators. I also understand that in times past it was the prerogative of The Professor, as head and chair of a department organized along the lines of British universities, to have his (a male, most likely) name included on any research conducted and reported by a member of the department.

I hesitate to examine such traditions out of context, but I do not think these are appropriate models for reporting qualitative research today. I encourage faculty to find ways to circulate and celebrate the qualitative studies performed by their students. Joint authorship is not the only way—and seems not the best way—to accomplish this. A synthesis of the work of others, reported with careful crediting in our own writing, is a commendable way to make our students' efforts better known. Co-authorship based on fieldwork conducted solely by subordinates is not. Whoever does the fieldwork ought to report the fieldwork; someone else can take it from there.

Another factor that contributes to a lack of independence in the fieldworker role is the (obvious?) circumstance that it is a role. As a role, it has its own built-in constraints. We all like to step out of our roles at times, often with a self-conscious effort to transcend role and simply be ourselves. There is a curious paradox here for the social scientist. Roles provide convenient ways to generalize about virtually everyone (else) with whom we have contact while we perceive ourselves essentially in terms of personality. We experience discomfort when others press role conformity (i.e., their role expectations) upon us; somehow they fail to recognize how marvelously we ourselves transcend them.

The role of the participant observer fieldworker has a seductive quality about it in that we somehow expect it to lift us above the role of ordinary researcher to become that role's antithesis, the non-researcher researcher, the person who acts (acts?) naturally, in order that those studied will act naturally as well. The role can both consume and sustain you, but it does not free you from being a researcher. It gives purpose to your presence, but in return you can expect to be expected to act like a researcher, even when you yourself are responsible for creating those expectations. While trying to be yourself, you may be tested for your ability to observe more intently and reflect more thoughtfully—literally to make something different out of the experience from what anyone else in the setting is obliged to do. Those are, after all, the qualities you have attributed to this kind of researcher. If you are beset by a strong work ethic—and people who are attracted to research are not the world's best hedonists—then you will be besieged by your own morality, pressing you to work harder, see more, record better.

An argument put forward on behalf of long-term fieldwork—and I trust you to keep in mind throughout this discussion that I take genuine fieldwork to be of no other kind—holds that the researcher must remain in the field long enough that those present cannot maintain a pose. Sooner or later, and probably sooner, you should begin to learn how things really are. But that works both ways. You will not be able to maintain a pose of your best self for long, either. No doubt you will want to be seen as neutral, objective, and equally fair to and interested in all alike. But you will be put upon, and you have your own appetites to contend with. In time, you may feel that in your role as researcher you are always on duty. Occasionally you might want to go off duty to catch your breath, gain a bit of perspective, perhaps simply enjoy some privacy. If you are really immersed in the field, you probably will find no easy escape, trapped in the very role that once seemed so natural, so inviting, so unencumbered.

What to do? Well, don't torture yourself with feelings that you are the first ever to find the role more difficult to sustain than you realized. Try to develop your own coping strategies. Rosalie Wax confessed to a noticeable weight gain during her first fieldwork as she literally ate her way into compensating for the stress and loneliness eating away at her (1971:72). If you can pass up the bonbons or equally tantalizing alternatives, such as unusually long hours devoted to sleep or escapist reading, and you really are as work-oriented as I suspect you are, you might try writing. Writing and writing. Sooner or later that is what you must do anyway.

For many individuals, researchers included, writing has therapeutic as well as professional value. Clifford states, "One of the ways Malinowski pulled himself together was by writing ethnography" (1988:104). That is a fairly candid assessment, the kind one makes years after the fact and after we are sure that the researcher did actually pull himself or herself together and pulled together a significant research account as well. (Clifford is less generous on the latter score, noting that "Malinowski never did pull together Trobriand culture; he produced no synthetic portrait, only densely contextualized monographs on important institutions" [p. 104].) In whatever ways writing helped Malinowski—and it did give us, among other things, both *Argonauts of the Western Pacific,* published in 1922, and *A Diary in the Strict Sense of the Term,* published posthumously in 1967— consider the possibility that it might also work for you. An important part of the discussion to follow (part III) will emphasize writing, especially the idea of beginning one's writing early in the fieldwork.

Fieldwork is unquestionably that aspect of qualitative inquiry over which one asserts the least control. One can be prepared, but that does not necessarily entail formal training. How one has learned to cope with all the exigencies to be confronted in the course of everyday life surely has more predictive power for fieldwork success than how many courses one has taken, manuals one has read, or ethnographers one has known. Having been an avid backpacker in my youth, I was intrigued to read that backpacking has proven to be excellent preparation for doing fieldwork; I note with interest that candidates for field schools today are asked about their camping experience.

One can probably prepare better for two major aspects of the fieldwork process to be discussed in the next chapters—conceptualizing what one is doing and getting on with the writing—than for the actual doing of fieldwork. Some measure of confidence should spill over to the field encounter simply because you have a good idea of where the work is leading. You are more apt to get there if you have an idea of where you are going, even if you are unsure of the way. But never delude yourself into thinking that the choices you will face along the way will be yours alone to make. You may really only be free to make a whole new set of mistakes and then decide how candidly you intend to report your efforts to deal with them.

Deception and Betrayal

Of all the risks inherent in fieldwork, none is more personally disturbing to me than the suggestion, and sometimes the outright accusation, that those whom we have studied feel betrayed by what we have said or written. And I know no more disturbing sentence addressing this topic than the one Miles and Huberman included in the first edition of their widely acclaimed *Qualitative Data Analysis* and staunchly reaffirmed in the expanded second edition a decade later:

> It is probably true that, fundamentally, field research is an act of betrayal, no matter how well intentioned or well integrated the researcher. One makes public the private and leaves the locals to take the consequences. [1984:233; see also 1994:265]

In further support, they add by way of footnote a quote attributed to writer Joan Didion: "I am so small, so neurotic, and so inoffensive that people invariably forget an important point: the writer will do you in" (quoted in Miles and Huberman 1984:248n).

Sociologist Maurice Punch goes a step further to suggest that if a latent aim of fieldwork is to create trust in the researcher, then the relationship actually involves "a double betrayal: first by them of you but then by you of them." As he puts it, "Often in fieldwork the subjects are conning you until you can gain their trust and then, once you have their confidence, you begin conning them" (1986:72–73).

Discomforting as it is, we must face the charge of betrayal head on. I do not subscribe to the idea that field research is always an act of betrayal, but the possibility is ever present. There is no way we can do this work without uncovering additional information, complexity, and linkages; no way we can claim to be in the business of finding things out without finding things out; no way we can report what we have understood without the risk of being misunderstood. The whole purpose of the enterprise is revelation. Our quest may be ennobled by our seeking understanding, but it aims at revelation, nonetheless. There is the likelihood that in what is revealed some party or parties will feel betrayed, which is always a matter of individual perception. That is not to suggest that betrayal itself is one of our darker arts; rather, our obligation is to attend responsibly to the art of revelation. That can be, but need not be, sinister business.

Closely related is another charge that we must learn to live with rather than deny. Our efforts to live our way into the groups we wish to study, and particularly our efforts to win over informants for extended and close collaboration, can be viewed not only as establishing rapport but also as seductions, and "massive seductions," a phrase suggested by cross-cultural psychologist David Gutmann:

We are too apt to play at being democratic "good guys" at the expense of our often very hungry and vulnerable informants. We think that we are being cool, and unconcerned with status; but they too often experience our transient gestures toward equality as *massive* seductions. . . . Thus, it is not enough that we develop sensitivity to our informants' motives; we should also be very sensitive toward and corrective of our own. [Quoted in Langness and Frank 1981:131]

Gutmann's recommendation was that "all fieldworkers in training should be supervised not only by experts in their particular discipline, but also by clinical psychologists or psychiatrists" (p. 131). In their *Lives: An Anthropological Approach to Biography*, L. L. Langness and Gelya Frank paired that notion to a need for life historians to "learn the rudiments of personality theory and clinical practice," a seemingly worthy if nonetheless unlikely objective. But the phrase "massive seductions" continues to ring in my ear. Like Blanche DuBois in *A Streetcar Named Desire*, fieldworkers must rely on the kindness of strangers to help them get where they want to go. On some of those strangers the fieldworker may press inordinately.

The issue raises uncomfortable questions: Is seduction one of our darker arts? As craftspeople, are we so crafty that others don't know when they are being seduced? Is there some ethically acceptable approach to, or level of, seduction appropriate for fieldworkers? Is seduction necessarily so one-sided, the powerful always overwhelming the helpless? When we ourselves are not doing the conning, are our informants conning us?

Many such interpersonal dilemmas are associated with fieldwork. There are situations in which the better the artistry used in confronting them, the less, rather than the more, we might admire the guile of the fieldworker. Maybe we are better off recognizing and confronting the fact that, however well intended, our work cannot transcend being a human endeavor, with attendant costs as well as benefits. We may as well acknowledge those costs and be alert to ways to minimize them, rather than deny them or be too quick to point an accusing finger at others.

No fieldworker ever has license to tell all. Is there an art to recognizing how much to tell? That is where trust comes back into play, haunting us with questions about discretion, which one might assume to be an implicit part of the bargain. The consequence for fieldworkers is that we cannot avoid a certain amount of deception. David Nyberg has defined deception as the artful deployment of the varnished truth (1993:7), re-minding us of a Caucasus proverb that a man who tells the truth should keep his horse saddled. Because the write-up may not be completed until long after fieldwork is concluded, fieldworkers who do not prematurely divulge the nature and extent of their proposed reporting do not have to keep their horses saddled. Not all of them dare ride off in the same direction twice, however.

Along with not knowing enough about the subject of an inquiry, you are also likely to discover that you know too much. The seriousness of the problem will probably be proportional to the quality of your fieldwork: The more successful you are as a fieldworker, the more likely you are to learn things that you did not intend—and possibly did not want—to learn. You will experience concern about what you should disclose, at what cost, to what audiences.

To a large extent, this becomes a problem of reporting, for that is when you make decisions about what needs to be made public and, of that, how much you take responsibility to report. Anticipating the problem will influence your thinking from the outset as you make choices about what to study and to what depth you intend to pursue your inquiries. The same people who may try to put you off may also unburden themselves once they discover that you are a good listener, particularly if you are perceived to be a non-judgmental or sympathetic one. Qualitative researchers may inadvertently find out too much of the wrong stuff while trying to learn more of the stuff that fills their own definition of how the inquiry is supposed to proceed. What to do?

I think fieldworkers should always have in mind the boundaries of their inquiries. At the same time, they need to keep those boundaries flexible. There must be room to refine or redirect the focus of a study, should that become necessary, and to accommodate personalities and circumstances on a moment-to-moment basis during the interpersonal processes of being in the field. You have to respect people's efforts to convey what they want you to hear, just as you hope they will talk candidly about what you want to hear. Your sense of courtesy will guide the extent to which you allow them just to go on and on. The limits set for the inquiry should guide the extent of extraneous material to record.

Whether and how often to caution those in the research setting about your presence and purposes is another judgment call. People not only need to know but periodically to be reminded why you are there. To whatever extent possible, you should also help informants maintain some sense of the scope of what you intend to report. When appropriate, you might help with the former by keeping your notebook or other recording devices visible, even though the content of what you record may be for your eyes and ears alone. You can help with the latter—foreshadowing the direction you plan to take in reporting—by commending information that is particularly helpful or remarking on topics clearly beyond the boundaries of your intended study. Such feedback may help to allay second thoughts among those who realize too late that they have talked too freely or divulged information they do not wish to see in print. Those signals also provide some hint about the kind of information most likely to make it into your final report.

Fieldworkers often discover to their surprise that informants try to use them as conduits for communicating problems and concerns to a wider audience. Those in the research setting cannot later claim to be disappointed in your work if, from the outset, you have made clear the limits of what you expect to do and to acknowledge concerns they may have that you know you will not address. I could assure my Kwakiutl friends that no matter what I put in my "memory book," no royal commission was subsequently going to be appointed to investigate their concerns about fishing rights. For that problem, they needed to understand that I simply was not their man.

An artful sense of discretion, plus a close reading of the social scene and research climate, will guide much of your decision making about what you report. You may feel torn being between the extremes of daily news coverage or television fare on the one hand and gun-shy colleagues and administrators warning you about possible lawsuits on the other. The personal guideline I draw is both a Confucian proverb and a restatement of the Golden Rule, to not do unto others anything you would not want them to do unto you.

My counsel is to be candid but discreet, a topic I develop more thoroughly in chapter 11. Whatever you do divulge, reveal accurately, but always stay within the limits of the research focus rather than fostering a reputation for selling diaries or telling tales out of school. Important points tangential to a particular inquiry can be flagged for reader attention by noting issues raised but not resolved in your study or by footnoting topics worthy of future inquiry. Similarly, sticky issues can often be alluded to in such a way that insiders recognize that you were being discreet, rather than simply naive, while outsiders need be no more the wiser.

Clandestine Observation

Exactly what motivates those of us who commit ourselves so wholeheartedly to be the self-appointed watchers of others? Do we engage in some special, socially approved form of voyeurism in which, through our insistence that we are attentive to all aspects of human life, we can also insist that no aspects of it are to be denied us?

Few fieldworkers (Van Maanen 1978:346 is one exception) have been so bold as to use the term *voyeur* in looking at our roles in research, but the least hint that our observations titillate us does not rest lightly. Nonetheless, exclusion is the enemy: We want to see it all. We search for arguments in support of claims about seeking knowledge for the common good to counteract the concerns of others about the rights of privacy. Demands for full disclosure of our research purposes among those whom we study rankle us, yet we express surprise and dismay to discover that something we have observed too closely or disclosed too fully rankles them.

We may vigorously deny that we are voyeurs, but we must face that accusation head-on to acknowledge whatever influence it may exert on our work and others' perceptions of what we are up to. Perhaps we are better off admitting to both personal and professional leanings in this regard—as fellow humans and as social researchers—making sure they are seen in context. Our interest in what others do certainly extends beyond a strictly prurient one—virtually everything that humans do is of potential interest to us. Whatever it is, we would like to see how they do it, especially if it is something that we also do, would like to do, or perhaps would like to help them not to do.

A fundamental curiosity about what others think and do, how they live their lives similarly to and differently from how I live my own, drew me to the study of cultural anthropology. I can live with being identified as a kind of licensed social voyeur, someone who wants to, and to some extent gets to, look at life in all (or much) of its intimacy. Maybe by simply bringing these aspects of fieldwork into the open we can keep them from seeming to be one of our darker preoccupations.

But I can and do draw the line between being a voyeur and being a Peeping Tom. A key word associated with the latter may help distinguish the darker dimensions from our everyday actions as fieldworkers. Although we sometimes use the expression "Peeping Tom" to refer to (or subtly reprimand) those prying into something not legitimately their business, specifically the label is directed at anyone who obtains sexual gratification by observing others surreptitiously, the chance of a glimpse of Lady Godiva replaced today with the caricature of an individual peeping through a bedroom window while someone disrobing inside remains unaware.

The catchword is "surreptitious." And that points to a darker, clandestine element in our work. It is not surreptitious observation itself that presents the problem but a recognition of when such observations are appropriate or acceptable and when they are not. As humans we are not above making surreptitious observations, but we certainly hate to get caught making them. If fieldworkers sometimes act like detectives, and are perhaps too often likened to spies, then a certain degree of stealth may be warranted. When those in the setting are observed and described naturally, we commend the stealth of the fieldworker.

In the name of ever-escalating national defense expenditures, huge sums have been directed in the past toward the development of stealth bombers and stealthy submarines that are difficult to detect. On the international scale, then, the art lies in knowing which side to get caught on! In fieldwork literature, it has not been many years since something as sinister sounding as "lurking" was presented as an appropriate fieldwork technique (see Strickland and Schlesinger 1969).

Issues related to disguised observation, both in general (e.g., Erickson 1967; Hilbert 1980; Roth 1962) and, in particular, the investigations of Laud Humphreys that culminated in *Tearoom Trade* (1989), have been part of the research dialogue for years. A realistic review and appraisal of the problems can be found in Richard Mitchell's *Secrecy and Fieldwork* (1993). Mitchell recognizes secrecy as "a pervasive feature of contemporary social life" (p. 1) and secrecy in research as "risky but necessary business" (p. 54). "If the social sciences are to continue to provide substantive, enduring insights in human experience," he continues, "timid inquiry will not do." Mitchell also cautions against confusing secretive research methods with harmful research results. He is neither an advocate of nor an apologist for deception; it is a fact of social life and therefore a fact of fieldwork life. The moral obligation of acting responsibly remains on the shoulders of the individual fieldworker.

Proceed with Caution

Of course there are counterpoints to be offered for each problem I have raised, just as it is tempting to insist Not me! to each accusation. Conversely, one might draw longer lists (see, for example, Gary Fine's "Ten Lies of Ethnography," 1993), or more damning ones. My purpose is achieved in emphasizing that our high calling has its own dark underside, especially as seen by outsiders put at risk because of our inquiries and sometimes amazed at both our self-righteousness and our audacity.

I think we had best soft-pedal our claims of righteousness. We do what we do, create what we create. We should take pride in doing it well. But it's not a bad idea now and then to take a look in that mirror we are so anxious to turn on others and to face some of the tensions in a role that we often need to explain and occasionally to defend. Our collective ambivalence can show up in the labels we apply or deny, as, for example, when anthropologists in the field refer to themselves as sociologists or linguists, yet take umbrage when journalists or others pose as anthropologists. We are all engaged with both the professional and personal dimensions of impression management.

In her monograph *Surviving Fieldwork*, Nancy Howell states that about 25 percent of her sample of cultural anthropologists report having been suspected of spying (1990:97), which, as she points out, is "a difficult charge to defend against when one is there in search of information." Far better, I think, to have a realistic picture of how others sometimes see us than the Pollyannaish one we might prefer to think we have created. As with others, our work and our ways of working must speak for themselves.

But understand this: To some degree deception is always involved in the research humans carry out with other humans. It is not something we try to rise above; it is something we must learn to live with. I return to it in the closing chapter to help you recognize it and cope with it, not as something negative, but as part of a broader talent each of us needs to develop—the art of discretion.

PART III
FIELDWORK AS MINDWORK

Without an ethnographer, there is no ethnography.

—Paul Bohannan, *How Culture Works*, p. 157

Fieldwork is a state of mind and something you put your mind to. Whatever goes on in your mind as you prepare for it, engage in it, reflect on it, and report it constitutes its essence. The previous chapters directed attention toward the more interpersonal, physical, and mechanical aspects of fieldwork—social courtesies, gaining access, observing, asking, leave taking—moving your body through space to get to a suitable place at a suitable time. Careful attention to such details can get you properly located with a willing informant or in an appropriate setting, perhaps a video or tape recorder at the ready, along with your trusty notebook. All very helpful, great for making you look like a fieldworker.

But what counts—the only thing that really counts—is what is going on in your mind, your sense of purpose among an infinite number of purposes that might be accomplished. I can't state it any better than the way I heard it years ago during the premier season of the TV series "NYPD Blue," when its redheaded protagonist, Detective Kelly, turned to another character and asked succinctly, "What do you want to accomplish?"

What do you want to accomplish? We have some slightly fancier terms—*problem finding, problem posing, problem seeking*—but they all address the same concern. Problem finding, rather than problem seeking, is at the core of the creative process—for artist and scientist alike (see Freeman 1993; Getzels and Csikszentmihalyi 1976).

My mentor, George Spindler, used to call this "the problem problem." During a period when he and Louise Spindler assumed editorship of the *American Anthropologist*, they became acutely aware of what other anthropologists were investigating and, especially, how those others went about reporting to their peers. The Spindlers were intrigued that drafts submitted for review often lacked focus, taking on the air of "haphazard descriptiveness" that is an occupational hazard for anyone who engages in this work. The Spindlers' writerly advice, included with the inevitable letter of rejection for such manuscripts, was that the author/researcher go back to the original problem statement, or refine or rework the problem statement that eventually evolved, so that it would bring the necessary focus to the process of revision. Their contributors needed to work through their problem problem.

Possibly the most serious misconception about qualitative research—and for those who harbor it, the biggest disappointment as well—has to do with how our research questions arise in the first place. What is the genesis of the problems we study? Somewhere out there lurks a wrongheaded notion that problems rise up before our eyes in a sort of intellectual equivalent of spontaneous combustion. That is not how it happens.

The problem problem is not embedded within the lives of those whom we study, demurely waiting to be discovered. Quite the opposite: We instigate the problems we investigate. There is no point in simply sitting by, passively waiting to see what a setting is going to tell us or hoping a problem will emerge. Yes, the Eskimo carver wonders aloud, "Who hides there?" but the answer is never "Ah! Giraffe" or "Ah! Missionary!" And there is no simple answer to the seemingly straightforward question, Just tell me the steps one follows in qualitative inquiry. What does one do first, what next? No theory. Just the steps.

When such questions come to us, typically disguised as questions of fieldwork technique, the answer is usually, It depends. The response is well intended but not always well received, for it is at once profound and exasperating. I have had occasion to use it often enough in these pages. The underlying point is that, except in the broadest of terms, fieldwork techniques cannot be distilled and described independently from the questions that guide the research. They are the tools of our trade. In the hands of an artist, tools of the trade produce art; in the hands of craftspeople, they produce craft. In the hands of the careless, they may even result in injury.

There are numerous fieldwork manuals, including those that outline explicit efforts to systematize fieldwork into neat sets of step-by-step sequences (see, for example, Fetterman 1989; Flick 1998; Kutsche 1998; Spradley 1979, 1980; Werner and Schoepfle 1987a, 1987b). Such manuals present some seasoned veterans' attempts to demystify fieldwork procedures and to guide novices in using the tools and techniques of field research. Regardless of how systematic such efforts may appear, they never achieve the meticulous algorithms and elegant formulae that give quantitative researchers an edge over what others perceive as our too-casual, too-vague approaches.

Not surprisingly, aspiring fieldworkers and seasoned veterans alike sometimes appear self-conscious about issues of method. They become defensive at any mention of a standard litany of conceptual issues such as reliability, generalizability, or objectivity. Therefore, the first problems I address in this section devoted to mindwork are matters for chapter 7, "The Art of (Conceptual) Self-Defense." I deal with these problems to offer both perspective and encouragement, for they seem forever to get in the way without any likelihood that they will ever go away. I then proceed (in chapters 8 and 9) to discuss the essential arts of conceptualization and write-up.

CHAPTER SEVEN
THE ART OF (CONCEPTUAL) SELF-DEFENSE

Certain problems keep recurring not only in the dialogue between quantitative and qualitative researchers but among qualitative researchers themselves. Fieldworkers need coping strategies for dealing with them. But they need not seek definitive answers that resolve such issues for all times, for these are the debates that surround the inquiry process itself. They are critical issues in the research dialogue, yet they are potentially subverting of that process whenever turned full force against any particular research effort, qualitative or quantitative.

My advice to beginning researchers is to be informed as to the substance of these debates rather than to be drawn prematurely into them. Leave them for others, or for yourself on a day when you are prepared to deal with issues on a grand scale rather than confronting a modest research task immediately at hand. Think of these issues as on a par with environmental protection, social justice, a world without war, or the ultimate answer to a question like, What is art? There are myriad issues, ethical, methodological, and philosophical, about which you may be asked or challenged to take a stand. When you are, you will be expected to have a thoughtful position, not to come up with the answer. Any of the dilemmas identified in the previous chapter can be posed either as a broad challenge to qualitative research in general or as a focused one addressing how you propose to approach your particular topic. The issues identified in this chapter are methodological in nature, the sort likely to occur in dialogue (or, sometimes, interrogation) between qualitative and quantitative researchers.

Do not get lured into believing that the entire rationale for qualitative approaches now rests on your shoulders alone or that until you have satisfactorily resolved each of these methodological perplexities, you may not proceed with your own research.

The issues to be raised here concern the scientific method, objectivity and bias, neutrality, reliability, validity, and generalization. The closely related issue of theory introduces the chapter that follows.

Scientific Method

There is not such a thing as a Scientific Method.

—P. B. Medawar
The Art of the Soluble, p. 148

In chapter 4, I inventoried some important techniques currently employed in the more scientific approaches to fieldwork. I did not inquire into the broader issue of "a" or "the" scientific method itself. What about the criticism one hears that fieldwork is the antithesis of scientific method, that quantitative approaches have all the method and fieldwork has none?

A method is a procedure, a technique, a way of doing something.

Fieldwork is a way of doing something.

As a way of doing something, fieldwork includes several rather standard techniques, all of which can be adapted for any particular setting as needed. All fieldwork techniques can be subsumed under the single heading "Participant Observation" or under two major headings if "Participant Observation" and "Interviewing" are paired off to become the dynamic duo of field research. The choice, as discussed in chapter 5, depends on whether one considers interviewing as the complement to participant observation or a major facet of it. Here I treat them separately.

The approaches to fieldwork are, in their almost infinite variations, alternatives rather than sequenced steps, choices among strategies rather than the selection of proper techniques. As George Homans observed years ago (1962), research is a matter of strategies, not of morals. Qualitative approaches avoid any semblance of the rigid, step-by-step sequence generally associated with tight research designs. They are intended to allow researchers to follow a suitable course of inquiry rather than to dictate in advance what that course should be. In essence, qualitative research, as Becker states it, is designed in the doing (1993:219). Although that makes fieldwork difficult to explain in the abstract, anyone who has engaged in it recognizes that in practice it can proceed no other way.

We should rejoice that we are not encumbered by the scientific method in pursuing our work, even while we may feel a bit of envy in recognizing how convenient and self-validating such recipes might be when trying to teach (or having to convince) others about how we proceed. It is easy for us to forget that scientists themselves are not particularly encumbered by the scientific method. As observers have pointed out, there is no particular incentive for those assumed to work under its aegis to tarnish their idealized reputation for systematic work, since it does not get in the way of practice. Paradoxically, the very idea that "real" scientists relentlessly follow the scientific method provides the cover that permits them to be more imaginative (and at times just plain bumbling), while the complementary idea that qualitative research is not guided by rigorous methodological doctrine is held up as one of our major shortcomings.

On the wall of my office I once hung a sign with the words of biologist Paul Weiss: "Nobody who followed the scientific method ever discovered anything interesting" (quoted in Keesing and Keesing 1971:10). It is hardly surprising that a biologist's comment about the scientific method is offered as solace for cultural anthropologists torn between wanting their discipline to be, as Eric Wolf stated years ago (1964:88), both the most scientific of the humanities and the most humanist of the sciences. Except perhaps when lecturing or conversing with colleagues outside their discipline, cultural anthropologists have emphasized the results of their studies, be they findings or interpretations, rather than their methods. In recent years, however, method has come to assume a more prominent role in their dialogue, a preoccupation that has tended to divide them into two camps, those concerned with methods and those concerned with those concerned with them.

Such methodological preoccupation has also found many anthropologists going farther afield, deeper into modes of analysis rather than deeper into fieldwork to achieve methodological sophistication. In the days when the phrase "participant observation" was explanation enough, advice as to how to go about it tended to be offhand: "Hang around." "Talk to folks." "Try to get a sense of what is going on." It was always pragmatic, sometimes too much so, as reflected in what Jean Jackson calls the "take-a-big-stick-for-the-dogs-and-lots-of-marmalade" jokes (1990:24). Sometimes these were humorously profound, as with Radcliffe-Brown's purported advice, "Get a large notebook and start in the middle because you never know which way things will develop" (quoted in Rubinstein 1991:14). Any such advice was intended to bolster confidence in the fieldworker. It was not intended to reassure fieldworkers or their critics that they were going about their work in the right way.

Nevertheless, fieldworkers do become self-conscious whenever method is at issue. Scientific methods in general, and the essentially mythical Scientific Method in particular, continue to hang as specters over our efforts. What is our equivalent? The unscientific or nonscientific method? The humanistic method? The rejection-of-method method or the absence-of-method method?

It may be comforting to keep in mind that even the most scientific of research procedures, regardless of how systematic and objective, can be neither perfectly systematic nor ultimately objective. Descriptive studies of how laboratory science proceeds remind us that on close inspection the investigative process is (of necessity) totally susceptible to human judgment, a product of social construction subject even to plain old down-and-dirty politics (see, for example, studies by Fleck 1979; Latour 1987; Latour and Woolgar 1986; Woolgar 1983). It is the insistent demand of outsiders for the guided tour of the laboratory and a proven formula for discovery ("just tell me the steps you follow") that traps researchers of all persuasions into portraying as a neat, linear, logical sequence what is, in fact, a dialectical process in which all critical judgments are made by humans. "All worldly truth," Jack Douglas states boldly, "rests ultimately on direct individual experience" (1976:6).

So exactly what are we being defensive about? Insight, intuition, imagination, luck—yes, even serendipity—each is critical to any discovery process, ours no more than theirs. The phrase "scientific breakthrough" nicely credits scientists for maintaining control, always knowing where they are going, although I recall Professor Aubrey Haan suggesting years ago that "scientific fall-through" might be the more appropriate phrase in most cases. The critical art in all observation is achieved not in the act of observing but in recognizing when something of significance has been observed.

Fieldwork proceeds that way, too, not simply through observation but in recognizing when something of significance—of potential significance—has been observed. The difference is that we try to exert as little interference as possible. We typically deny any suggestion of our own power and authority even when made uncomfortably aware of our advantaged status in the settings we study.

Tight research designs strike me as a good strategy for researchers who need to exert control over what they study, both control *of* and control *for*. Qualitative approaches represent a different way to achieve a different kind of understanding, one that appeals to those who find satisfaction in the discovery of what is going on without the hope of achieving the authority of cause-and-effect studies. Every way of knowing has its place. Science cannot proceed without controlled experimentation, but neither science nor controlled experimentation can reveal all we seek to understand about ourselves and our fellow humans.

Objectivity and Bias

"Objectivity" is perhaps best seen as a label to hide problems in the social sciences.

—Michael H. Agar
The Professional Stranger, p. 91

The process of forming links between ideas in the observer's mind and what one has observed is dialectical: Ideas inform observations and observations inform ideas. The prime mover in the process is the researcher. Whatever constitutes the elusive quality called "objectivity," mindlessness is not part of it.

Observation cannot proceed without an idea in the observer's mind of what to look at and for in qualitative research any more than in quantitative. This runs counter to claims made on behalf of objectivity (and, by extension, to warnings about the evil influences of bias) and stated in strong terms, such as this declaration by ethologist Konrad Lorenz, writing on behalf of an outdated position that claimed more for observation than it could ever hope to achieve:

> It is an inviolable law of inductive natural science that it has to *begin* with pure observation, totally devoid of any preconceived theory and even working hypotheses. [1950:232]

Another ethologist, C. G. Beer, my source for the above quotation (1973:49), cogently presents the counter view to that of Lorenz, whose position he dismisses lightheartedly as the "doctrine of immaculate perception." Beer cites philosopher of science Karl Popper, who argues that "preconceived theories or working hypotheses must always be involved in scientific observation to enable the scientist to decide what is to count as a fact of relevance to his investigation" (p. 49).

Malinowski tried to put preconceived ideas to rest more than eighty years ago, dismissing them as pernicious, in contrast to what he called "foreshadowed problems," which he endorsed as "the main endowment of a scientific thinker" (1922:9). For a long while the distinction caught the attention of other fieldworkers, but it proved too facile. Beer and other observers were more instructive in equating preconceived ideas with the working hypotheses essential to scientific observation. Scientists like the word "hypothesis." I take pleasure in substituting a different label, "bias."

Rather than dismiss bias as something we should guard against, I have come to think of it not only as something we must live with but as something we cannot do without. Bias reflects prior judgments that speed us along toward new objectives without having to reconsider every decision we have already made along the way. Think of it as comparable to selecting among the options in your computer's Preferences menu, allowing you to proceed without having to rethink every previous choice you have already made, choices that constitute your modus operandi.

Bias itself is not the problem, but one's purposes and assumptions need to be made explicit and used judiciously to give meaning and focus to a study. As long as it is fully explicated, bias should never get in the way. It offers an answer to the criticism voiced by insiders who claim that only they can understand their own group. Bias requires us to identify the perspective we bring to our studies as insiders or outsiders and to anticipate how that affects what we report.

Its counterpart, prejudice, is our true foe, judgment formed without examining its roots. If you can distinguish your prejudices from your biases, let the former guide you away from topics on which your opinions are likely to interfere with, possibly even obscure, your discoveries. But covet your biases, display them openly, and ponder how they help you formulate the purposes of your investigation and show how you can advance your inquiries. With biases firmly in place, you won't have to pretend to complete objectivity either. Try instead for what Margaret Mead described as "disciplined subjectivity" rather than a pretense of objectivity (quoted in M. C. Bateson 1977:71). No artist could wish for more!

Neutrality

Whereas traditional researchers cling to the guard rail of neutrality, critical researchers frequently announce their partisanship in the struggle for a better world.

—Joe Kincheloe and Peter McLaren
"Rethinking Critical Theory and Qualitative Research," p. 140

At one time I harbored the misconception that neutrality was another essential element in descriptive research. Neutrality held that in order to be fair, one had to regard all humans with equal esteem—the anthropological proclivity for "deferred judgment" run amok. An experienced fieldworker, John Connolly, raised for me the question of whether one really needed to be neutral in order to be objective. I was having enough trouble trying to sort out what being objective meant, especially in the subjective and sensitive business of humans observing and interpreting the behavior of other humans. But I admit I was relieved to realize that having likes or dislikes—a rather human quality in which I have been known to overindulge—did not perforce exempt me from doing fieldwork.

I recall my dismay that Jules Henry had allowed himself what seemed too free a rein in presenting his "passionate ethnography" of American society, *Culture against Man* (1963). A decade later, Colin Turnbull was roundly criticized not only for his negative portrayal of the Ik (Turnbull 1972; see also Grinker 2000) but for revealing personal disaffection for them, violating the anthropological canon of deferred judgment. Since those works were published we have seen innumerable instances in which personal preferences have provided anthropologists the impetus for writing their accounts.

A wave of postmodernists even insisted that the only understanding a fieldworker could gain in the course of research was of himself or herself. For a while, it seemed that anthropologists might become so taken with describing their own feelings that fieldwork would be nothing more than a vehicle for self-understanding. Perhaps a time of self-reflection (bordering on self-absorption) was inevitable after so long a period in which fieldworkers were not expected to demonstrate any feelings at all. In that earlier day anything recorded privately in diaries or personal correspondence was usually published as a separate memoir or remained privileged information forever (see Bruner 1993).

I take deep and genuine interest in the people and settings I have written about. I have learned to recognize and to appreciate in those feelings a source of energy for conducting my studies. My feelings have not always been positive, and I have never known any group of people that did not have its share of rogues and rascals, most certainly including some of my associates in academia. Nevertheless, I cannot imagine initiating a study in which I had no personal feelings, felt no interest or concern for the humans whose lives touched mine, or failed to find in those concerns a vital source of inspiration and energy. Neutrality is another of those topics we must be able to address without having to embrace.

Reliability

Reliability preoccupies those who hold anthropology to be a behavioral science, and who thus place severe limits on what the ethnographic method should include. It is a valuable quality in laboratory, medical and product safety research, and in some social research operations.

—Roger Sanjek
"The Ethnographic Present," p. 620

Reliability remains beyond the pale for research based on observation in natural settings. That is unfortunate, for it is difficult to escape the suggestion that if our work is not reliable, then it must be unreliable. Its technical meaning in the lexicon of researchers, as Jerome Kirk and Marc Miller define it, is closer to "replicability" or "consistency," "the extent to which a measurement procedure yields the same answer however and whenever it is carried out" (1986:19). In order to achieve reliability in that technical sense, a researcher has to manipulate conditions so that replicability can be assessed. Ordinarily, fieldworkers do not try to make things happen at all, but whatever the circumstances, we most certainly cannot make them happen twice. And if something does happen more than once, we never for a minute insist that the repetition be exact. As James Fernandez observes, "We anthropologists have long had the Heraclitean understanding that we cannot step into the same stream twice" (1994:136).

Reliability and its partner, validity (to be discussed next) are frequently cited as critical components of research and are sometimes described as complementary aspects of objectivity (Kirk and Miller 1986:19). It is awkward to have to admit to strict adherents of the quantitative tradition that fieldwork does not lend itself to reliability. But I have never been all that convinced that reliability necessarily serves quantitative researchers well, either.

The problem with reliability is that the rigor associated with it redirects attention to research processes rather than to research results. Similarity of responses is taken to be the same as accuracy of responses. The problem with equating them is that one might obtain consistent temperature findings consistently in error due to a faulty thermometer, obtain consistent responses to survey questions that make no sense to respondents, or obtain consistent ratings among raters trained to look for the same things in the same way, in each instance achieving a high degree of reliability because of unreliable data. The strain for identifying consistency in findings thus yields to establishing consistency through procedures. Reliability is, therefore, an artifact.

We need to recognize the circumstances that render reliability essentially irrelevant as a central concern in fieldwork; we do not need to apologize for it. Kirk and Miller recommend that we handle the problem through carefully documented ethnographic decision making (1986:73). I heartily concur as to the value of documentation, but I am not convinced that it solves the issue of reliability. Nor am I convinced that we need to address reliability at all, except to make sure that our audiences understand why it is not an appropriate measure for evaluating fieldwork.

That is not to say that reliability in this technical sense is out of the question. Certainly some of the systematic data we gather are amenable to statistical treatment. For anyone concerned primarily with reliability, however, I think the more systematic methods for data-gathering have far greater appeal than the kind of fieldwork I am advocating in which we try to be right but do not turn to statistical manipulations to validate our claims.

Validity

What the ethnographic method aims to achieve are accounts that support the claims they make. In terms of validity, there *are* better and worse ethnographic accounts.

—Roger Sanjek
"The Ethnographic Present," p. 621

Although fieldwork should yield highly valid results, I have argued elsewhere against the relevance of validity as a criterion measure in qualitative research (HFW 1990). Yet I find validity to be a more robust concept than reliability, one to confront boldly if we must confront it at all. Whether to confront it brings us again to the issue of whether we are willing to accept the language of quantitative researchers as the language of all research, or whether different approaches, like different art forms, warrant different evaluative criteria. To me, a discussion of validity signals a retreat to that preexisting vocabulary originally designed to lend precision to one arena of dialogue and too casually assumed to be adequate for another.

As originally employed in its technical sense, validity asks whether a researcher has measured what the research purports to measure. That issue is of vital significance, yet in practice validity is nowhere near as rigorous as reliability. Instead of generating coefficients that allow numerical comparisons, validity is more akin to a property like neatness, where one thing may be recognized as neater than another but nothing achieves absolute neatness.

But validity has taken on wider meaning; today it is associated more closely with truth value—the correspondence between research and the real world—rather than limited to measurement. To illustrate: The underlying question of the validity of an IQ test is related not only to performance as revealed by an individual's test score, but to the larger issue of whether the test has tapped into something as complex as intelligence.

Clearly, our "I was there" approach to research positions us well in terms of the potential truth value or warranted assertability of our reports. They should be substantially accurate and substantially complete—in spite of the fact that sometimes they are not. We can, and often do, make the validity claim. Anthropologists Pertti and Gretel Pelto offer an argument on its behalf:

> "Validity" refers to the degree to which scientific observations actually measure or record what they purport to measure. . . . In their field research anthropologists have invested much effort to achieve validity, for we generally assume that a long-term stay in a community facilitates the differentiation of what is valid from what is not, and the assembling of contextual supporting information to buttress claims to validity. [1978:33]

A question that remains is whether we need such a claim at all. Anthropologists like the Peltos have worked on behalf of a more scientific anthropology and thus a more systematic approach to fieldwork. They strive for validity. Fieldworkers as strongly committed to the *art* of fieldwork might instead be content to remind a reader that while their stay in the field was long, it could never be long enough. They would be less insistent about their ability to differentiate between what is valid and what is not, holding instead that whatever information they provide offers illustration but in no way constitutes proof.

Validity can be dismissed, but does not go away; qualitative researchers may find comfort in Russ Bernard's observation that validity is never demonstrated, only made more likely (1994b:42). Fieldworkers need to be able to speak to the issue of what they do on behalf of making the truth value of their accounts more likely or more *credible,* Egon Guba's suggested alternative term for internal validity (1981). Similarly, they must be able to address issues of external validity and generalization, or *transferability,* again Guba's suggested alternative term. Such issues can and should be addressed, but they are better regarded as an invitation to dialogue rather than as a barrier to research. We can demonstrate our willingness to join the dialogue; we need not be distracted or intimidated by it. Pulling off such a feat while one is still discovering which terms must be addressed requires some artistry at game playing. One needs time to figure out how the game is played before deciding whether and how to participate.

Generalization

Whatever the approach, ethnography is always more than description. Ethnography is also a way of generalizing. This way differs from the standard scientific model, however, and in some ways is closer to the arts. . . . As in good literature, so in good ethnography the message comes not through explicit statement of generalities but as concrete portrayal.

—James L. Peacock
The Anthropological Lens, p. 83

Although issues underlying any of the topics addressed here pose serious problems, debate about them often takes on a sophomoric quality, with neither side really listening to the other or appearing to comprehend the existence of an alternative view. Objectivity, for example, is often argued as being attainable or unattainable; there is no middle ground. Qualitative researchers need to understand what the debate is about and to have a position; they do not have to resolve the issues. As Howard Becker notes about all such epistemological issues underlying research, "If we haven't settled them definitively in two thousand years, more or less, we probably aren't ever going to settle them. These are simply the commonplaces, in the rhetorical sense, of scientific talk in the social sciences, the framework in which debate goes on" (1993:219).

Generalization is another of these epistemological issues, but I find it more worrisome than those already reviewed. It raises a fundamental issue in qualitative work where we invariably look at one of something or at a single case. Even when we are cajoled into increasing our *N*s, perhaps to do three, four, or five little case studies instead of devoting rapt attention to one, we are always disadvantaged by our inability to generalize. That disadvantage raises the critical question, What can we learn from studying only one of anything?

My immediate and perhaps too-glib answer to that question bespeaks my strategy toward all such questions rooted so solidly in a positivist orientation. What can we learn from studying only one of anything? All that we can!

The quick counteroffensive is a good device, and the response "All we can" is enough to cut short a diatribe, although admittedly it is only the beginning of an adequate answer. Most certainly we need to demonstrate how our cases contribute to some larger picture. We are particularly in need of such explanation, given the paucity of our efforts to date to aggregate myriad case studies into some bigger picture. Once again we find ourselves figuratively trying to fill the Grand Canyon with popcorn, one piece at a time.

Were the question posed in slightly different terms to ask, How do you generalize from a qualitative study? you might answer candidly and succinctly, "You don't." That is a safe and accurate answer. It is the basis on which American anthropology was founded under Franz Boas. With an empiricism directed toward rigorous historical particularism, Boas insisted that no generalizations were warranted from the study of any particular society.

As a discipline, anthropology was founded on the horns of a dilemma that committed it to the detailed study of individual societies while professing passionate concern for all humankind. The inevitable resolution was, and is, to maintain two camps, one more inclined toward postpositivist scientific practices that examine frequencies and distributions from which generalizations are deemed to be warranted, the other more attentive to interpretivist meanings and symbols played out in the course of individual cases and lives. Depending on purposes, to some extent the two can be reconciled, but a preoccupation with eclecticism obscures attention that should be directed toward purposes themselves.

I am inclined to treat generalization as something desirable yet always beyond my grasp. I have never studied more than one of anything and always at a particular point in time. Someone who recalled hearing me make that statement asked, "Didn't I hear you say you have never studied more than one person at a time?" With a major effort devoted to the ethnography of one school principal (1973) and another devoted to an account of the Sneaky Kid (1994b, 2002), that impression (generalization?) might have seemed warranted, but it was not correct. What I meant to say, and here make a matter of record, is that the unit of study in my various efforts at field research has varied: one individual, one village, one institution (urban African beer drinking), the implementation of one educational innovation in one school system. Whatever can be learned from a well-contextualized study of a single case is the contribution that each of those studies has to offer.

If you are interested in averages, frequencies, distributions, and the like, my accounts are not a good source. If you want to know about an instance of something I have studied, my reports should be a rich resource, and that suggests a reasonable criterion by which to judge them. In each of those studies I make a few generalizations, implicate a few more, and leave to readers the challenge of making further ones depending on their own concerns and prior experiences.

Years ago my attention was called to a statement about generalization that I have always kept as a guideline. It was penned by Clyde Kluckhohn and Henry Murray (1948:35) to introduce their coauthored chapter on personality formation and, except for now-outmoded gender language, still represents an elegant way to think about the individual and society, the nexus between the one and the many.

> Every man is in certain respects
> a. like all other men,
> b. like some other men,
> c. like no other man.

In any fieldwork I have conducted, I have substituted my unit of study into Kluckhohn and Murray's aphorism and thereby felt some freedom in offering whatever generalizations seem warranted. I regarded the Kwakiutl village and school of my first fieldwork to be a village and school in certain respects like all other villages and their schools, in certain respects like some other villages and their schools, and in certain respects like no other village and its school. There seemed little point in spending an entire year as a village teacher and a participant observer in village life, then devoting another year to writing up an account, if nothing was to be learned that might be of relevance to other villages and their schools as well.

At the same time, I did not want to claim that the village was typical or representative. There were many ways in which it did not seem typical even among other Kwakiutl villages, let alone villages in other First Nations communities. Nor was I able to exert any influence over my assignment other than to put myself in the hands of Lyman Jampolsky, director of Indian education in British Columbia at the time, to request an appropriate village placement for me: a single male teacher (thus a one-teacher school) in a region under Anglican rather than Catholic jurisdiction. To an American raised under the strict separation of church and state, it seemed shocking that my religious affiliation was a major criterion affecting my teaching assignment.

Like many qualitative researchers, I pretty much had to take potluck as to where I would be assigned, making the best of whatever opportunities the assignment afforded rather than trying to find a site that I could defend as typical. Instead I needed to specify how the village and school to which I was assigned fit within some broader set of categories. This idea, a sort of artful end run around the sampling problem, followed advice written by Margaret Mead in 1953 to explain how researchers in natural settings can address issues of sampling when sampling itself is neither practical nor possible. Her essay concerned the issue facing Kluckhohn and Murray quoted above: How can we arrive at statements about groups of people when we meet them only individually, and thus, how can we deal with representativeness?

> Anthropological sampling is not a poor and inadequate version of sociological or sociopsychological sampling, a version where *n* equals too few cases. *It is simply a different kind of sampling,* in which the validity of the sample depends not so much upon the number of cases as upon the proper specification of the informant, so that he or she can be accurately placed, in terms of a very large number of variables. . . . Each informant is studied as a perfect example, an organic representation of his complete cultural experience. [Mead 1953:654–55; italics in original]

Mead turned the sampling issue on its head, suggesting that in fieldwork we ask how the instances we have to report fit into some larger picture. Unable to control the sampling procedure itself, as fieldworkers we redefine the problem to fit the circumstances under which we are likely to obtain not only our informants but our research sites. We do not presume to identify the typical informant or village or setting; instead, we ask how our informant or village or setting fits into the larger scheme of things. To what extent is the one in some important ways like the many?

This way of approaching generalization asks the researcher to make what seems an essentially artistic choice between emphasizing how the single case informs more generally or how its uniqueness must be cherished. In my Sneaky Kid account, I came down on the side of the former, emphasizing that although his story was unique, it was not an isolated case. I drew on Clifford Geertz for the authoritative footnote: "The important thing about the anthropologist's findings is their complex specificness, their circumstantiality" (Geertz 1973:23). That "complex specificness" remains the heart of the matter, the characteristic of a fieldwork approach. While the effective story should be "specific and circumstantial," its relevance in a broader context should also be apparent. The story must transcend its own modest origins. The case remains particular, its implications broad (HFW 1983a:28).

Some fieldworkers play a more cautious hand, underscoring that they have not tried to find the typical informant and do not want to detract from the uniqueness of the case. I know of no better example than the way anthropologist Sidney Mintz introduces his key informant, Taso, in *Workers in the Cane*. This is a statement to which I referred students who got caught up in this question of typicality:

> He is not an "average" anything—neither an average man, nor an average Puerto Rican, nor an average Puerto Rican lower-class sugar cane worker. He has lived just one life and not all of that. He doesn't think of himself as representative of anything, and he is right. His solutions to life's problems may not be the best ones, either, but he seems satisfied with his choices. I have tried to put down his story in the context of what I could understand about the circumstances under which he lived and lives. [1974(1960):11]

It is interesting to realize how persuasive a powerfully written statement can be. Mintz steered clear of seeming to write about "some other men" in his portrayal; the story was Taso's own. When invited to write a preface for a reissue of the account a number of years later, however, Mintz confounded the question, seeming to want to portray Taso as average but not typical. (I think I might have wanted to write it the other way around: typical but not average.)

In fact, except for his very unusual intelligence, Taso might be described as quite average in nearly every way. This, then, is the autobiography of an average man. But I tried to make clear when I first wrote the book that this emphatically does not mean that Taso is "typical," representative of others, or ordinary; and in these regards, the book—and Taso's own words—must stand on their own account. [Mintz 1974:ix]

In preparing our cases we, too, want to have it both ways. Each case is unique, yet not so unique that we cannot learn from it and apply its lessons more generally. We are provided a way out of our seeming ambivalence if we resist the trap of an either/or position, keeping in mind Kluckhohn and Murray's aphorism, broadly restated, that every case is, in certain aspects, like all other cases, like some other cases, and like no other case.

Self-Defense versus Getting Defensive

I have identified certain topics—scientific method, objectivity and bias, neutrality, reliability, validity, generalization—because they are problematic in field-oriented research. Individually and collectively we need to be thoughtfully aware of them, to have a sense of the underlying problems they point to and a working resolution for them. My call is for fieldworkers to be well coached in the art of self-defense, intrigued with, rather than defensive about, epistemological issues.

Neophyte researchers also need to be attentive to the research climate in which they propose their inquiries. You are not likely to be lauded for your creativity in conceptualization if your audience is hammering away at you about objectivity and reliability. I have not meant to give false hope that such methodological issues can be brushed aside. When they are placed more like barriers than hurdles, challenges to help you achieve better clarity of purpose, you should weigh the wisdom of pursuing a qualitative approach at that place or in that moment. Artists and fieldworkers alike must find a receptive audience for their efforts.

The issue of theory follows hard on the heels of topics discussed here. Issues concerning theory cannot be sidestepped by the individual fieldworker, regardless of how basically descriptive or atheoretical he or she might claim to be. I turn to that topic to begin a new chapter and continue this discussion of fieldwork as mindwork.

CHAPTER EIGHT
THE ART OF CONCEPTUALIZING

In questions of art, learning is a sort of defeat; it illuminates what is by no means the most subtle, and penetrates to what is by no means the most significant. It substitutes theories for feelings and replaces a sense of marvel with a prodigious memory. It amounts to an endless library annexed to a vast museum: Venus transformed into a document.

—Paul Valéry
quoted in S. Price, *Primitive Art in Civilized Places*, p. 12

I defend my compulsion to collect ethnographic data. I believe it is done less by anthropologists today than by those of my generation, which was not so much concerned with theory. . . . Except those of recent years, my publications are heavy in ethnography, and much of the theory is implied, covert, or shyly presented.

—Simon Ottenberg
"Thirty Years of Fieldnotes," pp. 150–51

The original working title for this chapter included the words "conceptualization" and "design." Both words point to what I want to discuss. Yet it seemed strange to be discussing design, for in its research sense I associate the term with tight, formal experimental or "treatment" studies, the very antithesis of fieldwork. If, as Howard Becker suggests, a distinguishing feature of qualitative research is that our studies are designed in the making, then design has at least one special meaning among fieldworkers, to refer to an ongoing process rather than a fait accompli.

John Creswell, a colleague equally receptive to qualitative and quantitative approaches (see Creswell 1998; 2003), tells me that when discussing aspects of research design, he asks his students to think of research as involving choices and applications among compositional techniques. He sees the process of composing a study as akin to composing a piece of music or a painting. I like that analogy. Without diminishing the importance of assembling the necessary raw materials or having the requisite skills for blending them in a final composition, it underscores a critical component of inquiry, the ability to generate ideas that prompt and guide inquiry.

The analogy with music is also a subtle reminder that neither materials alone, nor skills alone, nor technique alone, is sufficient. Everything must come together under the genius of the composer or the artist at the easel. Stephen Sondheim's musical *Sunday in the Park with George* becomes *Monday at the Site with Mead* or *Malinowski:* Order. Design. Tension. Balance. Harmony. So many possibilities, yes, but someone must be able to bring them together to achieve a clear purpose.

"The Art of Conceptualizing" as used here refers to how fieldworkers put together—how they compose—studies in the absence of tight, formal designs. But no purposeful inquiry proceeds without conceptual underpinnings of some sort. So what is it that fieldworkers do that is comparable to what researchers of other persuasions call "design"? We can begin by looking at the role of theory.

Theories are always being contested in the social sciences. In art worlds, by contrast, I have the impression that more often it is theory itself—its role and significance—that is contested. Performance or product is what matters, not how one gets there. In Paul Valéry's words, one does not substitute theories for feelings. Artists whose work draws inspiration solely from theory or method raise suspicion that creativity itself may be in short supply.

The art metaphor invites that different perspective. At the least, the role of theory appears less heavy-handed when analogies are drawn to art rather than to science. The arts have their theories and their theorists, to be sure, but they also have their movements, periods, eras, and schools. There are many ways to categorize these styles and periods. We are more accustomed to hearing them identified with descriptive titles or historical periods—the romantic period, the impressionists, the Dutch masters—than with some latter-day scholar's efforts to impose a theoretical label on them. Postmodernism itself, today closely associated with music and literature, began as a style and movement in architecture, a rejection of an earlier modernist era with its "rules, geometric order, and austerity" (Kottak 1994:12n).

I find it refreshing to think of the preoccupation with theory as a relative newcomer, a recent era, rather than as what every fieldworker has been doing all along without knowing it. That is not to insist that old-time fieldworkers did not think about what they were doing. Nor were they reticent about using terms like *theory, hypothesis,* or *proposition.* They simply were not as preoccupied with making theory explicit as we are today.

This is not to suggest that the current preoccupation is a passing fad, for theory provides a kind of clearinghouse and lingua franca for inquiry across disciplines as well as within them, and we are entering the era of the Great Interface. The pursuit of theory has a unifying effect even in the absence of a unifying theory itself. Theory provides a focused way for us to talk to each other—and to ourselves—about what we are up to. It also provides a way of linking past and present, since we can attribute implicit theory to the lives and works of our forebears just as we can attribute implicit culture to them. But the self-conscious insistence on having and using explicit theory and using theory explicitly is *one* way, not the only way, to pursue fieldwork. That insistence is another reminder of how wholeheartedly we have bought into the scientific paradigm. It is the task that theory addresses, not theory itself, that must be attended to.

We do not beat upon, or beat up on, composers or painters or sculptors to declare their theories before we allow them to proceed with their works. Indeed, artists who lean on theory to explain what they are up to may raise the suspicion that whatever artistic experience they are about to introduce is more likely to be good for, rather than pleasing to, an audience. Theory offers no magic or guarantee of quality in the art world.

Reflecting on "Thirty Years of Fieldnotes," Simon Ottenberg refers to theory in his own writing as "implied, covert, or shyly presented," suggesting how recently theory has come to occupy so central a role (1990:150–51). The thirty years of Ottenberg's field notes are roughly the years of my field notes as well, and I, too, have boasted of the same theoretical nonchalance with which Ottenberg describes all but his most recent work.

The point of my foray into art worlds in chapter 3 was to underscore how the art that any individual produces is like the work of his or her fellow artists because it is produced in a social milieu. In a similar manner, today's fieldworkers scurry about in search of appropriate theory because that is what they are expected to do and what everyone else seems to be doing. But it has not always been so. I remember being startled to learn of a book by anthropologist David Bidney with a title that struck me as an oxymoron: *Theoretical Anthropology*. Apparently that book, although originally published in 1953 and reissued in paperback in 1967, never gained a wide audience among anthropologists, at least among the earlier fieldwork-oriented ones.

In those earlier days, theory was not so imposing and was never a prerequisite to fieldwork. But thinking was! In proposing a dissertation study in the early 1960s, I was expected to come up with a conceptual orientation, not a theoretical one. As a result, I have always been comfortable with the idea that conceptual frameworks are sufficient. I do not bully others about theory and am unswayed by those who would bully me. Acculturation studies were then in vogue; they provided sufficient links to a broad social problem and a body of ongoing work in cultural dynamics and culture change. Today that same research effort and setting would—and easily could—be translated into some highfalutin theoretical framework. But the essence is this: I had an idea of what in particular I would be looking at within the broader context of an ethnographic account of a contemporary Kwakiutl village and its school.

Ottenberg goes on to make an interesting comparison between broad ethnographic inquiries and the more problem-focused studies that began to take explicit form in the work of Margaret Mead, although they have always been inherent in the ethnographic task itself. Ottenberg offers this explanation as to why his own publications seem "heavy in ethnography."

> This suggests a hypothesis: those who produce ethnographic, nontheoretically oriented notes will produce ethnographic writings; those who produce problem-oriented or theoretically directed notes will produce like writings. [1990:151]

I don't know why Ottenberg felt that he needed to present his you-are-what-you-write idea in the form of a hypothesis (unless it was because everybody was doing it), but I liked the contrast he suggested between broadly descriptive studies and problem-oriented or theoretically directed ones. I think a clear distinction is warranted between these latter two as well; problem-driven and theoretically driven studies should not be confused with each other. One certainly holds different expectations for a broadly descriptive approach (perhaps ethnographically oriented, perhaps not), a problem-oriented study, and a theoretically driven one. At the same time, we dare not lose sight of the overlap inherent in all field-oriented inquiry. A theoretically oriented or problem-oriented study must provide enough of the same context one expects from a broadly descriptive one, and a broadly descriptive study must provide an adequate description of its orienting concept or problem.

In the early "salvage ethnography" days, when anthropologists raced to record what they could save of relatively intact, relatively isolated societies, the imminent extinction anticipated for such groups was deemed problem enough. Subsequently, writing at midcentury, John Bennett noted the tendency of American anthropologists to begin fieldwork with a particular problem and then gradually broaden their scope, while British anthropologists began with broad concerns and narrowed their scope as fieldwork progressed (see Sanjek 1990:226). Today's fieldworkers, looking more often into micro-cultural aspects of complex societies, can consider themselves fortunate not to have to fill the broad charter of producing holistic ethnographies as well. The fieldworker intent on producing a standard ethnography works with a set of categories that impose structure sufficient to set one purposefully at work for a lifetime. Painting by the numbers is still painting, at least by some definitions.

The art metaphor invites examination of whether we have alternatives to theory for positioning ourselves conceptually. I think we do employ other systems of categories, however informally or unconsciously. I noted earlier that we do not identify schools with the names of the great masters of fieldwork, yet we are not so far from doing so. Anthropologists and sociologists in some major departments exert enough influence that we literally tag their graduates and presume a certain likeness in their work, as, for example, among Columbia- or Chicago-trained scholars. If we do not exactly have a Malinowski school of fieldwork, virtually anyone whose work is discernibly functionalist tends to be regarded as following in that tradition. Recounting his own career history, George Peter Murdock once stated, "I have been, at different times and in different combinations, a cultural anthropologist, a functionalist, a structuralist, a comparativist, and even a historical anthropologist" (1971:17).

Although I enjoy tracing my academic lineage, I never regarded myself as belonging to a school. Perhaps that is not so much because of any conscious resistance to categories as to my uncompulsive nature about theory itself. Nonetheless, my categorizing colleagues are able to fit me into whatever schemes they propose, sometimes graciously discerning shifts in my work that seem to keep me current but actually remind me that I, too, am moved about by subtle forces. "For over three decades," writes one reviewer, "[Wolcott has] charted an interpretive, postpositivist approach to the anthropology of educational practices. . . . In this collection . . . he finally breaks from this tradition and openly embraces a fully post-foundational approach to validity and textual authority" (Denzin 1994b).

The approach I discuss will, I hope, reflect my casual attitude toward recognizing the role of theory as a driving force in fieldwork. I am tempted to match Ottenberg with a hypothesis of my own: The more strongly a researcher is drawn to theoretical issues, the less likely he or she will seek opportunity for sustained fieldwork; conversely, the more strongly one is drawn to fieldwork, the less one will look to theory for either orientation or explanation.

Theory

In theory, theory is as essential to the pursuit of qualitative research as it is to all research. Indeed, if we are to believe a pronouncement attributed to William James (noted in Agar 1996:75) that "you can't pick up rocks in a field without a theory," theory is precursor to any purposeful human activity.

In the abstract, the notion that theory underlies not only our activities as researchers but our every act as humans presents an intriguing way to interpret how we go about our daily lives. But enthusiasm for theory can quickly pale when a colleague, committee, or funding agency confronts you boldly with a suspicion posed as a question: "What is your theory?"

I see theory as another of the many issues that must be reckoned with by every fieldworker. There are several levels on which to address it. Theory is something like doing physical exercise or taking Vitamin C: Some people are hooked on it, even to excess, others give it as little conscious attention as possible, and no one can do without it entirely. That prompts a redefinition that at once elevates formal theory to what I call "capital 'T' Theory," or Grand Theory, and leaves numerous other terms more modest in scope—*hypotheses, ideas, assumptions, hunches, notions*—that also capture the essence of the mindwork that is critical to fieldwork.

As an ideal, "grand theory" stands clearly at the pinnacle. Grand theory offers the ultimate means to transcend the limits inherent in our modest individual efforts. It allows us to aggregate efforts, play them off against each other, and precipitate from our observations the essence of what is significant at some higher level of abstraction, perhaps embracing multiple cases by multiple observers over extended periods of time. It is the kind of activity for which we admire (and romanticize) people like Charles Darwin, whose contribution, Kluckhohn has noted, "was much less the accumulation of new knowledge than the creation of a theory which put in order data already known" (1949:23). Darwin was indeed a careful observer, but mindwork was his genius. Darwin himself reports that for his study *Coral Reefs*, his whole theory was thought out before he had ever seen one (Darwin 1969[1887]:98).

We must learn how to protect ourselves from being beaten down (or up) by insistence that every field study must be linked directly to theory. Theory is often employed as a sort of intellectual bludgeon, a killer term used to menace problem-focused neophytes and belittle efforts at applied or practical research. The theory question poses a dual challenge—on the one hand to come up with an original problem and a theoretically adequate approach to it and on the other to be able to demonstrate how a unique case is embedded in some larger concern related to a significant body of theory. For those not initially attracted to or comfortable with theory in the first place, nagging issues of what to do about theory never get answered to everyone's satisfaction, but neither do they ever go away. The essential thing is to learn how to deal with them in a professionally adequate manner to ensure either that theory serves to guide and clarify (rather than to intimidate) or that the orienting function that theory addresses is accomplished even in the absence of theory made explicit. As for using theory explicitly, however, my advice is, if it works for you, use it, but if it is only *making* work for you, get on with some more productive task instead (more discussion of this in HFW 2001:76).

The fact that you are reading *The Art of Fieldwork* may suggest that theory is not your long suit. You'd rather be out there doing research or wandering and pondering in a potential research site, not sitting in your office ruminating or grunting out some set of supposedly linked hypotheses that should subtly prove you right if they don't do you in by proving to be wrong. If so, strategies are indeed what you need. Let me propose some guiding questions, followed by a reminder of how theory can inform without intimidating.

First, you need to assess the nature and extent of your concern for (and commitment to) theory. Does theory embody the kind of contribution you want to make, as revealed perhaps in recognizing that you wouldn't mind having your name or work identified as So-and-so's [your name here] theory? If this is how you would like to be remembered, then you probably need to embrace the more systematic approaches to fieldwork and to evaluate critically whether there is much point in engaging in participant observation at all beyond its broad orienting function.

However, a concern for and intrigue with what theory is intended to do is critical to all inquiry processes. The descriptive task that anchors fieldwork is itself endless. Theory addresses the issue of sense making. It can keep us from getting caught up in rendering accounts dismissed as travelogues or personal diaries. As a fieldworker—a self-consciously self-appointed researcher—you are already in the business of sense making. Malinowski not only identified sense making as critical to the fieldwork task, but he made what anthropologist Edmund Leach has identified as "the theoretical assumption that the total field of data under the observation of the field-worker must somehow fit together and make sense" (1957:120, quoted in Sanjek 1990:211). That is what his concept of functionalism was intended to do. Functionalism still serves as a useful guide for fieldworkers, provided they recognize a critical distinction between asking how (and whether) things fit together and taking Malinowski too literally and insisting that everything does fit together, does make sense.

My sense of anthropologists in the days of old is that those willing to struggle with concepts and theory left more of a legacy than did those who got on splendidly with the natives. That is because they were struggling with the problem of sense making in the course of writing up their fieldwork, not making any particular theoretical contribution itself. Some of anthropology's brilliant writers did rather little fieldwork of their own (e.g., Ruth Benedict) or are reported to have failed at it miserably (e.g., Alexander Goldenweiser). Claude Lévi-Strauss must have surprised some readers with his candid revelation:

> Finally, why not admit it? I realized early on that I was a library man, not a fieldworker. . . . In the unforgiving landscape of central Brazil there was many a time I had the feeling I was wasting my life! . . . I did enough to learn and to understand what fieldwork is, which is an essential prerequisite for making a sound evaluation and use of the work done by others. [Lévi-Strauss and Eribon 1991:44–45]

To whatever extent the reverse is true—that there are successful in-the-field researchers who never published—there is, of course, little record, only apocryphal stories. Writers are still trying to correct a mistaken impression that Frank Cushing, an anthropologist often singled out to illustrate the dangers of "going native," never wrote anything about the Zuni among whom he lived and studied for four and a half years (cf. Green 1979; Sanjek 1990:189–92). Cushing is only one among many fieldworkers whose mostly unpublished accounts accompanied them to the grave.

In terms of personal careers, some field-oriented researchers have become more interested in applications of, and contributions to, theory with their own advancing seniority. That offers a nice balance as the youthful energy that drives fieldwork gradually gives way to more contemplative activities carried on at one's desk. I take solace from a few elders who have challenged the preeminence given to theory, similar to efforts directed at the concept of culture, not to eliminate it, but to cut it down to size. "Pete" Murdock, quoted above, was the first to come to my attention with his observation that good descriptive ethnography, which he lauded as "by far the greatest achievement in anthropology," has depended "remarkably little on the specific theoretical orientation of the observer" and manages to outlive whatever theory may have spawned it at the time (1971:17–18). Ottenberg asks, "Where are all the theories today that existed then (and some seemed quite exciting to me at the time)? They are gone, dead as a doornail" (1990:155).

A second question has to do with how one wants to play the theory game. At least one among my colleagues has made theory the driving force of an academic career and holds tenaciously not only to an evolving theory that has guided almost three decades of fieldwork but to a personal theory of careers as well—that one cannot make meaningful headway in a scientific career without a clearly conceived and carefully explicated theory. If such preoccupation with theory points to one extreme, my own seeming obliviousness to theory might be taken as the other. While my colleague has hammered away at grand (or "baby grand"?) theory, I have shied away even from what is known as middle-range theory, satisfied to work within conceptual frameworks like culture and, especially, cultural transmission and acquisition. I am pressed by journal editors and reviewers who insist that my writing should display greater theoretical sophistication. But I have seen too much phony theory and phony posturing about theory to feel defensive. I think theory is overrated in terms of what most of us actually accomplish through our research. In theory-driven descriptive accounts, theory is more apt to get in the way than to point the way, to tell rather than to ask what we have seen.

Watching a colleague wind up a career in which singular preoccupation with contributing a big theory may have misdirected more than it helped, I hardly advise others to follow that course. I remain fascinated with the potential of theory, but in my own work and the work of my students, I have been more than satisfied with, sometimes, a great notion, hunch, idea, or tentative interpretation. Maybe that is why I remain so respectful toward bias. I regard bias as entry-level theorizing, a well-thought-out position from which a researcher feels drawn to an issue or problem and seeks to construct a firmer basis in both knowledge and understanding.

A third question addresses when and how you want theory to play a role in your work. The logic crystallized in the scientific method suggests that it must come first, that everything proceeds from there. Committed believers concur. I have to agree, at least to the extent that we cannot initiate an inquiry without some idea of what we are looking for. But I am inclined to place those ideas along a scale of formality that reserves terms like *theory* or *hypothesis* for ideas formally stated. That leads me to propose a working definition: Theory is a way of asking that is accompanied by a reasonable answer.

If the research problem you intend to pursue is accompanied by a reasonable answer, you can proceed more or less theoretically, more if your answer is linked to some larger body of thought and prior work, less if the answer is your own modest hunch or hypothesis. Recognize, however, that you can proceed with fieldwork without a reasonable answer to the question(s) you are asking as long as you have a reasonable sense of how to proceed, how to focus attention. Descriptive research is purposive; it need not be pedantic. Something as casual as curiosity or uninformed bias might be sufficient to set off purposive inquiry. At the other extreme, so might a problem posed by a client or funding agency. Purposelessness—of the questions-asked-on-a-tour-bus variety—is the enemy. Explicit theory can be joined with fieldwork anywhere in the research process, from driving the inquiry in its initial stages to positing how it might help in situating a single case within some broader arena of concern.

When and how theory makes its real entry into the research process is often masked by the canons of reporting. This is especially so in the constricted format of thesis and dissertation writing, in which the typically tedious review of the literature in a traditionally perfunctory second chapter includes an equally tedious recital of relevant theory (see also HFW 2001, chapter 4). An alternative to this approach, one I have pressed upon students and recommended to colleagues, is to introduce theory into the account in whatever role it actually played during the field research and write-up. Because I have never badgered my students about theory, the issue of theory (and the review of related literature) often has been reserved for the closing chapters of a dissertation, where a self-conscious but genuine search for theoretical implications and links begins rather than ends. One unexpected dividend from paying more attention to how theory is used, rather than to how others say it should be used, has been the publication of a set of original papers in which qualitative researchers candidly review their personal struggles with theory in fieldwork (Flinders and Mills 1993).

I see this question of when to use theory as a choice between the alternatives of theory first or theory later. I state it that way to disabuse qualitative researchers of the notion that everything and everybody (else) begins with a full-blown and formally stated theory. Broadly conceived, little "t" theory, acknowledging the conceptual role underlying any purposive inquiry, has to be there somewhere in some form. That does not necessarily mean it can be, or needs to be, stated formally. When others, students especially, tell us they neither know nor would even recognize the theories that relate most closely to their research interests, we perform meritorious service when we point them in the direction we think their theoretical predilections lie. Or we can tease out—but only by way of example—where our own interests might lead. We should neither insist that students be able to orient themselves in theory—a creative intellectual endeavor in which we all continue to struggle, usually with limited success—nor impose our own pet theories. A student (or colleague) without a theory is in a far better position to discover (and eventually even appreciate) how theory serves than someone who has been given a theory by someone else, no matter how well intended the gift.

The fourth and final question is whether theory is better regarded in the singular or the plural. I find Johan Galtung's plea on behalf of theoretical pluralism refreshing. Galtung holds that our work should be guided by a family of perspectives, rather than by commitment to a single theory (Galtung 1990:101). And Fredrik Barth advises that theories are to be "explored and played with" (1994a:358), suggesting that even if we regard our theories as competing with each other, the competition need not be a somber one. Thinking of theory in multiples helps keep it off the pedestal that has made it so formidable for some researchers, beginners especially. It is tempting to offer the advice that if you are asked the killer question, "But what is your theory?" you respond, "I assume you mean what are my theories?" Whether you actually utter those words will, of course, be a matter of protocol. If you aren't in a position to say them, even thinking them may offer some comfort.

And how does theory serve the individual researcher? It serves in several practical ways, some of which are implied in the preceding discussion and all of which help to keep the focus and linkages of fieldwork and deskwork manageable. These objectives are also accomplished through citations to the relevant literature under circumstances when theory per se is not the issue as much as is the need for every researcher to be able to place his or her work within some broader context.

- Theory offers the convenience of labels that help researchers identify and link up with prior work, both their own and that of others, and to call their work to the attention of those who share common interests.

- Theory offers a way to gain a broader perspective or provide a broader application for single cases of modest scope, thus overcoming a major limitation of qualitative research that so often is carried out by one individual.

- Theory offers a way out of the dilemma of generalization by allowing researchers to join their work to some larger issue or accumulating body of data.

- Theory offers a critical perspective by calling up previous dialogues in which certain aspects of a problem may have been singled out because they have been inadequately attended to or have raised new doubts or concerns.

- Theory offers a useful way to harness the power of disproof. We can never prove anything through efforts at qualitative research, but we can disprove ideas by providing negative instances. Theory allows us to make better use of that power by inviting us to look at classes of events rather than only at single instances.

What theory does is call attention to, and offer strategies for coping with, the dual problems of purpose and generalization. It is also a reminder that we ourselves need to be thinking about the underlying issue tersely summarized in a two-word question always on the tip of some skeptic's tongue: So what?

Through drawing attention to the art of fieldwork, terrorizing questions like So what? or What is your theory? are somewhat disarmed. Theory is not so exalted in art worlds. We want to have it both ways, drawing now from science, now from art. Theory is part of the baggage that accompanies the role of the researcher as a scientific thinker. Theory is supposed to help researchers of any persuasion clarify and explain to others what they are up to.

Whether or not we are explicit about our theoretical dimensions, as fieldworkers we, too, must know and be able to explain to others what we are up to. When formal theory seems to offer no helpful answer, the search for theory at a more modest level can be turned into a provocative question: What would be needed by way of theory to help me organize and present my data and to recognize relevant aspects of my fieldwork experience? To be able to ask that question other than rhetorically, a fieldworker must be able to share effectively something of that data and experience. So one way out of an analytical or theoretical dilemma is to begin talking and writing in order to be able to enlist the help of others. When I take up that topic in the next chapter, I will suggest that such discussion can take place not only during and after fieldwork but preceding it as well.

Mental Set

I hope the above was helpful, particularly for anyone inclined to put theory on too high a pedestal rather than enlisting it as another tool, a conceptual one, for helping fieldworkers accomplish what they want to accomplish. I have now said about as much as I have to say about such tools and about fieldwork techniques. I have tried to keep them in their place. Fieldworkers themselves make the difference as to whether the tools and techniques are used imaginatively in the pursuit of a more interpretive account, more cautiously in the pursuit of a carefully analytical one, or in some appropriate combination of the two.

There is no formula for conducting unique and original studies, but there is more potential for realizing them if the tools and techniques remain just that. Mindwork is the essential element. I return to the working definition of art proposed in chapter 1 to underscore the critical need for an idiosyncratic human touch in order fully to realize the artistic potential of fieldwork:

> Art is achieved when the addition of an idiosyncratic human touch in any production, whether performance or artifact, is recognized by a discriminating audience as achieving an aesthetic quality exceeding what is expected by the exercise of craft skill alone.

A number of other practical matters relate to conceptualizing, particularly the need for a realistic assessment of the match between what a fieldworker hopes to accomplish and the talent and resources necessary to pull it off. The assessment must be candid, although much of what is assessed comes under the heading of attitude, or belief, or . . . faith.

Let me suggest some dimensions for any prospective fieldworker to consider before embarking on a field study. Such an inventory should result in a thoughtful decision about the extent of one's commitment both to the topic and to pursuing it through fieldwork.

Being Receptive

I begin by repeating cautions already expressed about ideas of immaculate perception in the doing of all research. No one can take even the first step toward "pure" discovery. Nevertheless, a distinguishing feature of the fieldwork approach is the need for receptivity or openness to the research setting. Such openness is exercised particularly in attention to context and the researcher's opportunity to work intuitively, in contrast to the quantitative researcher's need to exert control.

A fieldworker must rely on his or her ability to surrender to what the field observations actually reveal, rather than prematurely to superimpose structure upon them. In *Transforming Qualitative Data: Description, Analysis, and Interpretation* (HFW 1994b), I proposed a resolution for this tension by attending to whatever balance between analysis and interpretation best achieves the purposes of the research. There is no ideal ratio of description to analysis to interpretation. The relative emphasis devoted to each depends on what one wants to accomplish. But there is little point in engaging in a fieldwork approach if one cannot derive a sense of excitement and anticipation about finding out, coupled with a willingness to alter one's focus, should it become evident that either the problem or an effective way to investigate it needs to be better defined.

Strive not only to be open-minded but to be even more open-minded than you would ever dare reveal, both while engaging in fieldwork and when subsequently reflecting upon it. Become your own devil's advocate; argue with yourself about what is really going on, what you are really looking at, and whether you are really homing in on something significant in the fieldwork experience.

I realize that grant and dissertation proposal writers may feel hampered by requirements to present a carefully designed research sequence that will emphasize systematic analysis and allow only modest interpretation. Keep in mind, however, that a research proposal is only that: a proposal. It should not be regarded as a contract. Research that is designed in the making is research that can be redesigned in the making.

At the same time, it is foolish not to keep a client, a granting agency, or one's committee members informed or to negotiate changes as work progresses. The flexibility inherent in our approach is not necessarily matched by institutional flexibility on the part of others of authority who no doubt have their own expectations about outcomes. Graduate students, especially, are cautioned not only to weigh their personal capabilities for conducting and reporting relatively open-ended inquiries but also to gauge the receptivity of their committee members to such an approach. Even veteran fieldworkers have occasionally found themselves constrained by prior commitments that leave them unable to pursue a research problem in the way they might have preferred to define it. The analogy to art worlds reminds us that receptivity also functions to restrain what artists are free to do. Somewhere there must always be a discriminating audience, not only to be sought out but also to be satisfied.

Being Realistic

It seems reasonable to make a realistic assessment of one's strengths and weaknesses as a fieldworker in terms of the problem to be studied and, especially, the setting in which the work will be conducted. That may be difficult for the novice fieldworker anticipating work in a totally unfamiliar setting, but one ought to be able to project oneself into a setting with some idea about, and confidence in, being able to pull the whole thing off. Reportedly, Alfred Kroeber's assessment about doing fieldwork was, "Some can and some can't" (Wagley 1983:16). The good news, especially with the fieldwork part of fieldwork, is that most can. Essentially, fieldwork requires us to involve ourselves professionally in unfamiliar social situations, something we must certainly have had to do before. The new twist is to become more aware of the doing and, particularly, to be able to sustain the effort for an extended period of time.

One of the most difficult tasks for neophytes is to capitalize on the opportunity inherent in the participant observer role to act naturally, rather than to assume a stiff pose as observer or evaluator. Fieldwork offers such latitude that one can work from one's own interpersonal strengths and natural style to make it successful. A bit of resolve doesn't hurt, either; in your heart you must know that you can carry it off.

Unfortunately, graduate programs in general, and sometimes courses taught specifically to prepare qualitative researchers in particular, often generate apprehension rather than instill confidence. I am dismayed when I meet students who introduce themselves with ever-so-humble phrases such as, "I'm planning to do a qualitative study, but I don't have a clue of how to go about it." As kindly as I can, I try to assess whether their lament is prophecy or pose. It is usually the latter, as their responses to some "silly" questions quickly attest: Do you intend to go to a hospital, jail, church, or school to make your observations? Do you plan to go on a weekday or weekend? Do you plan to do a formal interview on your first visit, or will that come later? Will you conduct a survey? For how long do you intend to conduct the fieldwork? Even unorthodox questions such as, How many chapters do you expect to have in your study? or What would be your tentative chapter titles if you were to start writing today? usually lead me to conclude such conversations on a high note: "Sounds to me like you have quite a few clues!"

Novices are inclined to believe that their more experienced colleagues know exactly how to go about conducting a study. I think that impression is false. Veteran researchers may indeed appreciate the challenge that a new study presents, but they do not have a modus operandi as much as they have confidence in their ability to find their way into a study as it progresses. That is what I mean by resolve.

Resolve reveals itself through answers to questions such as those posed above, including anticipation of how the fieldwork will be initiated—thus designing a study one step at a time—and of what the end product will be. The latter includes not only the manner in which one expects to report but also a clear idea as to the kind of information needed to complete that reporting.

Taken one step at a time, the whole project must seem eminently doable, including a realistic assessment that the time and resources available are adequate. In the realities of the research world, genuine participant observer fieldwork may be the first casualty in delimiting options, with a few cursory site visits substituted instead. Or because of the researcher's own commitments, a level of sustained observation deemed highly desirable may, for practical purposes, be quite out of the question.

The important thing is to ensure that the research will be completed, which includes that it will be reported. Recognize here the possibility of being superficial, of merely touching the surface of a topic that deserves, and perhaps demands, more thorough attention; also, beware of trying to take on too much and ending up with nothing. Those darker arts are never far away.

Being Committed

The greater the commitment to pursuing in-depth fieldwork on the part of the researcher, the greater the need for a realistic appraisal of the return expected for the time, energy, and resources to be invested. A first concern is an assessment of the significance of the setting or problem to be investigated. What potential does the intended research have for producing significant results, assessed in terms of competing problems that might be investigated instead?

In a strict risk-benefit analysis, the physical risks inherent in fieldwork obviously depend on one's professional or disciplinary affiliations and on one's choice of problem and approach. The physical dangers, with vehicle accidents topping the list, are, as Howell reports in *Surviving Fieldwork*, "at once the most dramatic and probably the most easily preventable" (1990:101). Among my colleagues who have done research in exotic climates, some continue to do battle with medical problems contracted initially during fieldwork. There are fieldworkers whose research on drug addiction, cults, gangs, and so forth has put them at considerable risk. (See, for example, discussions by Mitchell [1993] or Lee [1995]. Lee's succinct advice in dangerous situations is straightforward: Proceed on the basis of a worst-case scenario [p. 36].) Working in dangerous situations is largely a matter of personal choice. I suspect that sometimes it reflects a conscious decision on the part of the more adventurously inclined to escape their placid institutional environments.

There are also psychological and professional risks inherent in fieldwork (see, for example, Descola 1996). These include broad concerns, such as finding and nurturing a supportive climate for one's endeavors while actually in the field. It is not uncommon for fieldworkers to overestimate the extent of enthusiasm toward both the research and themselves when initiating a new project. This can come about when we hear what we want (need?) to hear about the extent of interest in our work, when we have enlisted support from only a few or from unrepresentative members of the community, or when our presence begins to look more intrusive than the gatekeepers originally anticipated. Should this happen, the next fieldwork miscalculation may be to overestimate the extent of disaffection for the work, to about the same extent that affection was overestimated initially. More likely, no one in the group has been paying that much attention one way or the other.

In a psychological sense, fieldworkers can easily become their own worst enemies. One trap is referred to as the "paradox of intimacy," when a high degree of trust, achieved too quickly, actually curtails rather than enhances subsequent fieldwork (see Mitchell 1993:21). Many a fieldworker has walked unsuspectingly into a power struggle in which an initial façade of cooperation hides unexpected intrigue, inviting the researcher into alignments that may later threaten the success of the research. The overly sensitive researcher may be more at risk here, but regardless, you must prepare yourself for the awkwardness of overstaying your welcome.

Evaluating the potential return of a qualitative inquiry should include a frank assessment of outcomes not only for the research but for the researcher, including indirect benefits incidental to the research process but integral to one's career, such as pay, publication, and promotion. Here again we confront the issue of why we conduct research, who benefits, and whether our rewards for wanting to find out must come at a cost to those who are found out. More of the darker arts!

Always keep in mind that there are other, faster ways to obtain results to announce. In fact, it is hard to imagine a more cumbersome way than conventional fieldwork to conduct research for anyone anxious to obtain quick findings. Fieldwork lends itself neither to speedy discoveries nor to dramatic ones. By its very nature, it presupposes a commitment of both professional career and personal responsibility, an opportunity to demonstrate what the approach can accomplish, coupled with an implicit challenge to make whatever contribution might be made from attending to a particular set of circumstances.

Commitment to fieldwork is not any easier to demonstrate than commitment to one's research participants, especially in the early stages. Perhaps that is just as well; fieldwork is not well suited to anyone in a hurry. Still, the fact that through the years so many researchers have been willing to commit to the approach provides a constant reaffirmation to the research community of the importance of having some of its members devoted to studying problems in broad time frames and broad social contexts.

A Capacity for Judgment

Pursuing the art metaphor and thinking of fieldworkers, who like artists work in a community of scholar-researchers, one also recognizes the need for fieldworkers to develop a capacity for reflecting on and assessing their own performance at every stage, from initial conceptualization to final write-up. This is another aspect in which the art of fieldwork requires more than technical elements of craftsmanship and the coordinating of materials and techniques. My colleague and former student Tom Schram picked up on this idea so eloquently in correspondence on the topic that I quote him here verbatim:

> Becoming a skillful fieldworker goes beyond the acquisition of skills and extends to one's ability to *judge* his or her performance in concert with a *collective judgment* about what constitutes good fieldwork. So it takes a capacity for self-evaluation and a sense of appreciation that is developed and sustained in a community of other fieldworkers.
>
> Acquiring proficiency in the craft does require instruction and practice —as does art—and perhaps, as Werner and Schoepfle argue, "great art" is dependent on talent. For both art and craft, nonetheless, I think we need to attend as well to a capacity for judgment and a sense of appreciation that is sustained and defined at some collective level. [Personal communication, March 1995; see also Schram 2003]

We come full circle: the lone fieldworker grappling with theory (or, better still, playing with theories), vowing to stay the course, mindful of the difference between being open-minded and being mindless, addressing an infinite task with the most finite of resources, working desperately to maintain an independence of thought, and, in the end, surrendering to judgment reflective of the community of others similarly engaged. Art worlds. Science worlds. Fieldwork worlds. Worlds of human judgment, every one.

CHAPTER NINE
THE ART OF SELF-EXPRESSION

Writing has emerged as central to what anthropologists do both in the field and thereafter.

—James Clifford
"Introduction," in *Writing Culture*, p. 2

What the ethnographer is in fact faced with—except when (as of course he must do) he is pursuing the more automatized routines of data collection—is a multiplicity of complex conceptual structures, many of them superimposed upon or knotted into one another, which are at once strange, irregular, and inexplicit, and which he must contrive somehow first to grasp and then to render.

—Clifford Geertz
"Thick Description," in *The Interpretation of Cultures*, p. 10

Reporting is the visible and outward sign of one's accomplishments in fieldwork, revealing what the field researcher-cum-portrayer has made of it all. Clifford Geertz captures this two-step process in the phrase quoted above, "first to grasp and then to render."

Rendering is a particularly appropriate word choice, since it implicates a broad range of activities. In addition to writing academic reports, articles, and monographs or making lecture and seminar presentations, one can render through slide, film, and video presentations; photography and museum exhibits; ethnodramas; stories and poems; ethnographic fiction; accounts prepared for newspapers and popular journals; maybe even appearances on TV talk shows. All these options are, to borrow a badly overworked term, *viable*. Some of the discussion in this chapter is relevant to the full range of options. However, for at least two reasons, my focus will be on written accounts intended for professional journals and monographs, reflecting the print orientation pervasive in academia and government agencies.

One reason for a focus on writing is that my graduate training came at a time when writing was the only thinkable way to present the results of field research. Films and photographs were valued, but they augmented the standard ethnography; they were never intended to serve in lieu of it. A picture may be worth a thousand words, but words came first; pictures were optional. Franz Boas's 1897 account, *Social Organization and the Secret Societies of the Kwakiutl Indians,* is augmented with 51 plates and 215 additional text figures, but the text stands alone. Audiences were assumed to consist essentially of peers, and one wrote in scholarly fashion for them, with an emphasis on detailed description. Margaret Mead's colleagues had a difficult time understanding how she could contribute a regular column to *Redbook* magazine, drawing on her professional experience as a perspective for giving advice to American women, when most anthropologists were still preparing accounts in which fieldworkers themselves disappeared from their texts.

For all their efforts at situated listening while conducting fieldwork, anthropologists did little to develop a listening audience beyond the lecture hall. In the early 1950s, Walter Goldschmidt was involved in the production of a series of half-hour radio programs to bring anthropology into the home by examining facets of culture. These recorded programs were sponsored by the National Association of Educational Broadcasters and produced by the Canadian Broadcasting Corporation (see Goldschmidt 1954). The programs were directed at the listening public. Anyone who replayed them for a class had the same worrisome feeling one had when showing classroom films—that they were judged more for their entertainment value than for instruction. They were dubious entertainment at that, setting students at a listening task without an accompanying picture to watch on film or, eventually, TV.

There were also heroic efforts beginning about the mid-1960s to bring anthropology into the classroom, either as an identifiable subject area or as a major source of information for discovery approaches to learning (for example, the outstanding "Man, A Course of Study" project). And there has always been a vast repository of ethnographic films prepared essentially for use in instructional settings, although their didactic quality seems more conspicuous today with the invasion such films have made into the home via public-service television.

In spite of efforts to bring anthropology before the public or to experiment with alternative forms of presentation, the old ways die hard. For most ethnographers, and for virtually all others reporting fieldwork—except perhaps documentary filmmakers and the new video ethnographers—writing is still "where it's at." Reporting in print continues to be the dominant format, especially among aspiring academics. Whatever technological changes may occur in how we go about placing our words before others, tenure-seeking aspirants find the writing of books and articles pivotal to their careers. Contract-seeking researchers now customarily include plans for dissemination as part of a standard proposal.

Writing is the form of presentation with which I have struggled, happily as well as unhappily, for four decades. Writing has become more than just a habit; it is part of my definition of who I am and what I do. As noted, I do not consider myself an author—an individual clever enough to make his living by writing—but there is no question that I am a person who writes. More accurately, I can be described as a person who writes some and edits lots. An extended editing process allows for two other critical dimensions: ample time for reflecting and reworking ideas, and time for making judicious use of outside reviewers at critical stages along the way.

An equally important personal reason to focus on writing is that, thanks to an invitation from Mitch Allen, who was with Sage Publications at the time, I was given the opportunity to say what I could about the topic of writing up qualitative research. And those are the very words I chose, *Writing Up Qualitative Research,* for the title of the monograph I prepared for the Sage series on qualitative research methods. That monograph is now in its second edition (2001), and I need not reiterate its message here. But I do want to review three major ideas emphasized in it:

- Begin writing early.

- Anticipate how you will parcel out the study.

- Work beginning-to-end, but think end-to-beginning.

I underscore an idea expressed by James Clifford: "Writing has emerged as central to what anthropologists do both in the field and thereafter" (Clifford and Marcus 1986:2). You can make that central to what every fieldworker does, both in the field and thereafter.

Begin Writing Early

My first suggestion, to begin writing early, is echoed by virtually everyone who has something to say about writing. You cannot begin writing too soon! I will go so far as to suggest that you consider writing before even beginning a field study. Whether or not you actually do it, give some serious thought to the idea, which is sometimes called "prewriting." I present a brief on its behalf.

We never come to a study totally devoid of an idea of what we are about. Early writing invites us to make what we already know—or think we know—a matter of record. It also helps us recognize areas of inquiry in which our information is scant or nonexistent. Thus, it can help give focus and purpose to fieldwork still in progress.

Of course, the argument can be made that early writing might unduly influence the subsequent course of the investigation. But I think a more powerful argument can be offered in rebuttal: Early writing should help identify biases and prejudices in such a way that we deal with them explicitly at the outset of an inquiry, rather than having to fight them off as we go along. Through prewriting, you might even recognize when your proposed fieldwork only validates a previously held position. If you are searching for a soapbox, why not just skip the research pose? Cut immediately to the chase; write the essay you should be writing, instead of reported research that happens to prove you right.

Anticipate How You Will Parcel Out the Study

Early writing helps keep the research focused on outcomes, on the results of fieldwork. An early step toward achieving one's purposes is to develop a proposed outline or table of contents for the final report, including an estimated number of pages to be assigned to each of its component parts. It is critical to recognize from the outset that in all descriptively based research, our bigger problem is not getting all the data we can, but getting rid of as much extraneous data as possible, so that the corpus of data we work with is manageable. Stated more succinctly, we don't need to get as much data as we can; we need to can most of the data we get. Premature as it may seem, the rationing of pages among proposed subtopics can be an invaluable step in thinking about how to apportion the account. In even the most descriptively oriented accounts, the space available is necessarily limited, and the requisite attention to method, theory, literature review, analysis, interpretation, recommendations, or implications all compete for precious space.

I hope I have not left the impression that topics such as theory or literature review need not be addressed in field-based studies. I have suggested that they be drawn into the account to whatever extent, in whatever place, and in whatever fashion seem most relevant and vital to the account itself. They are not routine matters to be dealt with ritually and dismissed with dispatch. They need to be addressed in such a way that they are integrated into the account. It is important to recognize that each of these topics takes up precious space.

Transforming Qualitative Data: Description, Analysis, and Interpretation (HFW 1994b) was born out of my efforts to deal with the critical problem of transforming data from observation to final account. The three aspects that constitute the book's subtitle—description, analysis, interpretation—present a way to distinguish among what I see as the major options we exercise in organizing and presenting qualitative data. To ground my discussion in real data, I drew on several earlier studies for illustration (just as I do in this book in chapter 11). For more technical aspects of analyzing qualitative data, an ever-expanding shelf of resources is available (e.g., Bernard 1994b, 2000; Denzin and Lincoln 1994, 2000; Miles and Huberman 1994; Richardson 2000; Silverman 1993).

I propose that you resolve issues of narrative style and the organization of data in the early phases of a qualitative inquiry, rather than wait until you are buried in field notes to begin to dig your way out. From the outset, you need to have in mind some broad categories, however tenuous, that provide sufficient structure to guide both fieldwork and deskwork. Do not chastise yourself for imposing structure on what you are about to report. If you can't bear to impose structure, you will never be able to compose the account.

In selecting broad categories, try not to be tempted by all the categories that the text-management programs can handle. Look instead for as few major categories as possible, categories that subsume numerous minor topics yet keep important distinctions visible. A proliferation of minor categories or subcategories is not worrisome—the more the merrier if you like to have a place for everything. As your work progresses, you should discover categories that can be collapsed or eliminated as you begin to distinguish recurring patterns among one-time events. Just keep a tight rein on the number of major categories you employ, a number that ought to feel right intuitively as you continue your sorting. Recognize also the direction in which you tend most naturally to work, creating from raw material like the potter in whose hands something new is formed or carving away like the sculptor to reveal in fine detail what you felt was there all along.

In *Teachers versus Technocrats* I used an analogy to the two-part moiety form of social organization studied by anthropologists. Hypothetically assigning everyone in the setting to one of two moiety-like groups gave me two major categories, and subsequently describing them in interaction provided the third. I described the teachers in the setting as the target group. Then I described the technocrats as the donors. Next I turned to the interaction between them. That proved a satisfactory way to present a basically descriptive ethnographic account, accompanied by an anthropologically oriented analysis from the perspective of social organization. The target group–donor group–interaction setting sequence was suggested by George Foster's *Applied Anthropology* (1969). It strikes me as an excellent way to do some basic sorting.

Software programs developed for qualitative researchers are designed to utilize the remarkable capabilities of microprocessors, but they are not well suited to the more limited capabilities of the human mind. My proclivity for dividing things into sets of three serves me far better than a computer program capable of handling many categories at one time. In striving to keep the number of major categories as small as possible, I usually begin sorting by trying to work with only two categories, keeping an eye out for what I am missing that might necessitate a third (or, more reluctantly, a fourth, fifth, and so on).

Work Beginning to End, but Think End to Beginning

My third suggestion is an extension of the second one. I urge you not only to propose a tentative table of contents early on but to think through your entire study in the reverse order of the way you intend to carry it out. Begin with a careful consideration of where you want to end up, what you want to have when you finish. (I take this to be what John Creswell wants his students to do in thinking of their task as composing rather than simply doing their studies, as discussed in the previous chapter.) Try to anticipate as specifically as you can the outcomes you want to achieve. Then back up a step to identify the kinds of data and range of experience you will need to support or illustrate those outcomes. Then back up one more step to ascertain how to get that information.

Thinking finish to start invites a critical appraisal of whether your intended approach is really the best way to obtain whatever information you actually expect to use. One of fieldwork's temptations is that it presents the unsuspecting researcher with so much potential data that might possibly be of use, data often relatively easy to collect, that newcomers risk losing sight of what they are getting data for. In practice, it isn't a bad idea to maintain a running dialogue with yourself, asking, Why am I recording this? What use am I likely to make of it? My experience has been that the more clearly one can specify the data needed, the less likely a fieldwork "broadside" to collect everything possible is an efficient way to proceed. If data are what you seek, just get them. If data alone cannot provide what you need, then your investment in a fieldwork approach is more likely to be warranted.

You might as well back up even one step further. Reflect on how you have posed your problem in your purpose statement and whether fieldwork offers a reasonable approach to it. As posed, the problem ought to invite the broad scope of inquiry that fieldwork allows, permitting you to develop, test, and modify ideas as necessary, rather than binding you, right or wrong, to your original charter.

Alas, you may not enjoy ideal circumstances that allow you to alter your course and redefine your problem. Like the artist constrained by an art world, you need to recognize what you can accomplish under the conditions that guide your work, especially if you are conducting research in which the problem and parameters have been established by others. Because tension is more likely to arise over what you eventually report and how you report it than how you go about your inquiry, attention to early writing can help you anticipate your reporting problems and look for ways to resolve them.

None of this is intended to have you complete a study before you start. It is intended to keep you finely—and finally—tuned to what your study can reasonably accomplish, as well as to help you assess your research objective itself. The more you are able to flesh out your ideas, the better off you will be. You might even be able to write a draft of the entire study. Just for yourself. Should you feel too constrained by circumstances beyond your control, you might want to prepare two early drafts instead of one. The first draft can present the study as you feel it ought to be told; the second can present the study as it will most likely have to be told. That leaves you with a documented record of what you were thinking and feeling, an account to which you may someday return.

The quality of your early writing need not be of paramount concern. Five paragraphs into the preface to his book *Style*, Joseph Williams notes reassuringly, "We write a first draft for ourselves; the drafts thereafter increasingly for the reader" (1990:x). That you are writing demonstrates from the outset that you are thinking beyond the fieldwork experience to how you will render that experience to an audience. Perhaps Geertz dismisses such experience a bit too casually with his reference to "pursuing the more automatized routines of data collection" (1973:10, and quoted in the second epigraph to this chapter), but it is hard to take issue with his insistence that ultimately your work turns on your ability to render an account. There's neither help nor solace in his observation, but it is an accurate statement of the task that renders all previous steps worth the effort.

Writing with Panache

I turn now to writing with panache, drawing attention not so much to flair—the grand and flamboyant manner some actors evoke on stage—but to verve, as used to refer to literary vigor and, especially, literary style. Descriptive accounts often contain at least a dash of panache. When they do, however, it may not be due so much to our own latent talents as to poignant elements of the accounts themselves related through the anecdotes, vignettes, or expressive language of those whose lives we examine. "The subjects of ethnographies, it should never be forgotten," writes Robert J. Smith, "are always more interesting than their authors" (1990:369).

I do not suggest that everyone has or necessarily ought to strive for a light touch, giving each paragraph a sprinkle of wit or sparkle. I assume that writing with such a touch either comes easily or is best left to others. But I think most academic writers would like to season their work with at least a bit more panache and would prefer not to depend solely on informants to supply it. Sometimes that touch is realized in unexpectedly revealing footnotes, a descriptive opening paragraph that deludes the reader into believing that what follows will be a delight to read, or intimate dedications, acknowledgments, or postscripts that speak in an altogether different voice from the body of the manuscript. I encourage academic writers at least to lighten up, especially through editing stilted academic prose written under the ill-conceived idea that we have to be boring to be believed.

Yet I'm not sure exactly how to help anyone lighten up. A new self-consciousness about representation, especially concerning voice, has allowed (and even encouraged) authors to put more of themselves into fieldwork-based accounts, but little was gained for those bogged down in the jargon of postmodernism itself.

Writing in the first person often helps. It leaves authors no place to hide, instead inviting them to become part of their manuscripts. Sure, it can be overdone; I am aware of my excesses in this regard, of an unbecoming number of I's in almost every paragraph. On at least two occasions in my experience, however, I have had editors override my first-person style with a turgid third-person style of their own, sending a "corrected" manuscript to the printer without the courtesy of even consulting me. How anyone could look at what they did to those manuscripts and call it an improvement beats the hell out of me!

In any circumstances when authors are instructed to submit manuscripts written in the third person, I suggest one not submit at all if a first-person narrative is integral to the account. And in field-based research, it is hard to imagine how the author-researcher would ever totally disappear or why he or she would want to. There are enough editors who understand this; they are the ones to whom we should "submit."

For all questions related to style, I suggest carefully checking whether rigid prescriptions for academic writing really exist or are simply part of a lingering and often unexamined lore passed along in the halls of academe. We all observe and transmit rules that are not rules at all. Be suspicious of anyone who informs you knowingly that "journal editors don't like . . ." or "the graduate school requires . . ." Maybe they do, maybe they don't (do not?). Maybe the previous editor or provost was an old fogy, but the present one isn't. Check for yourself.

There is no point in trying to inventory all the ways one can add a dash of panache. Such efforts are like selecting the right seasonings from a kitchen shelf—we all have our favorites, know what works best for us, and occasionally reach for something different to add zest to a dish, just as we try to add zest to a manuscript. Natural storytellers introduce excitement, intrigue, surprise, even mystery. The more cynical work wonders seasoning their accounts with paradox or irony. Compassion seems particularly suited to our efforts as human observers, allowing us to temper our sometimes too analytical, too dispassionate observations with something from inside ourselves to remind the reader that we, too, are human. Compassion is a powerful ingredient, best used with discretion so that it evokes empathy, without tempting an author to become a bleeding heart. It might be likened to using just the right amount of cayenne pepper, curry, nutmeg, or any seasoning for which more is not necessarily better and the slightest excess can spoil the whole effect.

Another approach, seen perhaps too seldom in academic writing, is to make oneself—rather than one's subjects, one's readers, or the rest of the world—the fall guy. As researchers turned writers, we can better afford to be the naive ones, the individuals who completely missed the point or needed to learn a lesson. Better to point the finger at ourselves than to be pointing a finger at the world. Yet how infrequently do we read accounts from fieldworkers who admit to foibles of their own or seem to remain aware that, ultimately, it is ourselves we seek to understand?

Writing as Central to the Art of Fieldwork

At one time writing was so little associated with fieldwork—and with the social sciences in general—that to have a work cited for being especially well written raised doubts as to whether that was another of its attributes or its only one. Murray Wax was the first fieldworker of my acquaintance to insist that writing is not simply an adjunct to fieldwork but a critical component of it. Prior to hearing the importance he bestowed on writing, I was content with the more cautious observation that readers were twice-blessed when a fieldwork account proved not only to be of substance but also well written.

Those doubts linger on, for there is nothing that raises more uncertainty for me than to have something I have published commended for being well written. Such doubts did not spring full-blown by themselves. When I first encountered anthropology some twenty-five years after the initial publication of Ruth Benedict's *Patterns of Culture* (1934), her book was still one of the anthropological accounts read most widely among lay audiences. The book was touted for its elegant style, which was often explained away by peers anxious to point out that Benedict was also a poet. By implication, as a poet she could be forgiven for writing well; conversely, as a poet she might not be the most authoritative source for a rigorous anthropology. By her book's second paragraph, Benedict herself was quick to point out, "It may be that I have carried some interpretations further than one or another of the field-workers would have done" (p. vii). Oscar Lewis's *Children of Sanchez* (1961) was greeted similarly, its literary style so highly regarded as to cause concern among his peers about the extent to which the account was authentic.

The ability to write well is now recognized as an essential element in fieldwork. Our accounts are meant to be read. We do not have neat findings, conclusions that can be summarized or reduced to tables and charts, or tidy hypotheses instantly e-mailed to colleagues around the world breathlessly awaiting reports of our results. If nobody reads our studies—virtually in their entirety—our efforts are doomed to obscurity. We need not apologize for efforts to make our work interesting.

Anthropologist Gerald Berreman expressed concern years ago that ethnographers were likely to diverge into a majority who would "take refuge in scientism," seeking rigor at the expense of "content, insight, and understanding," while a minority, with no pretense at being scientific, would become "essentially creative writers on anthropological topics" (1968:369, quoted in Sanjek 1990:242–43). One could do worse than being an essentially creative writer on anthropological topics. For openers, how about being an essentially uncreative one?

None of us has been drawn to this work because of a demonstrated capacity for writing. Many people aspire to become writers, some of them do write, and some of what some of them write makes its way into the public arena. But I have never met anyone who turned to fieldwork because of the opportunity it presents for writing, and I have spoken with numerous individuals who cannot imagine doing fieldwork because of the writing that it entails.

One does not ordinarily think of researchers of any type as true authors, and there are certainly more efficient ways to go about telling a story than spending the time necessary or trying to reach the depths ordinarily sought in fieldwork. Fieldworkers become writers out of necessity, drawing on personal resources never tapped except perhaps in preparing class assignments. They may not have been required to do enough writing to become proficient even in that. Only as a doctoral student did I have the opportunity (that is the word I use now; I may have used other words at the time) to write major term papers. I had no idea how one went about writing a book (i.e., dissertation). By the time I was ready to write the dissertation, however, I did have two things going for me, as I have noted. First, I had time itself. When the opportunity came, I gave dissertation writing top priority in my life, and I devoted myself almost exclusively to the task. Second, I felt I really had something worthwhile to say.

Opinions vary as to which stage is the most difficult in the writing process. The initial hurdle is to overcome inertia, to get something written without becoming discouraged by the quality of the product that ensues. I have struggled with and at the same time delighted in the problems of organizing and finding my way into each fieldwork account. The art is to present material in an engaging yet coherent manner sufficient to hold the interest of a reader who may not expect to be entertained but hopes not to be bored. In most cases, we have just one chance to capture the interest of a reader. (We might borrow a motto from people who sell Christmas trees: "Never let a customer leave the lot without one." Neither customer nor reader is likely to return.)

Choosing how to get into the account, in a manner intended to draw the reader along, provides the toehold I need to get the writing started. Of course, I sometimes get off on the wrong foot and find myself on a tangent instead of on target. That produces a second problem, resolved either by throwing out material that I have written (which I do only reluctantly) or becoming frozen into a particular way of conceptualizing an account and remaining unable to shake loose from it.

Sometimes we simply must make a fresh start. It may take an outside reader to tell us to do just that. Among your invited early readers, you ought to have one or more whom you can count on to tell you like it is, before you get to the stage where rejections start to close out options.

It is important at this point to keep clearly in mind that the final product must be written well, not the earlier drafts. It matters not how many drafts it takes to arrive at an acceptable final one. Therein lies hope, for what an experienced old hand or gifted newcomer may achieve in a single draft, the rest of us can still achieve through the processes of minor editing or major revision. It may take iteration upon iteration before we get a version that satisfies not only critical colleagues—reviewers, journal referees, editors, dissertation committees—but also ourselves. If we have chosen our problem well, conducted our fieldwork well, and organized our data in a form suitable for analysis and interpretation, then we owe it as much to ourselves as to our readers to keep polishing until we come up with a satisfactorily written account to present it.

Once I have a draft in hand—the completed draft of the entire manuscript, so that I know where it is (or was) heading—I begin editing and revising. Editing and revising with a passion! From then on, both figuratively and literally, things have to get better, and they do. I cannot stress too heavily that my manuscripts improve through sustained efforts at improving them, draft after draft after draft. I am not embarrassed by the number of drafts I go through before I reach what I consider an acceptable standard. I admit to dismay in realizing that the initial writing—my sentences as I first put them on screen or paper—seems not to be improving in spite of all the years I have worked at this. Still, with the help of time, prodigious editing, and feedback from critic-readers invited to review drafts at various stages, things usually end up okay.

I have never been preoccupied with quantity in my writing. I was astounded while being introduced to an academic audience overseas to hear that I had written 157 books and articles, until I realized that a busy administrator summarily recruited to introduce me had simply counted every entry on my curriculum vitae, whether book, article, panel presentation, or conference attended. I recommend turning a deaf ear to anyone who claims to know the number of books or articles required to achieve tenure, promotion, or fame. I am unimpressed by colleagues who crank out what amounts to academia's equivalent of motel art.

Although writing may be an art—and even the "primary art," as the English poet Samuel Taylor Coleridge claimed—my writing has not made an artist of me. What I have become is, I think, a skilled craftsperson. I have to work at it. My pride is essentially craft pride. Mine is careful work, carefully presented, perhaps envious of art but without any pretense of achieving it.

As to feedback from others, it helps if among your invited critic-readers you include some with technical knowledge about your topic, but not all your readers need to be specialists. One effective way to solicit nonspecialist help and to recruit readers over objections that your work is "much too technical" (or some other excuse that can be taken more than one way) is to ask them to read your manuscript aloud to you. That will enable you literally to hear for yourself how your words read to someone who shares neither your specialized knowledge on the topic nor your intimate knowledge about how your sentences are supposed to be read.

You are not likely to find anyone willing to read back every sentence of every draft. Therefore you must learn to read your sentences as though they were being read by a stranger. Imagine that stranger to be easily led astray by ambiguous references, convoluted sentences, or insufficient attention to headings, paragraphing, and punctuation. If I have any secret to reveal about my editing, it is that I try to attend to every sentence in search of possible traps for an unsuspecting reader. I don't mind writing a tricky sentence now and then, but I pore over my sentences to search out ambiguities and eliminate needless words. Writing has to communicate. Right?

Finding the appropriate level of detail is a major concern in preparing accounts derived from descriptive fieldwork. How much detail should we present, in what manner, to make our case without unduly burdening the account with inconsequential facts? To me, such questions get back to purpose, to that carefully worded (and pondered, and revised, and pondered some more) guiding statement intended to get us on track and to keep us there.

Style—panache—can neither cover nor make amends for a problem of focus. Style is necessary but not sufficient. It is highly personal, a mark of every individual's idiosyncratic human touch, most certainly an element of art rather than a practice of science. Even styles identified by their lack of style—academic writing, for example—become habits we acquire and observe without critical thought. There is too little testing of the boundaries, too little effort to employ a wider variety of styles appropriate to the topic and acceptable to an audience. Keep an eye out in your own journals to see if everybody is writing the same way. Do academic editors really insist on turgid prose, or do they publish turgid prose because that is mostly what they receive?

Much has been written about style, but in seeking after it you are probably better off to spend time editing another version of your own work than devouring another style manual. If I had to pass along one bit of advice that strikes me as helpful, it is this, also from Joseph Williams: "The secret to a clear and readable style is in the first five or six words of every sentence" (1990:52). Clear and readable style is the name of the game. If Williams insists, as apparently he does, that style is set and revealed in the first few words of every sentence, consider taking him at his word(s) and attend to your own first few words. Then, just in case he has miscounted, attend to everything that follows, in that and every other sentence as well.

Giving special attention to the beginning of each sentence, paragraph, or section provides an excellent starting place for anyone serious about style. If you are not sure how to begin your editing, begin with beginnings. If more academic authors did that, we might end up with fewer opening sentences that discourage rather than entice. Style cannot save a manuscript any more than it can save a sentence, but it can greatly enhance the chances that a manuscript will go on to have a life of its own.

Having put so much emphasis on style, have I skipped too lightly over the haunting specter and crippling effect that not being able to get anything down on paper poses for the researcher who cannot, or will not, get the writing started? The anxiety associated with not being able to start writing is fearsome, and one may succumb to some darker art in defense. Self-deception is one. Frequently such fear is camouflaged by endlessly extending time in the field or at the library under the pretense that there is still so much to be learned before one can be so presumptuous as to begin writing.

I do not know how to help anyone who cannot, or will not, start writing. That is a problem I do not have. I start by looking for a way to take a reader with me into the account, which also gets the writing process itself underway. But I can pass along some oft-repeated tips, accompanied by further reflections so they are not mere clichés, that may help you get started:

- *Set aside time for writing each day.* I'm sure no one disagrees with this wonderful idea. I also realize it may not be practical for people whose writing must be sandwiched into busy schedules that preclude time for it. Nor is it likely to seem helpful to anyone who has experienced just sitting there. You must admit, however, that you are unlikely to get anything written unless you have paper or a keyboard at the ready and have made writing your top priority for the moment. To overcome inertia that finds you just sitting there, how about listing all the things that seem to be getting in the way and then examining each in detail—in writing—along with any ideas about possible ways to overcome each of them?

Consider the possibility that your dilemmas themselves offer entrée to the account you are trying to present: "As I sat down to begin this account, I realized several dilemmas that confronted me," or "From the moment I was first able to conceptualize the problem addressed here, I realized I faced a comparable dilemma in bringing it before a wider audience." By the second or third draft you may even be able to drop those awkward beginnings and get to the point.

- *Begin writing too early.* As already discussed, you should start writing soon, the sooner the better. Recognize that writing must be joined to the research; it is not a final step to be held off until everything else is finished. If necessary, write to discover what you have to say about what you are experiencing and how you are going to say it.

- *Write what you intend to use and use what you write.* Whether your note making is brief or elaborate, don't make every entry something that would need to be rewritten before you could incorporate it into your final account. Take particular care with your descriptive passages, the write-up of complete, richly detailed vignettes. Your own musings as your fieldwork proceeds warrant similar care and elaboration. Such entries might find their way into the finished account at a later date, their location to be determined as the manuscript takes shape.

- *Begin writing at an easy place.* When you are ready to begin drafting sections of your final account, start with sections where the writing should come easily. Method, perhaps? How you happened to pose this problem? Some first impressions or common misperceptions? Draw together some purely descriptive sections, incorporating or expanding on original field notes, as described above. It is never too early to begin writing the final draft. But there is no reason you must begin with the hardest part of the writing when there is so much else that must be written as well.

Sometimes it is helpful to recognize or reaffirm what you already should know: Your writing problems are not all that different from what other writers experience. I was surprised to learn that even my set of private distractions was not all that unique: clearing my desk instead of turning immediately to writing when I know that first thing in the morning is my most productive writing time; hitting the cheese and Triscuits early on; spending an unusually long time combing the cat. I would like to be able to report that I am so well disciplined that while I was teaching I still found time to write every day. In truth, the best I could do was to arrange writing days when I had at least an entire morning without interruption. But during those periods, if I was on a roll, I might not even have answered the telephone.

Simply stated, the only antidote for not writing is to write. And you can always improve something you have written previously, editing the good stuff and tossing the rest. Until you have words in front of you to edit, thoughts can jump around forever in your head in so abstract a form that they can neither be communicated to others nor sharpened to your own satisfaction. Of course I mull things over before I write, and of course I jot down ideas, phrases, and questions as they pop into my head anytime, day or night. But my best mullings, like my best scanning for related ideas and relevant citations in the literature, seem to come after I start to capture my thoughts on paper, not before.

When you are not writing, be honest with yourself and others; don't make the claim to be writing unless some words are in place where you can actually look at them. But if mulling ideas is the way you like to begin, don't let me rush you through that stage. Do whatever works for you and enables you to get the account written, one draft at a time.

This book serves as a good example of writing in order to find out— or in this case, squeeze out—what I had to say on aspects of a topic I had not addressed previously. The work was entirely a think piece, a reflection on practice rather than a report of research. I believed that I could easily make a case for the art of fieldwork and that the writing would simply flow. Until I began to identify the various aspects I wanted to discuss (my tentative table of contents, subsequently revised and revised), I found myself working with unbridled but also undisciplined enthusiasm. I wrote a complete draft before I discovered the need to make a crisper distinction between two complementary, but distinct, dimensions implicated by my title, one examining a perspective for looking at the work of fieldworkers, the other examining the art of doing fieldwork much as one might talk about the art of conversation, fly fishing, or restoring antiques.

Once I began writing (rather than just ruminating), ideas began to form, to reveal their strengths and weaknesses, and, alas, to contradict each other. With writing came better questions that offered a better way to consult the work of colleagues, rather than reading or rereading everything anyone had written on the topic before attempting to capture my own ideas.

Let me note a certain comfort I gained from the realization that a book like this can also be revised after it is in print. Even as work on the first version came to a close, I entertained the idea that the opportunity to prepare a second edition might someday present itself. For the time being, I had taken the ideas as far as I could go. Now, a decade later, I have an opportunity to take a second look.

A distinction needs to be made between revising a fieldwork-based account and revising an extended essay such as this. I have never revised my field-based accounts, a conscious decision I made the first time the opportunity arose. Fieldwork accounts are best left intact as historical documents, corrected only for errors of fact or abridged to meet publication requirements. New information, alternative or enhanced analyses and interpretations, and follow-up accounts can be appended or published separately. For example, the chapter "A Kwakiutl Village and School 25 Years Later" was added to my original *A Kwakiutl Village and School* (HFW 1967) when it was reissued in 1989, and a new preface, bibliographic addendum, and previously unpublished autobiography were added to the updated AltaMira version published in 2003. But these additions supplemented the manuscript, which remained as originally written.

I think publishing further editions with additional (supplemental) information has become standard practice, beginning perhaps with

William F. Whyte's classic *Street Corner Society* (1943). The second edition of his book (1955), with the addition of an appendix on method, became an even more valuable resource for urban fieldworkers than the original publication. The reissue of many of the original monographs in the Spindlers' Case Studies in Cultural Anthropology series in a subsequent Fieldwork Edition added a section on method and enjoyed similar recognition.

Writing as Disciplined Activity

The emphasis I have placed on writing, especially on early writing, gets words recorded, the process begun. Admittedly, however, there is not much quality control beyond one's own criteria for what constitutes an adequate sentence. No writing at one extreme is countered by the excesses of overwriting, where writing processes get in the way rather than facilitate reporting. This can happen when wordsmithing takes over so that style becomes a preoccupation, leading to "slick" instead of "thick" description. Efforts at good writing need to be coupled with having something worthwhile to say.

Academic pressure to publish or perish interferes by insisting that whether or not you have something important to say, you had better get something into print anyway. The system is not likely to change. The best solution seems to be one suggested earlier, to address your research efforts toward topics of genuine importance to you. You'll need to bolster your energy and morale as necessary to convince yourself that your work does matter and is worthy of your effort. Take personal responsibility for work that bears your name. And see that your work does bear your name. Consider your name on a manuscript as your hallmark.

In an effort to develop a personal style and to contribute original work, you may be distressed at the influence others can exert over your writing, especially if you had anticipated that, like any self-respecting artist, you would be free at last to do your own thing. Where you may have anticipated many possibilities, you seem instead to encounter constricted choice. The message you wanted to tell seems lost or redirected, your own style subordinated to the preferences of your dissertation committee, journal editor, or funding sponsor. I must console with little consolation: Welcome to the club!

If it wasn't clear at the time, maybe now you realize why chapter 3 examined art worlds and the cultural milieu in which artists work. Realize that if the circumstances are not good, at least you are in good company. If your committee or an editor or publisher offers little by way of options to their directives, you probably need to knuckle under and do what they ask you to do. A Chinese proverb suggests, "When the door is low, bow your head." Survival is a first order of business and that includes more than mere survival during fieldwork.

The power to withdraw a manuscript is about the only power you have, short of some overly dramatic action such as dropping out of a degree program or changing your career line. These are never attractive alternatives, especially if you have invested months on a particular project and some part of a lifetime acquiring competence in fieldwork. Withdrawing a manuscript may bring modest personal satisfaction, but you are in a position to exert rather little force when virtually all journals have manuscripts competing for space and all publishers have more on the table than they could ever print. In general, I recommend that you accede to whatever requests and suggestions you receive if they are likely to lead to having your work accepted. Just think of yourself as comparable to struggling artists in their studios, knowing what they would like to do but doing what they must.

But always write for yourself first—tell the story you want to tell, the way you want to tell it. Be willing and prepared to make deep, painful changes when circumstances seem largely out of your control. But keep your original ideas—and manuscripts—intact. There may come a day when you will be able to return to your original script, to compare your critics' comments with your own reassessments, and decide whether you still wish to develop your material as you had originally planned.

Regardless of how heavy-handed they seem, most people who offer suggestions are well intentioned. Your immediate perception may be that others are placing roadblocks in your path, but they are more likely trying to help you with your writing (or, at worst, endeavoring to save the rest of us from poorly written or poorly researched accounts). Points conveyed as directives also may be more negotiable than they appear initially; editors do not like to be accused of dictating to authors, especially authors writing for journals in their field. Non-negotiable items may reflect publishing house or institutional policies over which even your seeming adversaries have little control. You may feel the urge to challenge such policies, but consider doing so at an appropriate time in your career—such as after, not instead of, getting your degree or publishing your book. (I could hang tough and insist on a footnote of explanation and apology when one editor replaced my first-person pronouns with his awkward third-person ones, but that incident took place twenty-one years after I completed my doctorate! Now, there's a thought: Perhaps you can enlist some old-timers to fight your battle for you.)

Your experiences with publishers and reviewers might also be of interest to colleagues. You may be able to vent your anger and turn out an insightful piece on academic publishing at the same time. However, don't be surprised if, after the passage of time, a manuscript you were willing to defend tooth and nail no longer looks as inviolable as you were once ready to insist. One of the most difficult kinds of objectivity to achieve is that toward what we ourselves have written. I noted that I take pride in what I write and enjoy rereading earlier pieces, but that is personal and subjective. In cold, hard fact, nothing I have written is destined to become a runaway best-seller.

Publishing, like everything else about fieldwork, can be highly political as well as involve a high degree of chance and luck. An author can most effectively exert a positive influence in attracting an editor's attention to a manuscript by carefully matching the material to the publishing source. This involves a certain amount of networking, and newcomers can seek help from old-timers who may have a broader view of who is interested in publishing what. Be selective in asking others to help with the critical editing of a manuscript, but remember that it is not unreasonable to inquire whether a distant scholar might be willing to read your manuscript and render an overall judgment as to its suitability for publication. Perhaps you can even solicit suggestions as to possible journals or publishers.

Along the lines of matchmaking, the best place to inquire about publication is with a journal or publisher known to publish material similar to what you have prepared, much as artists exhibit where comparable works already have been shown or performed. Although publishers and journal editors (like gallery and museum directors) may prefer to think of themselves as open to anything new and different, they must specialize in order to define any audience at all. The journals most likely to publish a paper reporting a qualitative study are the journals that have been doing it all along. The journals most interested in an ethnographically or an ethnomethodologically oriented study will be the journals that have already published such pieces.

You should be able to find clues as to likely journals from looking at the citations in your own reference section. If a journal you are considering is not already cited, look at recent issues and think about adding some "politically correct" references to your list. "Window dressing!" you cry. Perhaps it is. Window dressing can be a highly developed craft. Edward Bruner reminds us,

> The bibliography, as much political statement as scholarly reference, cites some authors and omits others, thereby positioning the writer within particular networks, schools, and traditions in the academic discipline. The politics of the bibliography has yet to be written. [1993:3]

Sending material out for review brings another reminder that style alone is never enough. Academic reviewers and editors are likely to regard a manuscript in hand as a draft, not the polished manuscript you intended it to be, which means that quite likely it will need still further editing for style. My experience is that the most prevalent problem with submitted manuscripts is the lack of clear focus, the author going off in too many directions rather than developing a well-honed and logical argument or case. So we end up full circle, back at the "problem problem" where we started. Well begun is half done. Indeed, maybe more than half!

PART IV
FIELDWORK AS PERSONAL WORK

For many of its zealous practitioners, participant observation is an art form and almost literally a way of life appropriately constituted as an oral tradition.

—Danny Jorgensen
Participant Observation, p. 8

Implicit in most *Art of...* books is the assumption that as we discover how to do something, or how to do it better, we will derive greater satisfaction in the doing. Some *Art of...* books make that assumption explicit, as does Irma Rombauer's forever popular *Joy of Cooking*, its title calling attention to the pleasure to be gained rather than to the how-to nature of the book.

I am hesitant to write about the joys of fieldwork. Not everyone who engages in it is overcome with joy. Most who have a major engagement with it make that engagement only once, usually in the course of conducting dissertation research. Some never quite get through, or over, the experience. The editors of a collection of essays presenting an "inside view" of qualitative research" introduce the book with this stark appraisal:

> Fieldwork must certainly rank with the more disagreeable activities that humanity has fashioned for itself. It is usually inconvenient, to say the least, sometimes physically uncomfortable, frequently embarrassing, and, to a degree, always tense. . . . Field researchers have in common the

tendency to immerse themselves for the sake of science in situations that all but a tiny minority of humankind goes to great lengths to avoid. [Shaffir and Stebbins 1991:1]

Further, I am not sure that those of us who enjoy and derive personal satisfaction from fieldwork—at least in the recounting of it, if not necessarily on a moment-to-moment basis at the time—want to give our detractors more ammunition by suggesting that one reason we do it is that we like it. Still, there has been an analytical cast to the discussion to this point, and I may have dwelt unduly on fieldwork's complex problems, contextual constraints, and paradoxical dilemmas. My intent has been to present a rounded view that meets fieldwork's frustrations and complications straight on, from the perspective of doing art rather than science.

I have also tried to keep the discussion grounded in practical concerns, and that may have given the foregoing more of a how-to cast than I intended, although that would underscore the doing of fieldwork as meticulous art and craft, not something artsy-craftsy. In any case, I have devoted enough attention to how-to matters and to considerations of what we can learn from looking at how artists working in other media for other audiences do what they do.

It's time now to ask why, with a look on the bright side, touting some of the personal satisfactions in fieldwork. Chapter 10 offers such a review. Chapter 11, new to this edition, looks at another personal dimension of fieldwork, the critical role of discretion. This is the personal resolution each of us must make about all that we observe and what we decide to report. To accomplish that with real data, I take a look at three of my own studies and consider some things left out of the final telling and why they are not there.

CHAPTER TEN
THE SATISFACTIONS OF FIELDWORK

For some readers of ethnography—myself included—the apparent freedom from rigid methodological rules associated with fieldwork and the blissful disregard that many ethnographic writers displayed for high-flying abstractions in their papers and monographs seemed to provide a wonderful excuse for having an adventurous good time while operating under the pretext of doing serious intellectual work.

—John Van Maanen
"An End to Innocence," in *Representation in Ethnography*, p. 2

The claim to attention of an ethnographic account does not rest on its author's ability to capture primitive facts in faraway places and carry them home like a mask or a carving, but on . . . the power of the scientific imagination to bring us into touch with the lives of strangers.

—Clifford Geertz
"Thick Description," in *The Interpretation of Cultures*, p. 16

All art requires presentation and representation; nothing is exactly as it seems. Fieldwork joins other art forms in that regard. It, too, is necessarily partial and incomplete, sacrificing some elements to enhance others through presentation and representation. Its accomplishments are what we behold.

We do not expect to be regaled with every dilemma each fieldworker has confronted, any more than we are bound to accept an artist's personal plight or unbridled enthusiasm when making our private assessment of the finished product. We no more seek out poor or incomplete reports of fieldwork than we seek out discarded canvases or unfinished musical scores simply to gain a deeper appreciation of the good ones. We do, however, give undue attention to trying to discern the genius in, or isolate artistic elements of, the scores or manuscripts or canvases of famous composers, authors, and painters, just as we return repeatedly to a small corpus of fieldwork classics.

It may be reassuring for the novice practitioner of any art form to keep in mind that even the best of potters throws away some pots, the best painter paints over unsatisfactory canvases, the published author admits to poems or manuscripts that have never been (and are unlikely ever to be) published.

Failed fieldwork is more elusive still. It simply disappears. If there is no written record except in private notes, and the fieldworker makes no further mention, it may in the long run be of no more consequence than a forgotten summer holiday. As a result, the only models available to the beginner are of successfully completed fieldwork as reported in successfully completed accounts, and of those the same few are held up to generation after generation of students. As with other art worlds, we, too, place the masterpieces on so high a pedestal that they tend to inhibit when they are meant to inspire. Consistent with his notion of the integrated professional, Howard Becker suggests that as a consequence "people tend to denigrate routine science and art work, when that's what practically all of it is" (personal communication, April 1995).

Three anthropologists who joined forces to edit a collection dealing with fieldwork as human experience made this observation in the text they did produce about another text that got away:

> It must be mentioned at this point that not all fieldwork has been successful: there have been failures. All anthropologists know about them through the cocktail circuit, but they are rarely written up. As editors we first wanted to do a book titled *Failed Fieldwork*, thinking that much could be learned from such a book, but we could not get anyone to contribute chapters. [Lawless, Sutlive, and Zamora 1983:xv–xvi]

In examining fieldwork processes, my intent has been to encourage researchers to become bolder in the art of their work just as they are

214

admonished to become more exacting in its science. One might think of that part of the discussion as attending to the professional side of fieldwork. As a professional, the researcher self-consciously draws from both science and art to create a role unique to fieldwork. In this chapter, I review personal aspects that can make fieldwork not only professionally but personally satisfying.

I do not mean to divorce the personal from the professional; one attractive feature of fieldwork is the way it links the two. This is especially so for researchers who buy into a mainstream work ethic, as I suspect most do. They find salvation in a correspondence between what they feel obliged to do professionally and something they find personally satisfying. Although fieldwork is not a career in itself, it can become the focal activity in a career oriented toward research and writing.

The word "work," embedded in the compound "fieldwork," suggests a productive, effortful activity, although perhaps a rather curious form of it to outsiders. Most of us who pursue fieldwork have been called on to explain, both to disbelieving relatives and to skeptics in our research settings, exactly what the work part of it is. This is difficult to convey to those who restrict their definition of work to physical activity involving some degree of exertion. In practice, the term *fieldwork* is probably used most comfortably everywhere except when one is actually in the field. At a research site, the word "study" rests a bit more gently. That term frees us from having to defend why we are not at a workplace of our own. How else can we explain why we are free to come and go from whatever else it is that we do, in some other place that is apparently not too insistent that we be there to do it, to join in the activities of others among whom we appear to have few obligations, no responsibilities, and often rather limited skill, including even the ability to communicate?

Qualitative researchers resent the suggestion that their methods are easier than quantitative ones; they are likely to insist that fieldwork is hard. Of course, we don't mind when colleagues commiserate with us about the long hours, risks, inconveniences, and uncertainties associated with fieldwork. For anyone with a strong work ethic, those hours, risks, inconveniences, and uncertainties underscore claims that fieldwork means hard work, if more of an emotionally stressful than a strictly physical nature.

Commiseration for all we go through in conducting our work is heady stuff for anyone who likes to be recognized as a hard worker. Yet I become uneasy whenever quantitatively oriented researchers assuage me by insisting that qualitative research is even harder than theirs. I prefer the argument that it is difficult primarily because it is fraught with uncertainty. As with explanations about teaching, it is not easy to communicate to a casual onlooker exactly what makes such hard work of it. Perhaps our most convincing argument deals not with fieldwork itself but with the concomitant responsibility of reporting it. Novice fieldworkers may share the same concern. They may anticipate the thrill of having an adventurous good time without a clue as to how one goes about writing it up afterward.

I trust that experienced old-timers will agree that conceptualizing and reporting are fieldwork's biggest bugaboos, but any aspect of the fieldwork process can strike terror in the heart of the inexperienced researcher. There is no end to the list of potential what-ifs. Those who feel overwhelmed by every aspect are well advised to seek another line of work or to pursue their inquiries in a more systematic fashion. But each step along the way also offers potential satisfaction to those who see opportunities rather than obstacles.

I have singled out for discussion five such sources of satisfaction. One might regard this as a list of suggestions for deriving the most satisfaction out of the fieldwork investment. Better still, these might be thought of as guidelines for living the fieldwork experience.

Being—or Becoming—a Sociable Social Researcher

An interesting role we play (often inadvertently) is a strange combination in which we serve at once as *ambassadors for* and *detractors of* research. Our fieldwork excursions ordinarily take us among ordinary people likely neither to have been the subjects of research nor to have encountered a researcher in action. What we do is not all that mysterious, and thus we give the uninitiated a peek behind the research veil. They see research performed by, with, and "on" humans like themselves. Granted, they see a special type of researcher, quite different from their presumed image of someone peering through a microscope. Our very presence on-site detracts greatly from the mystery, in the same way that government scientists are demystified when we read about them or see them interviewed on TV.

I think it valuable for people to have this realistic glimpse into how research operates. In reality, research is a fallible human endeavor, neither totally trustworthy nor totally beyond any layperson's comprehension. We read often enough about researchers in high-stakes efforts who have falsified reports, announced results prematurely, or taken credit for work that was not their own. Although we are sometimes made painfully aware of fieldwork's shortcomings, the breadth and depth of all knowledge should remain suspect. Too seldom is the public made aware of the huge leaps researchers sometimes make between what they observe and the possible implications for human safety or well-being. In a modest way, the on-site researcher performs a public service by exposing inquiry for what it is, rather than fostering its image as the mysterious doings of an unseen group of relentless truth seekers referred to collectively as "scientists." We bring research to the people in more ways than one.

Unquestionably there is an aura and a status associated with the term *researcher*, but it is not the image of a fieldworker. Perhaps reflecting my own generation, I envision the researcher at work as a white-coated chemist carefully pouring a liquid from one test tube into another. (NB: The liquid in one of the two vials should have a reddish cast.) Granted, that image is probably better suited to the local pharmacist; the only research chemist of my personal acquaintance sits in front of a computer most of the time. I do not envy his work, although paradoxically I, too, spend a great deal of time sitting in front of a computer. I don't mind borrowing something of the scientist's aura and status. I do that by appropriating the label "researcher," careful to emphasize—as though an obvious plus—that the kind of research I do is conducted not in the laboratory but with *real* people in *natural* settings.

As with most qualitative researchers, there is an implicit equation in my mind: The realness of my settings compensates for the lack of a laboratory that might otherwise validate my claim. I conduct my inquiries in the real world, a world that the laboratory researcher attempts to manipulate, control, and even replicate with computer capabilities ironically labeled "virtual reality." I study in real reality; my efforts are devoted to describing and understanding that world just as it is. And yes, that is research.

In the fieldwork part of fieldwork—that period in which the researcher is engaged with the individuals being studied—one can actually be in role as a social being while remaining totally immersed in one's work. For those inclined toward sociability, you can't get much closer to having your cake and eating it, too. For those not naturally outgoing, fieldwork provides—and to some extent demands—a level of sociability they might envy in others but would not otherwise achieve were it not for the requirements of the role. In short, fieldwork lauds natural sociability and insists on some effort in this regard among those for whom sociability does not come easily.

It is the *role* of fieldworker that is social. Humans are innately social, but those attracted to academic careers are not necessarily the most social of humans. The role sometimes helps fieldworkers achieve what they seem unable to achieve through personality alone. That may explain why fieldworkers who seem distant and aloof at home sometimes write with such fondness about "their people" or "their informants" at more remote field sites.

The fieldwork role has often necessitated my pursuing one social activity I particularly abhor: visiting. (I'm not much on attending weddings, graduations, or funerals, either.) I am perfectly capable of carrying on a conversation, but I go to great lengths to avoid having to sit and visit. In part this may be because I am a listener, and obsessive talkers seem to take advantage. But dignify such visiting as an essential element of fieldwork—small talk and endless listening done in the line of duty—and I can do it. The knowledge that not only must I carry off the visit but will later have to write up my notes makes my effort all the more heroic. Such sacrifice—all in the name of research.

A Hint of Adventure

Fieldwork can provide an invitation to adventure underwritten with a sense of intellectual purpose. Of course, not everybody seeks adventure or wants to devote the time necessary to engage in it. Fieldwork can be a terrible nuisance to anyone simply checking off the obstacles to academic tenure or otherwise anxious to get permanently settled. Under such circumstances, it can make an already potentially unsettling experience even more so, literally and figuratively. But young people whose lives have been lived essentially in schools, or tenured faculty feeling hopelessly trapped in the presumed security of their institutions, may long to escape the deadening routine of too-settled lives. My impression of the academic career is that to get somewhere one shouldn't really go anywhere. Fieldwork offers an appealing resolution to that dilemma.

For the tenured academic, the tradition of sabbatical leave provides the opportunity to engage in fieldwork throughout a professional career rather than only at its outset. Sabbatical leave—ordinarily taken during the seventh, or sabbatic, year of service—has surely been one of the special dividends of a teaching career, at least in the past. For a field-oriented researcher, it presents not only an incredible research opportunity but also the possibility of a periodically recurring one. For faculty not financially dependent on summer teaching, sabbatical leave may be parlayed into as much as an uninterrupted fifteen-month period every seventh year, making extended fieldwork a possibility even at mid-career. Of course, it is not all that easy to drop everything and take off for a year, even for those unencumbered with working partners, children in school, and the host of other complicating factors in our complicated lives. Yet the sabbatical makes field research compatible with teaching and offers the possibility of adventure in an academic career that might not otherwise seem destined for it.

My fieldwork experiences have literally taken me around the world. An involuntary tour of duty in the early 1950s with a see-the-world army got me no farther from my hometown of Oakland, California, than Fort Lewis, Washington, although at the time that seemed preferable to being sent to fight an unpopular action in Korea. Fieldwork conducted in British Columbia, Canada, for my doctoral dissertation took me only a few hundred miles farther north. But on subsequent sabbaticals I have spent the major part of a year in Rhodesia (now Zimbabwe), another in Malaysia, and two extended periods in Thailand, all made possible by the sabbatical tradition (and salary subsidy) augmented by other funds (a subsidy from Daystar Communications in Africa and two Fulbright awards in Thailand).

Once actually in the field, descriptives of a more mundane nature are quickly substituted for the word "adventure." Adventure is, in fact, something most fieldworkers would rather have happen to someone else. But both before and, especially, after, the fieldwork experience tends to be glossed in a quasiromantic fashion. I confess that my collective memories of fieldwork give far greater pleasure than the day-to-day experiences themselves necessarily did.

No matter how difficult it is living in the field—when and if it is possible and appropriate to make so total a commitment—or going to one's research site for repeated visits of a shorter duration if that is the realistic alternative, fieldworkers may be surprised to feel ambivalent about departing when the time comes to depart. At the end of my initial twelve months spent among the Kwakiutl, I felt at once emotionally drained yet intellectually invigorated by the opportunity to have observed and participated, however marginally as a white male teacher in an Indian community, in a culturally different way of life. (As I discuss in the final chapter, I also departed with little idea of how I would go about writing it up. It was far too close as personal experience; the dissertation assignment was what had become unreal at the time.)

Conversely, even if the experience itself has brought the fieldworker little joy, sometimes the departure brings both joy and a sense of relief, and one's anger or frustration provides impetus for the reporting. Anthropologist Hortense Powdermaker described her joy at leaving Hollywood after the fieldwork on which *Hollywood: The Dream Factory* (1950) was based:

> I was never totally immersed in Hollywood as I have been in other situations. . . . As I left Hollywood after a year and drove past a sign marking the boundaries of Los Angeles, I burst into song, as is my habit when feeling joy. But even that reaction did not make me realize how deeply I had hated the place. [1966:224–25]

Whatever the outcome of the fieldwork itself—and negative experiences can prove as powerful as positive ones to motivate subsequent reporting— the critical test is how deeply one has felt personally involved and affected. If it is hardly surprising when ethnographers at their sites for a year or more feel this way, the nature of fieldwork can produce such a reaction after even a modest project. I always reminded students that they would probably remember their too-brief fieldwork encounters long after they had forgotten the class sessions, the texts, alas, even the instructor.

Problem Setting as Intellectual Challenge

The conceptualizing that accompanies field research affords a major worry for some but a stimulating intellectual challenge for others. Fieldwork presents an unusual opportunity for the truly contemplative life, not only figuratively, but literally, through living fully contextualized research. Regardless of how the experience is later written up, the thinking that accompanies fieldwork must be one's own: Everything is filtered through what Geertz calls "I-witnessing" (Geertz 1988:73ff). The self becomes the referent against which all others' actions are played out, all others' meanings discerned.

There could be no more nurturing circumstances for the self-reflective individual than in the mindwork that must accompany fieldwork. The entire previous section examined fieldwork as mindwork, and I underscored that the conceptualizing that precedes, accompanies, and follows fieldwork can be highly satisfying, personally as well as professionally. Mindwork is the creative dimension in fieldwork, the reflective product of a maturing scholar. There are no child prodigies in this endeavor.

When engaging in fieldwork, we observe something that has never exactly occurred before and would not now be an object of study were we not doing it. Our work is always unique in time and place. Today many researchers are also breaking new ground by introducing qualitative inquiry into disciplines and professional arenas previously receptive only to rigid experimental approaches. Even when our research topics are similar to what others have done or are doing—studies of new immigrants, the urban homeless, those suffering with AIDS, drugs and violence—the exact combination of ourselves as observers and the specific settings in which we work stand as one of a kind, a fleeting moment that we capture. Every start is a fresh start, rife with potential for seeing new possibilities, gaining new insights.

We are, in a sense, freed from the onus of replication studies because we can never exactly replicate the conditions of a field-based inquiry. There is no excuse for fieldworkers to crank out the equivalent of motel art. Every study ought to reveal something significant that expands our efforts at understanding. I so like to hear researchers embarking on their inquiries who say genuinely, "I'm really excited about this study!" Why shouldn't they be? Why ever undertake what Margaret Mead described as the "deep involvement" of fieldwork without that sense of excitement:

> The ability to do good fieldwork still depends, as it always has, on a deep
> involvement with a task so exacting that no efforts, no amount of brilliance
> or imagination, no battery of technical aids, no depth of commitment and

sense of responsibility will ever be enough to permit any individual to do what is there to be done. Those who are attracted by the inexhaustibility of the task will continue to be so. [1970:258]

The fact that for years we continue to reflect on our fieldwork experience offers consolation, even compensation, for the inevitable frustration of finding ourselves unable to bring a study to the level of sophisticated insight we would like to achieve. As discussed earlier, we abandon our studies rather than complete them. We come to a point where we must give them up in order to get on with other pressing obligations.

But we need never totally abandon them. One's fieldwork experiences cannot help but be cumulative if they have been deeply lived. We have the opportunity to mull them over and over, to bring new understandings to bear on earlier problems, to seek fresh perspectives. I feel fortunate to have accumulated a lore of research experience that I continue to ponder and to mine. One way or another, I return to review the lessons of my experiences and to reflect on my efforts to draw lessons from them. An envious office-bound colleague once reflected, "You fieldworker-types are lucky. You never run out of things to write about."

The Authority of Authorship

Writing is another facet fully as capable of providing satisfaction for some as it most assuredly brings a sense of panic to others. Writing is creative in two senses, its figurative one entailing an originality of thought and expression and its literal one of creating something in a new form through re-creating prior experience. Accomplishing the task cannot help but bring personal fulfillment as well as professional recognition as the fieldwork cycle comes to fruition. For myself, writing has become a fulfilling activity in its own right. Deferred gratification though it certainly is, I derive a sense of accomplishment from the writing I have done and an exhilarating sense of challenge while doing it. (Well, at least on most days.)

I do not suggest that fieldworkers must necessarily have a love of words or take particular delight in sitting at their desks forging sentences at their fingertips from ideas not all that clearly formed in their minds. Nor is there necessarily great joy to be gained from endlessly editing what one has drafted in the effort to generate sentences that better convey intended meanings. Rather, I think personal satisfaction is gained from having something important enough to say to warrant saying it well enough to call to the attention of others. This is not fieldwork's long suit—our accounts never signal dramatic breakthroughs of the kind that hit the evening news or morning papers. But it is heady stuff nonetheless to be able to report well on topics of social significance, to bring them to life. However modestly, that is how we make our individual contributions toward human knowledge and understanding. As researchers, that is why we try to get things right as well as get them written.

I noted that I have never heard of anyone who became a fieldworker simply to exercise his or her writing talents. Yet field research does offer an alternative way to slip into a writing-dependent career without having to study journalism, become an English major, or take courses in scientific writing. That may explain why fieldwork accounts are often tedious to read (a feature they share with certain literary classics), but it is gratifying to recognize a growing library of accounts that are as satisfying for their style as they are profound in their insight. And sometimes we come out well simply because we try to tell it like it is.

When our efforts extend to giving voice to others while learning to mute our own, we sometimes succeed in bringing different voices into arenas where they would not otherwise be heard, offering support for claims of what we do and perhaps do best. "The art of the ethnographer," Paul Bohannan writes, "is to learn, then to translate, a foreign people's stories without inserting his or her own pattern" (1995:77). He continues,

> Fieldwork was a first attempt to recontext ideas as they are actually held in the real world . . . into the emerging world of social science. It is the best way so far discovered, in spite of the fact that it remains an art with many built-in traps. [P. 148]

Looking at Life

As a form of legitimate voyeurism, fieldwork can delight anyone hopelessly attracted to people watching, in spite of the risk of censure for practicing a darker art. In its social science sense, voyeurism implies more than a preoccupation with sexual activity, referring in an inclusive way to the fact that fieldwork not only permits but requires one to observe other humans at work and at play. Consistent with their charter to study all facets of human life, fieldworkers have an implied license for doing what most people do only covertly—to examine whatever they find intriguing about the activities of their fellow humans.

Most certainly, sexual behavior falls into that domain. An incidental dividend of fieldwork is that one is not only allowed but expected to have more than passing interest in matters sexual. In pursuit of that "intimate, long-term acquaintance" discussed in chapter 4, fieldworkers have in fact often been conspicuously conscientious about detailing the sexual practices— or at least the stated beliefs—among whatever groups they have studied, while remaining conspicuously reluctant to discuss their own sexuality. Only recently has this topic been broached in the fieldwork literature, with such studies as Karla Poewe's candid *Reflections of a Woman Anthropologist* (published in 1982 under the pseudonym Manda Cesara) or collections like *Taboo* (Kulick and Willson 1995), or *Out in the Field* and *Out in Theory*, two volumes edited by Ellen Lewin and William Leap (1996; 2002).

One of my first impressions about the study of anthropology was that some of its sources were kept under lock and key in the library at the University of California, Berkeley, a fact so tantalizing that it is a wonder my horny undergraduate fraternity brothers did not all become anthropology majors at least long enough to check those books out. One of the books so guarded must surely have been Malinowski's *Sexual Life of Savages* (1929), its promising title endorsed in a preface contributed by Havelock Ellis. Even today, social scientists seem especially attentive to reporting whatever they can about sexual practices among the "natives." Michael Moffatt's *Coming of Age in New Jersey* (1989), for example, is a study of college student life that seems to have been especially adapted for the market by devoting two of its seven chapters to that topic. (In an earlier day, I might have wondered why *only* two chapters were devoted to a topic so central to the life and thought of twenty-year-olds.) My point is that our focus on natural settings is seen as giving us license to delve into sexual matters that might not otherwise be deemed any of our business.

We are probably not as subtle as we think in seeming to pass quickly over our interest in such topics. This was brought home sharply by the observation of a social scientist in Thailand who remarked, "We don't need any more researchers coming over here to do studies of Thai prostitutes. There are far more important issues that confront Thai society than that."

Her observation in 1985 kept me from revealing a topic I had considered for investigation, the life history of one or more young Thai male prostitutes. With the subsequent spread of AIDS in that population, perhaps I had a defensible topic after all. My point is that fieldworkers do feel they can exercise far-ranging choice in the problems they address or look at broad contexts in problems more narrowly defined. They appear able to indulge their whims in the line of duty.

It is problematic with all inquiry that researchers find what they are looking for. My focus here concerns personal satisfactions in fieldwork. Finding something that one is interested in can indeed increase personal satisfaction. Such satisfaction need not get in the way, especially for researchers who also derive satisfaction in a strategy for living their personal lives.

Another aspect of trying to figure out what human social life is all about, of being able to understand something new, is the pleasure many find in the role of a learner who actively regards others—people of all stations—as one's teachers. Fieldwork is not well suited for individuals who thrive on authority and expertise and feel they must know everything about whatever subject they touch. Nor is it comforting for anyone obsessed with maintaining control. But fieldwork is wonderfully suited for those who find satisfaction as lifelong learners, ever appreciative of how much others know and have experienced, rather than in need of parading their own knowledge before audiences. An old adage advises us to learn as though we will live forever. That seems good advice—or fair warning—for fieldworkers. The human condition does not remain static long enough for the work to be completed, even for an instant.

Fieldwork is a learning experience, and neophyte fieldworkers need to recognize their preferred learning styles in contemplating how best to make the experience personally satisfying. Some people like to meet new experiences head on; others prefer a gradual immersion, anxious to gain both knowledge and experience before undertaking independent work. I do not think that training or formal coursework are absolutely essential preparation, for I do not think of fieldwork as a mysterious process so much as a matter of good sense, sound judgment, and adaptability. Still, there is no reason for anyone not to benefit from guided experience. It seems counterproductive to begin an inquiry without some sense of what others have learned. Surely not every neophyte fieldworker needs to reinvent participant observation or interviewing all over again!

Courses and workshops offered today under such titles as ethnographic research, field methods, or qualitative inquiry provide an opportunity for guided practice in participant observation and interviewing. Funded research and large-scale projects also create opportunities for entry into fieldwork, with project staff working cooperatively on large issues or training assistants to continue or extend the work. Thus, there are ways to acquire fieldwork skills through apprenticeships as well as formal coursework. Both approaches tend to focus on fieldwork techniques, but that is what novices are most concerned about, and there is nothing wrong with taking first things first. Note that in arranging the chapters in this book, I followed the same logic, discussing the fieldwork part of fieldwork first. The essence of fieldwork, however, is the mindwork that guides it, from inception to publication, and mindwork is mostly caught, not taught.

In the days before we became so self-conscious about method, help was there for the asking and the occasional complaint was raised even then that supervision in the field was excessive, although it was handled entirely through correspondence. Written memos sent from the field do force one to keep up with the reporting, however, and they may eventually find their way into the final account. Sometimes these exchanges have provided substance for volumes in their own right (two examples already cited are the fieldwork dialogue between Solon Kimball and William Partridge [1979] and the correspondence of Robert Redfield and Sol Tax, compiled by Robert Rubinstein [1991]).

In the course of the fieldwork experience, many students have established satisfying collegial relationships with their mentors, relationships that extended well into their professional careers. This may be especially prevalent in anthropology, where attention to kinship among the peoples studied has made anthropologists more aware, and more appreciative, of their own academic kinship. Although four decades have passed since I completed my doctoral studies at Stanford University, George and Louise Spindler continued to exert an influence on my work through encouragement, ideas, and constructive critique. I trace more than twenty of my articles and books directly to their support, including my first two major fieldwork studies and the monographs in which they were reported.

Human social life is our focus, and fieldworkers able to see themselves as learners and actors in the social settings they study, rather than hiding behind the role of distanced onlookers, are in a better position to realize the potential of the disciplined subjectivity the approach allows. Although fieldwork requires some sense of detachment, it not only allows but calls for involvement as well, making room for compassion and understanding. Ideally, one ought to be able to escape roles completely and just be oneself, participating in and enjoying life by seeing how it is lived by others. The focus of field research ought to be on topics and groups where this potential can be realized. Those among whom you conduct research ought to be glad to see you each time you appear, and you ought to be glad to see them. A spirit of joie de vivre should prevail. Fieldwork is an activity one can engage in with passion and without apology.

Writing enthusiastically on its behalf, sociologist Danny Jorgensen confesses that participant observation "is for me an abiding preoccupation—if not a way of life—and an important component of my social identity" (1989:8). Jorgensen does not insist that everyone must become so zealous a practitioner: "You need not make such a commitment, however, to use participant observation appropriately and profitably" (p. 8). He's right; you need not make such a commitment, but why not make it? Fieldwork beckons, even dares, you to become part of what you study. That is the difference between observation and participant observation.

There is always the hope, the ever-so-slight possibility, that what we uncover and report from our fieldwork will in some small way enhance our understanding of the lives of others and of ourselves. Geertz describes this as "the power of the scientific imagination to bring us into touch with the lives of strangers" (1973:16), although my underlying premise is that science alone is not equal to the task. The roles of emotion and imagination—viewed as essential elements in artistic endeavor—are examined in the final chapter.

There is even the chance, perhaps slimmer yet, that we do actually help bring about beneficial change in the lives of those strangers. We can't measure such outcomes, at least not in the full context and long term that really count. But there is satisfaction that comes simply from recognizing the ideals to which we aspire. (Strange that social scientists are often so hard on missionaries for their zeal, so apparently unaware of their own.)

I remember a comment offered by one of my earliest doctoral students, Ray Barnhardt, reflecting on what he had gained from the anthropological spin I had introduced into his orientation as an educator, much the same way George Spindler had done for me. On completing his dissertation,

Ray took a faculty position at the University of Alaska, Fairbanks, where he has devoted some thirty-five years to programs creating new opportunities for Alaska's Indian and Eskimo populations. I assumed that he would extol the virtues of studies in cultural anthropology for providing insight he needed into these communities. But instead he reflected on how his studies in anthropology gave him insight and perspective into his own life and work. He could take it from there. His perspective provided me with a fresh perspective of my own. We do well to examine the extent to which whatever we would like to see happening to and for others is happening to us.

THE ART OF DISCRETION

I am left with a loose end, part of the wistful sense of unfinished business that seems inherent in fieldwork.

—Peter Metcalf
They Lie, We Lie: Getting on with Anthropology, p. 109

Every choice is also a sacrifice.

—Susanne K. Langer
Feeling and Form, p. 122

It has been a dozen years since I began work on the first edition of *The Art of Fieldwork*. My enthusiasm for and commitment to fieldwork as a research approach are unswerving, and I am happy to be able to report its ever-widening application. But I now temper my enthusiasm with a more realistic view of what a fieldworker can accomplish, both in terms of what can be learned and, especially, what we report of all that we observe.

Thus there has been a slightly different emphasis in this edition of the text. I have come to the conclusion that a critical aspect of the art of fieldwork, if not the core issue, lies in how we depict or portray what we have observed and what we consciously choose not to portray. And that issue resides totally outside the realm of science. Science can help support the decisions we make by lining up evidence for the action we have taken. Ultimately, however, questions of discretion are up to each individual fieldworker. Only that individual is aware of all the professional and personal dimensions to be factored in, subconsciously as well as consciously. Here, of course, I deal with the conscious ones—they are far-reaching enough.

And so I conclude this second edition by examining elements of discretion: how it works and how the choices keep changing, leaving each fieldworker to wonder if he or she still is getting it quite right. To accomplish this, I will look in closer detail at three of my own studies already mentioned in these pages: my first, my most recent, and one that lies between the two. Chronologically, they are *A Kwakiutl Village and School*, originally published in 1967, *Teachers versus Technocrats: An Educational Innovation in Anthropological Perspective*, originally published in 1977, and *Sneaky Kid and Its Aftermath: Ethics and Intimacy in Fieldwork*, published in 2002 but telling a story that began in 1980. If I am able to lure you into reading them, don't think I have done so without design, but I can say enough here to make my point about how they illustrate issues of discretion. This is not to say they are exemplary examples, but only to put before us some real cases. That means you now have to learn some of the things that were left out of each study or that were glossed over or examined with a special, light touch.

I examine what a researcher (me, in this case) did in these specific instances and ponder what more that tells us about fieldwork as an art. A brief synopsis of the three studies is followed by both personal revelation and a reflection on the times in which each was written.

A Kwakiutl Village and School

Looking at a beginning researcher leaving the field in September 1963 and dedicating himself wholeheartedly to the organization and writing of a dissertation, one would think that we might have exclaimed, "Here's a young man who knows exactly what he is doing. He is writing a dissertation that will become a scholarly monograph and will remain in print for the rest of his life. He's one to watch!"

Except that is not how it happened, not at all. Teaching my class of as many as twenty-nine Kwakiutl Indian pupils sorely tested my patience and resources, and living as a bachelor in an isolated village took time and energy. I knew that I had to make and keep field notes, but they were mostly anecdotal and diary-like, complete enough to remind me of what happened but seldom penetrating with any depth into aspects of village life beyond the walls of the school. I wanted to be perceived as sociable, but it seemed that whatever I was doing, several other things also needed doing at the same time. Often it was note making itself that got skipped for a day or two.

After the school term finished in June 1963, I stayed on in the village, living in the empty teacherage for the summer. (The Indian agent was more than happy to let me occupy the building until the next teacher arrived.) Summer allowed time to join villagers in commercial fishing. That took big hunks of time as well, although in those days (and continuing today) the work week usually lasted only two or three days, the "weekend" the balance, so there was some respite, at least when we returned to the village rather than stayed at a distant fish camp. Then suddenly the summer was over. The teacherage was going to be occupied, and I headed home to begin writing.

Writing? I didn't have a clue what I would write about, except that school would be the focus of one part of the study, and village life would be the other part. Did I plan to emphasize art over science or science over art? I don't think either was the driving force for my work. I felt that I could render a plausible account of daily life and a plausible account of my experiences as village teacher, period. I did not know how to make my account scientific other than to try to make it objective. As for art, it, too, eluded me. Literally, there was no art work going on in the village in the form of handicraft that was present in some villages, and figuratively there seemed to be nothing artistic about the way people lived except for the sheer art of survival.

I took my momentum from fieldwork observations and devoted myself to description. That was probably a wise choice, although I saw no real alternative. I might have examined some esoteric aspects of village life from an anthropological perspective, but my background was not that sophisticated. Such an excursion would also have led me into a massive literature on the Kwakiutl dating back almost seventy-five years to Boas's early reports, rather than to dealing with the villagers as I had come to know them.

I outlined four chapters ("Introduction," "Life in the Village," "Life at School," "Analysis") and projected a writing schedule of a chapter a month beginning in October 1963. The first month would be devoted to an introduction surveying Indian education in North America and looking at site selection and method of reporting on a contemporary case of it. This would be followed by two major descriptive chapters. A final chapter would look at what was emerging as my central theme, cultural barriers to classroom performance. In that chapter I would put my own two cents into the study, pointing to some problems and posing a few alternative solutions.

It will come as no surprise that I soon fell behind schedule, but I did get the brief first chapter completed by the end of October, and that did a lot for my confidence. The second chapter, about village life, took far longer and became far bigger than I had planned (310 typed pages!), but by then I was on a roll. More importantly, I felt that for the first time in my life I had something important to write about. Even if my advisor and dissertation committee at Stanford objected to the length or to the approach I was taking, I would have my original version to return to later. (As I recall, Spindler worried only about my opening sentences, and the others made only minor suggestions. I had lost track of the fact that they had their own work to get on with; they were not waiting breathlessly to read mine.)

I say I did not see how science influenced my study, but that is taking the idea of science quite literally, as we tended to do in the 1960s. In organizing my huge second chapter, I turned to some standard categories from cultural anthropology to help me focus on key elements of village life, especially the idea of an annual cycle of economic activities that allowed me to divide the year into manageable segments. The end product did not result in extraordinary ethnography, and it was organized in such a way that real people kept getting in the way of generalizations, yet the chapter did have the ring of truth about it. Since it preceded the chapter on the school, it set up that chapter at the same time that it helped me to keep school activities separate.

The school chapter began with an overview of the education of village children in the recent past. Next I described my teaching year. I concluded with brief case studies of five of the school-age children. In developing those profiles I began to realize how important individual cases can be, bringing everything to bear on a few actors rather than floating some generalizations that pertain to no one in particular. Getting personal seems to allow for a more artistic approach, perhaps because ideas of comparison yield to how things work in each particular case. My subsequent studies have more often taken a personal perspective, but at the time I recognized that my dissertation needed to look like other dissertations. Although there were some celebrated life histories in anthropology, they were not being done by junior people, and they were not being done in interdisciplinary endeavors like anthropology and education.

From the moment I began writing, discretion became a haunting problem. I felt I was doing a balancing act in the way that I portrayed the village and individuals within it. I recognized that I did not hold the fate of the village in my hands—I wondered whether anyone would read the entire dissertation, even whether the members of my committee would do that—yet I felt a responsibility toward documenting village life without making things more difficult if villagers chose to continue living as they were doing. Personally, however, I felt that the village was in a state of rapid deterioration. There were strong indications that the government was hesitant about continuing to staff the school, and signs of social disorganization were rampant. I did not feel that it was my job to slant a report one way or the other, but I realized that writing about anything invariably is to evaluate it. I proceeded with caution.

By the end of my year in the village I had witnessed firsthand or been told about things that had happened that would not show villagers in a flattering light. I decided to mute such incidents with nothing more than a hint that life went on there as elsewhere. To me that boiled down to reporting honestly without feeling an obligation to report everything. I made decisions that I could live with; that has remained my style. As I reflected years later, my indiscretions have been debated ever since the study was published, but my discretions remain unremarked.

My dissertation put the Spindlers in somewhat of a quandary in terms of how best to publicize it. They were always publication minded and were enjoying success as editors of a new series initiated in 1960 entitled Case Studies in Cultural Anthropology. They also realized that my study and those being written at the same time by three of my fellow students in anthropology and education did not fit the existing format. I was present when Louise Spindler had a brainstorm about developing a parallel series of studies focusing on schools rather than treating them somewhat incidentally, as had been the case with the earlier series. It was my good fortune to come along at the right time and to have the Spindlers looking after our mutual interests. The idea for the new series was born right then. As with art communities, so with publishing ones: It takes luck as well as perseverance to get something going.

All the time I was in the village I felt a vague sense of frustration at being locked up with the school-age children when I felt I should have been with the adults observing what they were doing. Having anticipated a Kwakiutl assignment, I had done a great deal of reading before embarking on my odyssey. I knew far more of their culture than did the pupils in my class! And so I gave up the greatest opportunity of my life—to learn how Kwakiutl children of ages six to fifteen were learning their culture and what they knew of it at different ages. It simply did not occur to me that I was in a living laboratory and that I should try to find ways to assess what the children knew, individually and collectively. The idea did not fit the dissertation format; it could not be neatly bound like the study that I produced. It was impractical. Oh, the idea was artsy, all right—way too artsy to submit. I had chosen the road more traveled by.

The good news is that I completed the study. I did not even consider the opportunity of looking at cultural acquisition. If I had, I might never have finished. There's another kind of discretion in that—keeping one's academic pursuits sufficiently modest that they are attainable, or at least there is a reasonable chance of attaining them. Addressing any problem through fieldwork is a straightforward approach indeed, and the rationale for taking that approach should not get tangled up in wordy or technical explanations. The answer to the "problem problem" described earlier does not lie in obfuscation, but in stating as clearly as you can what you plan to do and how you intend to proceed. If you lack discretion at the outset, you will pay for it later when your final report will inevitably lack the grandiose claims you originally made for it.

Raymond Firth has suggested in *Elements of Social Organization* that a work of art makes a selection among experience, imagination, and emotion (1951:156). That provides a good starting place for examining the art in *A Kwakiutl Village and School*.

Experience is the long suit here. My account clearly has the stamp of "I was there." As I began writing the dissertation that would become the basis for the monograph, I could not see any plausible alternative except to describe village life exactly as I had witnessed it in 1962–1963. Although I spent hours in the classroom every week and hours at routine household tasks, the sum total of my travels during the year seems remarkable. I flew to Vancouver a couple of times, got as far north as Namu with the fishing crew, hopped a flight all the way to Prince Rupert with a missionary group during a holiday, sailed deep into the coastal waters of Knight Inlet, and visited most of the other villages in the region. The travel provided me with context and perspective. Eventually I realized that although I could not go everywhere and do everything that villagers did, the school-age children did not get to do everything the adults did either. Like me, they were locked up in school. But they could tell me what was going on, and they did.

The printed account might seem quite lacking in imagination, but as I reflect back on getting started with the writing, I give myself credit at least for an amazing amount of chutzpah—utter nerve—to think that I could write an ethnography at all. I did not feel that I had the command that other ethnographers seemed to exude in their ethnographies. In addition, my study needed to devote considerable attention to the school, a topic that most ethnographers of the day simply skipped because it was irrelevant to the life—the "old ways"—they were intent on describing. As a matter of fact, schooling in any form was apt to get in the way.

I am quite sure that imagination escaped me. The idea of making up any element that I had missed to make my account more complete was unthinkable. As I perused the customary headings familiar to cultural anthropologists in those days—economic organization, social organization, world view, social control, political organization—I decided that it would be better to skip topics on which I had too little information rather than go to the literature to document things that I had not actually observed. Anything that I include in the study occurred as I reported it. The perspective obviously has a bias—mine—but whatever did happen, I said what I made of it. Mostly.

I gradually began to realize that although I intended to provide an account of village life, I was not going to report everything I saw or heard. My reporting was going to be selective. I was going to have to exercise discretion even in the absence of any mandate or criteria for doing so. I was there to paint a picture of village life, true, but it was to be a picture made on a sunny day. Whatever an ethnography is, it is not an exposé, not a license to tell all. I would characterize this as keeping one's account close to the ground, but screening everything through a filter, a filter of respectability.

Emotion was the enemy. Hovering in my mind was the idea that I was a scientific observer. I wanted my dissertation to meet critical standards for ethnography, which, although more implied than stated, held that ethnographers are scientists who carefully document what people say and do . . . and then *selectively* report what they have observed. Although ethnographers were assumed to have human qualities like the people they studied, they also were assumed to be able to check them at the door to carry out their work.

I found it relatively easy to rise above emotion in transforming my notes into a coherent account. I revealed few emotions of my own. The emotions of villagers were displayed through words and deeds and the reflections of others. I attempted to offer no judgment. I strove to keep everything even, like Sergeant Friday's reminder, "Just the facts, ma'am." In the dissertation you can see how this approach is evident in everything reported. The times were affecting me, and I tried to remain true to what I saw as ethnography's high calling to objectivity.

Apparently I not only succeeded but succeeded too well. As I rewrote the dissertation for publication, the Spindlers, as well as Dave Boynton, Holt, Rinehart and Winston's editor for both education and anthropology, asked and subsequently had to insist that I write a bit more. They wanted me to reveal something of how I felt and any ideas I could share about what might be done to improve things, especially to broaden the opportunities for children in school.

Twenty-five years after the original fieldwork, I was invited to write the afterword for the Waveland reprinting of *A Kwakiutl Village and School.* At that point I did have more to say, extending my original discussion to give new emphasis to the process of cultural acquisition. In the afterword, I felt I finally could bring the account to a conclusion, although the village itself had long been deserted. The material that I added was interpretive, more humanistic, more personal. I no longer had to worry about whether a committee would allow me to say what I felt or to express personal feelings. I mention this to underscore that one is quite unlikely to bring a descriptive study to a close within the time frame of writing a dissertation. It took twenty-five years to write a satisfactory conclusion. Like a mature painter, by then I felt that I could paint what I wanted. But I had internalized the norms of my vocation; my personal style fit nicely within the boundaries of ethnographic writing.

The original monograph had been kept to 132 pages, consistent with the Spindlers' insistence that everything in the series be short enough, and thus the monographs inexpensive enough, that students could purchase several case studies rather than a single text. By 2003, with the AltaMira reissue, the monograph had long been separated from the series. Publisher Mitch Allen encouraged me to add an autobiographical piece that had been written by a villager in 1963 while I was still teaching there. At the time her statement seemed too personal, but after forty years I was beginning to fear that it might never appear in print.

In much the same way that my afterword seemed to add a needed note, the autobiographical statement provided insight into village life from the perspective of a village woman able to tell her own story. Her words complement and enhance mine. Today I would label her account an "ethnographic autobiography" (see Brandes 1982; HFW 2004). That might help to avoid confusion with the label "autoethnography" often given to accounts in which the researcher not only has a role but is often the principal figure. I advise neophyte fieldworkers to err on the scientific side, to be cautious about filling pages with their personal feelings or hopes for the people they study. But a whole new genre has evolved around the concept of autoethnography for those who see their own role as central to the stories they tell (see, for example, works co-edited by Carolyn Ellis and Arthur P. Bochner). As we shall see, my most recent work moves in this direction to an extent I would never have anticipated in the 1960s.

This is not to say we could not write about our concerns, but we kept them separate from our scientific studies, and we placed them before different audiences. For example, I wrote a separate piece about my Kwakiutl classroom that has often been reprinted titled "The Teacher as an Enemy" (HFW 1997). There I suggested how the classroom might look from the students' point of view. The article took its data from my Kwakiutl study but turned the question around to ask how much cultural know-how a child could learn from a culturally different teacher and whether that would ever be enough that he or she could "pass" in the teacher's society.

Teachers versus Technocrats

The second study to be examined was the result of a somewhat arbitrary assignment to a project in the research and development center where I worked. Neither the project nor the center was arbitrary, but my assignment seemed more to answer the question, What are we going to do with Harry? than to meet the needs of a federally funded research center. My appointment to the center had provided the original impetus for accepting a position at the University of Oregon. By 1971, in addition to writing up the Kwakiutl material for publication, I had spent two years assisting on one project, completed a major study of my own in which I was both figuratively and literally the principal investigator (*The Man in the Principal's Office*), and enjoyed the experience of my first sabbatical leave.

However, the research center to which I returned from sabbatical was not the same center to which I had been recruited seven years earlier. Washington—referring in general to the source of federal monies and specifically to the Office of Education—was now calling most of the shots. What had started out as an institution oriented toward basic research was now under a far stricter mandate to help with educational development. Where I originally had been encouraged to propose and carry out a project that led to my earlier study, the question now arose as to whether my approach to research had any place under its refocused mission.

I was assigned to a project involving a variation of a program-planning-budgeting system (PPBS) designed specifically for schools. However, the director of the center recognized that serving on such a project was not exactly my cup of tea. He tailored the assignment by charging me with writing an independent report chronicling what had gone on in the school district during the implementation. Project developers were working closely with central office personnel, but my report was to be separate, an account of what had actually been happening out in the schools. The anticipated duration of my study was roughly six months, coinciding with the formal termination of the project. My report was to be submitted separately, perhaps circulated only as an in-house document.

That seemed about the best anyone could come up with. It did not present a very exciting opportunity, but it did give me something anthropological to do. I was lucky that the director found—or perhaps made up—an assignment that could accommodate an ethnographer, even if it did not specifically call for one.

I made my first visits to the school district in the company of the project director. He introduced me as someone from the center who had recently joined the project. I sat in on a couple of meetings and asked no questions, so my presence caused no concern. But during those meetings I began to get the impression that things were not going as well as we had been led to believe. It looked like the people with whom we met at central office were waging a battle with the teachers over demands the project was making on them. Teachers were objecting strongly to the amount of time required for detailing their objectives, for pretesting, for post-testing, and for record keeping, activities that the project seemed to call for in the extreme. I suggested that I might visit a school or two to see the project in action. I inquired as to which might be a good school to visit and was referred to an outlying school that seemed to be making progress implementing the program.

The impression I was supposed to get from meetings with the central office staff was that everyone was satisfied with the program except for a few recalcitrant teachers. "And you get that with anything you try to introduce," I was assured. But if the school I visited was at all representative, it did not boast high acceptance; it only had fewer disgruntled teachers than most. In short, teachers throughout the school district were in revolt. Any difference that I discerned between schools seemed to relate to how heavy-handed each principal had been in support of the project.

Apparently the superintendent of the school district and the director of the project were in cahoots in a well-intended, but misguided, effort to improve the schools by implementing the study as a demonstration project rather than as a pilot test as originally advertised. The project had been slipped into the curriculum so quietly that at first teachers hardly noticed. But this was now year three of a three-year project, and it was time to get serious and to begin to recruit other school districts to join the implementation effort. While pressure was mounting from the school district central office (and at the research center) to get the system fully implemented, the spirit of revolt was also mounting. As one teacher later summarized, "It took THEM about three years to get this project implemented; it looks like it is going to take US about three years to get rid of it."

Without a mandate either to help or hinder the project, I worked to make my independence as clear as possible. However, my sympathies were with the teachers, and sensing the power struggle that was going on, I became the teachers' advocate. I must admit to being chary of heavy-handed implementation, for I had been a classroom teacher and easily took the teacher's side in resisting efforts to dictate conformity. Back at the center we had no idea of the uproar the implementation was causing. I am not sure either the project director or the superintendent fully realized how the project had rent the school district. I had stumbled into a full-blown dispute, one whose source was, at least in part, the center that employed me.

By the time I was assigned to the project at the beginning of its third year, a group of teachers had organized to try to mollify the impact of the program. The committee did not operate in secret, so I went to its chairman and asked if I might be party to its deliberations. Committee members had to take my word that my study was independent of the project. Although I assumed they bought that idea, they may have figured that whether I revealed the extent of their dissatisfaction or not, my presence might lend validation to their efforts.

In time they realized that I was not a pipeline back to the project director. However, that realization also had a downside: My effort to chronicle what was going on would not produce any immediate benefits, since it would not be available until the project was history. They decided they could live with that. Perhaps by then they had begun to feel that it was nice to have an anthropologist around to document what was happening, even if nothing was to come of it in time to be of immediate help.

Alternatives for writing up the account might have included presenting the data as a fable or play, but I am not given to such writing, and my role as academic observer had been established from the beginning. The idea of finding something in the anthropological literature that I could draw on for perspective appealed to me. I hoped I could find some conceptual apparatus through which I could look at what was happening and maintain a balance in my reporting. I planned to make my personal biases known, but the reporting had to be more evenhanded.

As noted in chapter 9, I found such a concept in the anthropological notion of *moiety*, a word derived from the French that refers to a social system divided into two (and only two) parts. The parallel between a group consisting essentially of teachers, on the one hand, and their counterpart technocrats, the nonteaching administrators, along with researchers at the center, on the other, seemed a good fit. A preliminary review of the moiety literature proved encouraging. I asked Professor Philip Young in our anthropology department to provide an independent appraisal of the concept and its appropriateness for this purpose. His response was most encouraging. He lightheartedly began his written summary, "The quality of moiety is not strained."

My casual assignment to the project had evolved into something bigger, more ambitious, even more defensible, except perhaps to a project director who began to see the project unraveling before his eyes. Initially I planned only to mention the moiety concept as a possible analogy, but as I began writing, the idea of analyzing the players on each of two sides as the modern-day equivalents of the parts of a moiety system intrigued me. I ended up with a book that had three major sections, a first describing the events, a second introducing the moiety concept, and a third using the concept to analyze how the behavior of teachers and technocrats could be examined and understood from that perspective.

I was feeling more the artful dodger than the artist as I introduced a concept from the traditional anthropological literature to a contemporary case of resistance to change. I realized that I was becoming an advocate for the teachers in a day when there was not much precedent for advocacy. I employed the moiety concept in an effort to present a fairly balanced picture because in a moiety system members in each moiety must be present to perform duties both for the opposite moiety and for the system as a whole. The problem in this case was that the technocrats, with the resources of the school district's central office and the university's research center behind them, had gotten a bit rambunctious. With the flow of resources into the district and the lure of national attention, everyone had forgotten to look closely at how the teachers really felt about what was being demanded of them.

My completed account, now a book-length draft, was judged to be sufficiently evenhanded by a committee of peers. They recommended that the center publish it. I worked with the center's attentive editor, Jeff Grass, to get the manuscript ready to publish. Jerry Williams in our university's theatre department drew two knights jousting to create a splendid cover. The book was published in 1977. The center did a good job of announcing and distributing the book under its own auspices, but the center itself was floundering. Further, its audience consisted primarily of school administrators, hardly the group that would be excited by a report in which they appeared as the bad guys.

The book's advocacy comes through loud and clear. Its artistry will not, for that entailed finding and employing an analogy that allowed me to organize and relate the account without getting in the way. I am delighted to have the book in print again, since its story is as relevant today as it was in the 1970s. The schools will always be in need of improvement, and there will always be people with a gimmick or an idea for improving them. This is what happens when the movers and shakers of education lose touch with the people who do the work. As I wrote in the preface to the new AltaMira reissue (HFW 2003d), "How can we keep this from happening again?" I also supplied what I believe to be the answer: "We can't."

I felt that I had to have a defensible position in maintaining my silence during the heat of the fray. Of course, I could claim the anthropologist's concern for the underdog, which in this case was clearly the teachers. As well, I needed to rise above some personal animosity I had developed toward the project director, whose private motive seemed to be success at all costs. Whether it was imagination or just blind faith that I could produce a readable monograph out of the experience was a question that only time could answer. I banked heavily on an anthropological perspective to maintain a perspective of my own.

It was probably an act of imagination on the part of my colleagues when they decided that the center should publish the work, a decision that gave the monograph a chance at life yet doomed it to relative obscurity. The decision was based on the feeling that in spite of what had happened we were still a university-based research center. We had an obligation to track and report our failures in addition to touting our successes. I think it was courageous on the part of the center and its director to publish the account. But make no mistake—the report documented a failed project, a project destined to disappear from the face of the earth, leaving no visible trace.

Given the circumstances, there was little incentive to try to make my reporting artful. I tried making it as factual as possible. Fairness became a major consideration. Was I treating both sides evenhandedly enough when I found myself rooting for the teachers and disappointed in the ethos of project development for what one inside observer called "whoring after federal dollars?" Perhaps there is some art in that, an art of a devious sort designed to keep readers from suspecting your own one-sided view.

I decided not to hide anything, not even my distaste, although I did a final editing to see that I had not maligned anyone, for this was not a vendetta. I introduced the monograph with a surprise chapter that one would not ordinarily expect to find in an anthropologist's account of his or her people (although see Turnbull 1972 or Grinker 2000 for an exception). The chapter was titled "Caution: Bias at Work." Before I offered a word about the project, I needed to spell out my personal feelings.

Discretion took a decidedly political turn with this study. Instead of protecting all the players, I took sides. If I was evenhanded, I was only enough so to get the book published. In the ensuing years, researchers have become advocates in many instances. I did not feel at the time that I was pioneering a new role for qualitative research; it just didn't seem that there was any other way to go.

Sneaky Kid and Its Aftermath

Twenty-five years passed between the publication of *Teachers versus Technocrats* (1977) and the final study to be discussed, *Sneaky Kid and Its Aftermath* (2002). Those intervening years were productive ones, but as elders are inclined to do, I turned my attention to writing about the doing of research rather than conducting substantive studies of my own.

I had also discovered that I was uncomfortable doing the kind of research I preferred under institutional auspices that seemed to preclude any adverse findings. So just as educational research was getting bigger, I decided that any future efforts on my part needed to be smaller and conducted independently of an institution.

I had also made a conscious decision that with my fiftieth birthday (1979) I would give my professional career a new thrust that coupled anthropology with education in the study of cultural transmission. I was pleased to have pulled off *Teachers versus Technocrats,* but I did not want to risk being compromised again in studying something that was not of abiding interest. To me, that is how what follows makes sense in terms of a logical progression. If you prefer, you may chalk it up to serendipity, but note that Frederick Erickson had already set my course with some sound advice about how to look at the learning process from an anthropological perspective: "First of all, you'll need to get yourself a learner."

This story begins with an article published in 1983, "Adequate Schools and Inadequate Education: The Life History of a Sneaky Kid." It was followed by an article published in 1987, another in 1990, the three appearing together in an edited collection in 1994. So the story has been unfolding for more than twenty years now, and if you prefer you can watch it unfold by referring to the three articles as they appeared separately or to the collection in which they appeared together (HFW 1994b). An expanded account is contained in the book, and it is the book that I discuss here. I was going to describe the book as the "full account," but I assume that you get the gist of these remarks: There is no such thing as a full account—of anything.

As I noted in the previous chapter, in the years since I first set foot in a Kwakiutl village, I have had several opportunities to live abroad. Yet, ironically, the setting for this final account is not only in the state and city of my permanent residence for those same years but literally in my own backyard.

Although my mailing address is Eugene, Oregon, I reside outside the city limits. My backyard is roughly twenty acres in area. It sits on a slope abutting a wilderness that provides an important landmark at the southern end of town. And one day, after I had lived on the property for almost sixteen years, a neighbor telephoned to inform me that his young son had met a "hobo" who said he was living on my property on a site almost inaccessible from my house. Apparently he had built a cabin out of sapling trees and materials requisitioned from construction nearby. I did recall having heard distant hammering, but I had dismissed it as echoing from that same construction. I now realized it must have come from my own property.

Sure enough, after a somewhat arduous climb, I discovered my new tenant, although the label "hobo" did not fit the then nineteen-year-old youth who already had been living on my property for the past five weeks. He gave an adequate account of himself, including that he had been raised in the area, that his father, from whom he was estranged, still lived in town, that he was out of school and out of work, even that he had been in reform school. ("But it wasn't my fault," he hastily added.)

Time for a quandary of my own. I was uncomfortable allowing him to remain, but neither could I find sufficient reason for throwing him off the property when it was clear that he did not have a welcoming alternative. He said he had believed he was not on private land, and it was true that a couple of hundred yards would have made a difference.

I let him stay. And stay he did. For more than two years. I saw little of him the first year, leaving him free to go his own way while my partner Norman and I went ours. However, there were times when I needed help around the place, and I knew he could always use ready cash, so our paths crossed occasionally. Then for five months I was a guest lecturer at another institution and my partner Norman, with his aversion to "losers," probably saw him not at all.

Upon my return, one of my projects was to run a new water line to the house from a spring on the hill, as the old line often froze in winter. One day when I was getting a bid on the work, my unofficial tenant surprised me with a bid of his own, making a convincing argument that by hand he would make much less of a mess than anyone operating a backhoe. My immediate concern was that he would start the job but never finish it, so I offered to pay him by the foot, figuring that if he dug only part way before losing interest I would not be out all that much. However, I added an incentive: If he completed the entire trench and helped me install and bury the new water line, I would triple what I offered to pay.

And so the work started, slowly but steadily. I helped in places where rocks or roots made the going difficult. As we worked, we talked. I became fascinated with his lifestyle, with his story, and with him. Eventually our relationship became physical as well. He continued to make improvements on his cabin and found a part-time job with a landscape gardener who lived nearby, so his circumstances seemed constantly to be improving.

But just as he seemed, in his own words, to be getting his life together, he seemed to be losing his grip . . . on everything. I watched with despair as he gave up a sometime job that seemed to suit him fine, lost interest in everything going on around him, and seemed to be headed toward a mental breakdown. I was able to talk him into visiting the county mental health facility, but he did not find the options they offered attractive. For a couple of days local recruiters seemed an answer, but the fact that he had not completed tenth grade worked against him. The only option he saw was one he had exercised before, to hit the road and start over again in some different place.

A tearful farewell marked the moment he was ready to leave, and he promised to write or phone to keep me posted. To my surprise and dismay, he returned that evening in a more somber mood to collect things he had put in storage under my house, informing me he had a vision that when he returned I would be gone and his things were not safe. He could take on the road only what he could carry with him, but later I learned that he had stopped at a pawn shop the next morning before leaving town.

After we became physically involved, there seemed to be no subject that was off limits, and I pondered whether, in spite of his natural reticence, he might be willing to let me tape his life story. I felt a deepening sense of affection for him and was intrigued with his ability to eke out a living, in his words "to survive."

On that call I received from Washington, I had been invited to contribute a white paper—a think piece rather than a report of research—on educational accountability. It occurred to me that his story might add a new dimension to the issue of allocating additional federal funds for education should they become available. Instead of writing the white paper, I proposed doing a brief life history. Here in my own backyard I had found my learner, a young man whom the schools were no longer able to reach. Was his education part of the equation?

He agreed to give the idea of recounting his life story a try, and we conducted a number of taped interviews, for which he was paid. I submitted my report, after first passing a draft by him to see if he found anything objectionable. He suggested only a word change or two and even offered the opinion that it "might help people understand," although he never elaborated on what he meant.

I felt that his life story as someone lost to formal schooling was powerful. I was disappointed to learn that instead of reaching the wide audience I had anticipated, the article was going to be buried in a federal report on school finance. The report would mark a dead-end for the story. I began looking for some other way to bring it before a wider audience.

He was almost twenty-two and had been gone a year by the time I published the article (HFW 1983a). I had changed the subtitle of the original report to include an apt nickname he told me his mother had used when she caught him sneaking a piece of cake: Sneaky Kid. I was oblivious to the fact that referring to him as a kid would make him appear younger in the eyes of some readers. I was also oblivious to the importance of clarifying that he lived on my place for more than two years and that our sexual involvement preceded his taking the role of informant by many months. Neither of these points seemed deserving of attention at the time. Our consensual relationship was a matter between the two of us. That for awhile he was my informant also seemed irrelevant. But these facts came back to haunt me later.

In casual reference to the original published account, I mention that he returned only once after his departure and let it go at that. When my focus has been on this story, however, I elaborate in detail, for his return introduced a note of tragedy into my life and his own.

It was two and a half years before I saw him again, an interim in which I heard from him only once or twice by telephone but during which his mother and I communicated several times. She reported that his condition had worsened to the point that shortly after he turned up at her home in southern California, she had him voluntarily committed. She resigned herself to the fact that he was "insane" and would remain in need of support and supervision "forever." Through his mother I kept trying to reach him, but she insisted (later) that he did not want to hear from me. Then one day, out of the blue, I received a warning telephone call from a health official in San Diego advising me that he had been making threats about returning to Oregon to do me harm. I also learned that he was under regular psychiatric outpatient care.

The next thing I knew, he was back. He had broken into the house and was waiting in ambush for my return from the university one evening. He had spent the day preparing to set the house afire. Had Norman not returned shortly afterward to upset his carefully laid plan, I must assume he intended to kill me or to kill us both. The house and everything in it was totally destroyed by the fire. While I was whisked off to the hospital, the police began looking for him. They had him in custody within a few hours. He confessed to the arson the next morning.

Then things seemed to come to a standstill. His plea changed from guilty to guilty by reason of insanity. A period of eight months elapsed during which a trial and a sentencing hearing were held. Although ostensibly he was the one on trial, the trial seemed to be about me and my lifestyle. The nature of our relationship became central to his plea, an insanity that the defense implied I had fostered through my advances.

In the end the insanity plea did not fly. The ordeal left a lasting impression on me as to the convoluted and devious ways of our legal system. It was almost twenty years before I learned that the trial, from which Norman and I were formally excluded at the time, had been transcribed and was available for inspection in the state capital. In part this is what the Sneaky Kid book is about, continuing with what happened from when he first left my place to his incarceration several years later. (He received a twenty-year sentence, but with no minimum time. As was the custom in the state in those days, he was "matrixed out" to make room for inmates facing more serious charges and with longer periods to serve.)

It was the trial that made my sex life public, and it was Sneaky Kid himself who caused the trial to occur. "But why did you have to tell all this," some have questioned, "and why did you have to write a book about it, when otherwise no one would have known?" I address that issue here, how Sneaky Kid gets mixed up in my fieldwork ethics and my obsession with his influence on my life since 1980, the year he first arrived on my property.

Until the trial I had lived my life in private, watching even the American Psychiatric Association gradually give way to allow that homosexuality is, if not a commendable way of life in the eyes of some, no longer to be regarded as a mental illness. The trial, and the innuendos of both the prosecutor and the public defender, made public homosexuals of both my partner and me. And as friends advised, once you are out of the closet, never let them put you back in. If news of my homosexuality was not a nationwide event, it nevertheless was well publicized. I needed to confront it boldly and to make sure the facts of the case were clear. Once again, writing provided a way to do that.

After Sneaky Kid left, but before there was any hint that the mental problems were going to develop into something so serious, I drafted a sequel to the original story, titled "Life's Not Working: Cultural Alternatives to Career Alternatives." I did not have a publication in mind for the article, but I needed to write it, if only for myself. I wanted to describe the problems faced by someone who saw a completely different set of alternatives to mine, thus the cultural alternatives to my concept of career alternatives. By the time that piece did get published (HFW 1987), Sneaky Kid had of course returned and wreaked havoc on my house and life. But I did not want to detract from the message of that article, how different a future he envisioned for himself from what I would have projected. In a footnote I hinted at what others had already suggested, that he would someday return.

The occasion of his return prompted a third article (HFW 1990), this one discussing the nature of our relationship, his mental breakdown, his return, and the subsequent trial and its outcome. At the time I first began writing the third piece, he was still incarcerated, but he was routinely reviewed for parole. My candor in that piece shocked and dismayed a few who took it on themselves to dismiss not only the article but everything I had ever written. I had also begun using the original Sneaky Kid article as an example of ethnographic work, especially of the strength of the life history approach, and as an illustration of what one can do with a chapter-length article. That story, too, is retold in the book.

This is a tragic story as it evolved, but it is also a love story. I cared deeply about Sneaky Kid. I listened as he talked through his problems, and we survived more than two years with him living in close proximity. From the first it seemed highly unlikely that he would stay forever, but I wondered if he really could turn his life around and we might establish a bond that would last forever, and that he would feel he had a home in addition to his makeshift cabin.

Once he turned up at his mother and stepfather's home, other events took on emotional meanings. Those meanings might possibly have helped him dispel his demons. Instead, they exacerbated them to the point where a return to Oregon to resolve a reputed wrong seemed to him the only possible alternative. I am not privy to what he felt as the trial continued or during his prison experience. I do know my own soul searching. I remain as torn today as I was twenty years ago when he came back to burn the house down, still wishing we could go back to halcyon days and get a fresh start. At the same time, the threat he posed then might resurface at any time.

Sneaky Kid is not a study in homosexuality. It involves a homosexual relationship, but it involves a host of other emotions as well. And it involves not only establishing a relationship with a younger person but circumventing an ongoing relationship with my long-term partner. If such entanglements are completely foreign to you, then you, too, may feel shocked and betrayed, if not by my actions, then by my willingness to make them public. Many people are uncomfortable with such talk: Some might find it acceptable in a novel, or if they did not know, or know about, the person involved, or if it were not about a social scientist, or if it had happened long ago (e.g., Banner 2003; Grinker 2000). But this case is all too close. On second thought, muses anthropologist Don Kulick, who in his review of the book wonders if I remain a little too preoccupied with Sneaky Kid twenty years later, "If somebody you cared about and had written about tried to beat your brains out with a 2-by-4 and burned down your house, and if your whole life and career thereafter were colored by that experience, then hell, you'd be preoccupied too" (2004:118).

Although I consider the entire book a candid bit of reporting, only the first chapter, reprinting the original Sneaky Kid article, seems deserving of the label "ethnography," and specifically that of "ethnographic autobiography." The balance of the account reads more like a memoir. It was written from a social science perspective and is academic in intent, but it is too personal and too one-sided. I have only my part of the story to tell. I make no attempt to present it as ethnography. But it vividly portrays dilemmas of ethics and intimacy in fieldwork.

The Sneaky Kid book also includes an element of art in a totally different format. I received an inquiry from a professor of theatre at Arizona State University, Johnny Saldaña, informing me that he would like to write a play about Sneaky Kid and me (there was no question that there were two of us in this now). He wanted to know if I would be amenable to the idea and, if so, were there constraints I wished to place on the enterprise.

My feeling was that he should write the play in whatever manner he wanted; I would have to take my chances with his sense of discretion. When I realized he intended to stay close to the actual story, producing a true ethnodrama rather than a fictionalized account, I agreed to serve as dramaturg, helping with an adaptation for the stage. The play was performed in February 2001, first at his institution and then at the Advances in Qualitative Methods conference in Edmonton, Alberta. Although Johnny felt (and still probably feels) that the phrase "Sneaky Kid" should have been in the title, I argued for "Finding My Place: The Brad Trilogy" because the sequence of articles had been called "The Brad Trilogy" from the moment I first drew them together for publication.

With the encouragement of three people, publisher Mitch Allen, playwright Johnny Saldaña, and my longtime colleague in anthropology and education John Singleton, I next set out to write the book. Johnny gave permission for me to include the play (Saldaña 2002). The play has been the boldest step I have ever taken toward finding an alternative way to present a qualitative account. Note, however, that I was not the one who took it.

An Assessment

Other than the ethnodrama, for which I was but a minor collaborator, how does the Sneaky Kid book serve as an example of the art of fieldwork?

And if I am making a case for discretion, where exactly is the discretion in an account in which there seems to be so little of it?

There are always limits. Jules Henry described as "cut-off points" those places where we recognize that we are not to ask further questions, not to probe more deeply (1955:196). Have I transgressed here, or only pushed the limits? Such transgressions are not totally unknown among senior scholars who caution that things are never what they seem and then cite personal experience as evidence.

My point is not what I did, but what I chose to reveal in a case where I truly brought fieldwork home. Am I still being discreet or have I crossed the line? In all fieldwork, how much do we reveal of what we have experienced and observed? There are myriad forces to contend with; there are no precise guidelines.

Jean Lave observed in a published interview titled "What Is Anthropological Research?" that she relates only "some aspect of peoples' lives that is much smaller than the whole context of what I have come to know about them" (Lave and Kvale 1995). She explains, "I know that there is much more beyond it that substantiates and supports what I am trying to say. As an anthropologist, I never want to write at the edges of my own understanding of what life in the community is about" (pp. 226–27).

I wondered at first whether Lave hadn't made an unfortunate admission at a time when qualitative researchers were heeding the politicians (disguised as scientists) nipping at our heels because we do not report enough of the Truth. Lave was suggesting that fieldworkers write only about the solid core of what they are concerned with. She insists that there is a vast amount of work "in the margins" in every study, material that we are not prepared to deal with, that we are not prepared to reveal, or that we feel our audiences are not ready to receive.

My initial reaction was that if any category of researchers had the complete story, it was those who did fieldwork and who told all. I hold a more realistic view today. Fieldworkers often understand and reveal more of the intricacies of a story than do researchers following any other approach. But I would never argue that fieldworkers intend to reveal everything, even if they could. That is not what they set out to do.

I now understand why an earlier group of anthropologists was so taken with the idea of psychoanalysis; they recognized that they needed first to understand themselves before trying to understand others. It was not that psychoanalysis was the answer, but that they recognized the problem. Today, modesty about what we have reported, coupled with more attention to the standpoint from which we report, seems to have replaced the need for each of us to become such a perfect observer.

Discretion in Fieldwork

The critical aspect that I address here lies in the decisions each of us makes after we accept a fieldwork assignment: how much to tell of what we ourselves have seen and tried to understand and how best to present our observations. I don't mean everything we have observed, but what we feel is relevant to the case we are making and to the audience we assume we are making it to. And not in deciding what is relevant in every case of that. There are some obvious things that we intend to report because they relate directly to our purpose. And there are some things that we do not intend to report because fieldworkers never (never!) report them. From the outset, fieldwork allows and tolerates only selective reporting.

The conscious part of this is in deciding which categories and events are discretionary and, of those, which to report and which to omit. The problem is embedded in a human quality that we conveniently but consistently overlook—no one is totally honest and forthright with anyone about anything. We express shock and dismay to learn of corporate misdeeds and large-scale institutional cover-ups; we forget that we are all engaged in interpersonal cover-ups all the time. I do not mean that we are no more than a profession, or a community, or a nation, or a world, of liars (although there are days when we seem to be heading in that direction) but that it is impossible ever to be totally candid, not just about some people and some things but about everything and everybody.

Anthropologist F. G. Bailey refers to such sustaining lies as "life lies" or "saving lies" (2003:2). It is our human nature to buttress ourselves with saving lies. The problem is not peculiar to fieldworkers; it is universal. It becomes fieldworkers' special problem when we take up the challenge of describing someone else's way of life.

Thinking back on the three studies under review here, let me be a bit (but only a bit) more revealing about elements I chose not talk about. You can supply the why for yourself. Forgive me if I stretch to make a point, but I must try to encompass a wide range of behaviors that include what human social life is all about, behaviors that far exceed the bounds of field-work reporting. I reach among a selection of life's more distracting behaviors for my examples.

Murder. There is murder aplenty in the daily news. How has it managed to escape qualitative study in general and my three studies in particular? Well, hold on there—it was I myself who was the intended victim of Sneaky Kid's ambush. I never dreamed I would someday write about an attempt on my life. It still seems so remarkable that I invariably minimize that part of the telling, turning the story more on issues concerned with mental illness. The police did not have to be so discriminating; they charged him with attempted murder. The charge was subsequently dropped in favor of arson and assault, but only because attempted murder would be too hard to prove.

How about in the Kwakiutl case? During the partying when we tied up at a fish camp one weekend, the chief's grandson presumably was murdered, pushed overboard during a late night drinking spree. The body was not recovered for days, and the case was never satisfactorily resolved. I was asked to be one of two people to identify the body; no blood relation was willing to do it. The chief went to his grave absolutely certain that his grandson was a victim of foul play. I did not note this in my monograph and have never before mentioned it. Why not?

Even while I was studying the school implementation project, there was a tangentially related murder. Several of the teachers who taught in the district lived in the community where I live, some distance away. To our mutual surprise, I encountered one of them one night in a local gay bar. He asked, "Did you know?" meaning did I know that he was gay. I told him I did not, although I could have added, "But I suspected." He was murdered by a transient pickup, leaving both communities in shock. The murder itself happened after my report was completed, and there was no way or reason to include it in *Teachers versus Technocrats*. Still, there is a connection and a glimpse into the personal life of teachers. This glimpse was incidental, but not totally irrelevant because the teacher had been something of a model adopter in the implementation effort. But in the mid-1970s, a homosexual teacher in a small town had other pressing concerns.

Violence and abuse. With the inclusion of the autobiography in the reissue of *A Kwakiutl Village and School*, I made public the rape of a village woman. The incident is muted in her story: "He took advantage of my auntie being asleep and had his way with me." But the event so impacted her life that although she subsequently married him, fourteen years elapsed before she forgave him. She and her husband drowned in a tragic boating accident near the end of my year at the village. Her story turns more on personal triumph than tragedy, but it has haunted me ever since I first read how the experience of rape haunted her.

There was also at least one case of incest in the village during the year, reported second-hand following an all-night orgy. I had no reason to probe into it or mention it. There is no such thing as enough positive information to offset the negative cast that reporting a case of incest might create.

There were also at least two cases of physical abuse during my year. In one case a husband beat his wife so badly that for several days she did not make an appearance. She couldn't—she was unable to move from her bed. In the other case an adult man pushed his aging mother onto a hot wood stove during a scuffle; she had to be hospitalized for the serious burns she sustained.

In the Sneaky Kid book, I hurried through discussing the sex, dutifully noting yet quickly skipping beyond it. And it was I who was shocked to think that counsel for the defense would make such a big deal of it. Unlike fieldworkers, who must constantly make discriminating choices, the courts know no discretion. None at all! But get this—I was flabbergasted to learn that a rape charge was considered against me as a result of my involvement with Sneaky Kid. The matter was never pursued, but that it was even contemplated dumfounded me. How far do lawyers get to go in drumming up charges and countercharges in probing a case? I have noted that the trial seemed to be much more about incriminating me than putting Sneaky Kid behind bars. On that issue my opinion of our system of justice hit a low from which it will never recover, yet I had to keep even my own anger in check in published accounts.

These stories do not tell well. I had no reason to tell them then and would not be telling them even now if they weren't critical to making this point. They are true horror stories. No one wants to read about them in an ethnography. The violence in both the Kwakiutl and the Sneaky Kid cases is coated over. For another example, I mentioned only that I was "whisked away to the hospital." Did you need more?

Fear and insecurity. Fear is another dimension that is hard to introduce objectively. There certainly were times in the village when my sense of apprehension was high, when it seemed unreasonable to be out and about while everyone else remained prudently indoors. On two occasions, terrified villagers actually sought refuge in the school for fear that harm might come to them. I didn't mention it. And on the political plane, the village itself seemed to exist moment to moment as the government sought to consolidate outlying villages and move everyone to sites more convenient, more accessible. Within a year the school was closed permanently, the village deserted.

Any fear in *Teachers versus Technocrats?* Well, not of the "whites of their eyes" variety. But in any large group of teachers (or employee group of any kind), there are always those who feel a lack of permanence. There was no question that there were teachers who were afraid for their jobs, afraid that their principals or the central office staff did not view them favorably. A system ostensibly designed to "improve" them had produced exactly the opposite effect, giving voice to concerns that the technocrats were gathering evidence to prove their incompetence. Collectively the teachers were eventually able to get rid of an implementation they described as "the superintendent's baby" and to get things back to normal, with normal defined from their point of view. The end result was that the superintendent's days in the district were numbered; he quickly moved on. At the center, the head of the project also moved on. Our accounts end; the ramifications of the events they describe may be felt for years.

Sneaky Kid's long slide into mental breakdown was terribly sad to watch but seemingly impossible to head off. I do not know where it has led for him. Nor did I dwell on what Norman and I felt in the moments in our house when Sneaky Kid seemed to have the upper hand. As a result of the fire, Norman and I lost every possession we owned. Everything! The fire was so hot that it melted a cast-iron stove in our farmhouse kitchen, there mostly for looks but quite serviceable. We lost all personal possessions, my professional library, two automobiles, all our memorabilia, all field notes from the three studies described here. We had only the clothes we were wearing, and at the hospital mine were confiscated as evidence. ("Well," as Norman remarked later, trying to be cheerful, "no more dusting.")

The love/hate relationship. Straight talk about my sexual relationship with Sneaky Kid seemed to catch readers by surprise—sex is not ordinarily introduced into social science accounts, certainly not when one of the protagonists is the author, most certainly not if the other person is of the same sex, considerably younger, and the relationship is carried on through the better part of a year. Was that something you definitely needed to know, or definitely something you did not need to know? For myself, I find it more difficult to talk about my caring for Sneaky Kid than about the sex—that part of our relationship is too intimate, too personal. Even for me.

In what I thought was a neat case of having it both ways, the counsel for the defense in Sneaky Kid's trial lampooned my lifestyle. Then he explained to the jury how in establishing a new relationship I had not been faithful to my long-time partner. I was condemned as a homosexual, then condemned again for being unfaithful to my homosexual partner! Infidelity or human nature—who gets to choose?

The relatively dispassionate story of teachers and technocrats seems not to involve deep emotional feelings, at least beyond the workplace. Is that the only kind of study where we can depend on the fieldworker to report with candor? Yet even there we catch a glimpse of complicating facts, and I know I could never have inventoried all the personal agendas in the events that transpired.

Among the Kwakiutl I know, I have always felt ambivalence, torn between great admiration for some and disaffection with the malevolence of others toward even their own kin. And after all these years, even my partner does not fully understand and does not want to hear how I felt about Sneaky Kid, or at least Sneaky Kid the Younger. Nor does anyone want to hear how I felt (and to some extent still feel) about the role the university played in *Teachers versus Technocrats*. Apparently it was my ability to distance myself from the analysis that made that account acceptable. With Sneaky Kid, did I get too close? The Sneaky Kid story has magnified my ambivalence thousandfold between genuine affection and an eternal question of how anyone could hate me so much. Is there room for such all-out display of love and hate in an ethnography?

Who knows what meanings the incidents we choose not to reveal have in the full and complete accounting of events. I was hardly a disinterested observer to the incidents I describe above; I was a party to them. What would a full and complete account of such cases look like, were we humanly capable of rendering it? I obviously have exercised conscious judgment to leave certain unsavory details out in some cases and presumably made unconscious judgments in even more. Where did that sense of discretion come from? And think how it has been exercised—too much for some readers, too little for others.

The Management of Discretion

What is the point of examining studies in terms of what has been left out? It is to make us all aware that every case involves complicated relationships, that humans are far more complex, their lives far more intertwined and overdetermined, than meets the eye. The artist and the fieldworker alike render judgments as to how to portray their subjects. As Susanne Langer pointed out more than fifty years ago, "Every choice is also a sacrifice" (1953:122). She continues, "Every articulation precludes not only its own alternatives but all sorts of developments they would have made viable." Our so-called scientists are lucky if they are able to escape such complications. I can't help but wonder how they do it.

The world I live in, observe, and occasionally have tried to portray is infinitely complex. There is always plenty that is unquestionably relevant that I do not report, in addition to what I do disclose. And you, the reader, render a judgment about my judgment—whether you feel I have included what seem to be the right aspects, related to the right degree. Even so, only I know whom I believe I have shielded, what more I might have said, or if I made adequate decisions in the way I told what I told.

Not even I can believe that some of these things happened to me or are based on firsthand experience. In chapter 1, I note satisfaction in what I call "the art of living," which for the most part has entailed a relatively quiet life as a professor in a pleasant semirural community. The events I have described require me to go beyond the image I ordinarily convey. I have not attempted to live dangerously, yet the events reported are part of my real life. "We live," as Robert Nisbet observed, "by images and symbols" (1976:57). But only some of these images are those by which we would like to be known.

How do you feel now about all that you have learned? Are you glad to have more information so that you have a better picture of the events of each case? Do you bring more to each study and understand it better? Or do you wish that I had not burdened you with all this, raising doubts when I might better have spent my time reassuring you that I got it right the first time? Are you suspicious, now that you have a bit more context, that there must be far more to each story than I have told? And far more yet that I myself do not understand or am unlikely ever to know?

In revisiting these studies, I realize that the art of discretion lies behind every decision a fieldworker makes about what to reveal of his or her observations. We dismiss much unconsciously, but that still leaves a huge burden of casting out what we are aware of but do not intend to reveal, a burden that falls to each fieldworker individually. I have seen the issue raised in terms of distinguishing between ethnographers and journalists. The latter ordinarily enjoy a freer hand in reporting because they do not protect their relationships at the cost of misleading readers, but to do so, they ignore context (Harrington 2003:100). The social science perspective focuses on what sustains life in the face of the bumps we encounter, not the bumps themselves. And there is always the question of the audience for the completed account. Is audience appeal great enough or powerful enough for the occasion? Neither the journalist, the artist, nor the fieldworker can ever fully anticipate the reaction. For the fieldworker, there are no precise guidelines, only what Peter Metcalf calls the "wistful sense of unfinished business" inherent in this approach.

A Kwakiutl Village and School has remained in print so long that it appears about to become a (minor) classic. I told the story honestly, but now you know that I did not tell everything that I could tell and realize what you probably suspected all along, that I had only part of the picture. For the most part I left my personal feelings out of that account. Did I exercise a proper amount of discretion? With *Teachers versus Technocrats* I tried to mute my feelings with an analogy. Did that work? With Sneaky Kid, I put my personal feelings in—to the extent that some insist it is not a work of social science at all, only a confessional tale. Yet it is the story I know best.

I have been candid in what I have reported. That is a claim I make and the advice I give to others. But I have never reported everything. We can live the ethnographic life—taking a somewhat analytical orientation to what goes on about us—but we must contain ourselves in our qualitative reporting. There are untold constraints. We wade through our personal and professional lives for the most part unconscious of them, following decisions already made for us by circumstances we accept as a condition of life itself. We carry our own morality with us. We manage to submerge it a great deal, but it is always there, sometimes wreaking havoc with the public image we would like to convey. We accept as inevitable most of the circumstances under which we work, perhaps softening a bit in old age if we don't simply succumb to convenient forgetting. We do all these things because we are human, and we have put ourselves in the unenviable position of humans who report candidly on other humans. We do the best we can, even putting some of the blame back on the reader. We recognize that we could say more, but we really don't think the reader wants to hear it . . . and because we think we know the answer, we do not bother to ask.

I have been captivated by a phrase suggested by anthropologist Richard Fox urging fieldworkers to attend to the everyday life of persons rather than the cultural life of a people (1991:12). That seemed to be the distinction I wanted to make, to assure that we maintain our everyday concern for the behavior we actually observe rather than set our sights higher in order to make generalizations about something as lofty as the ways of mankind. We do and we should concern ourselves with the everyday life of persons. But in our work we do it far more partially, far more selectively, even far more purposely, than I fully realized.

We never for an instant pretend to tell all that we see and surmise about the individuals and groups we study. Nor do we see everything, even in ourselves. It is not just a suspicion that we are not getting it all or "not quite getting it right," as Clifford Geertz reminded us (1973:29). At best we get an incomplete picture; of that, we never understand everything of what we see; and of that, we are left to decide whether, and how, to portray what we have experienced.

Discretion cautions and informs our reporting. It is neither an ally nor an enemy; it is simply a condition of fieldwork. We do a remarkable job with the best of our studies, with what we are able to capture of human social life and how we go about linking things and making sense of it all. But portraying what we have experienced presents a daunting task. It confronts us with countless decisions that reside only with the individual who carried out the fieldwork and who alone must determine how much to tell and how best to tell it. Whatever the outcome, such decisions are weighed artistically. There is always art in fieldwork.

REFERENCES AND SELECT BIBLIOGRAPHY

Adler, Patricia A., and Peter Adler
  1994   Observational Techniques. *In* Handbook of Qualitative Research. Norman K. Denzin and Yvonna S. Lincoln, eds. Pp. 377–392. Thousand Oaks, CA: Sage.

Agar, Michael H.
  1996   The Professional Stranger: An Informal Introduction to Ethnography. 2nd ed. New York: Academic Press.

Atkinson, Paul, Amanda Coffey, Sara Delamont, John Lofland, and Lyn Lofland, eds.
  2001   Handbook of Ethnography. London: Sage.

Bailey, F. G.
  2003   The Saving Lie: Truth and Method in the Social Sciences. Philadelphia: University of Pennsylvania Press.

Banner, Lois W.
  2003   Intertwined Lives: Margaret Mead, Ruth Benedict, and Their Circle. New York: Alfred A. Knopf.

Barnett, Homer G.
  1953   Innovation: The Analysis of Culture Change. New York: McGraw-Hill.

Barth, Fredrik
  1966   Preface. *In* The Social Organization of the Marri Baluch. Compiled and analyzed from the notes of Robert N. Pehrson by Fredrik Barth. New York: Wenner-Gren Foundation.

1989　The Analysis of Culture in Complex Societies. Ethnos 54:120–142.

1994a　A Personal View of Present Tasks and Priorities in Cultural Anthropology. *In* Assessing Cultural Anthropology. Robert Borofsky, ed. Pp. 349–361. New York: McGraw-Hill.

1994b　Comment on "Cultural Anthropology's Future Agenda." Anthropology Newsletter 35(6):76.

Bateson, Gregory
1958　Naven. 2nd ed. Stanford, CA: Stanford University Press. [Originally published 1936.]

Bateson, Mary Catherine
1977　"Daddy, Can a Scientist Be Wise?" *In* About Bateson. John Brockman, ed. Pp. 55–74. New York: E. P. Dutton.

Becker, Howard S.
1980　Role and Career Problems of the Chicago School Teacher. New York: Arno Press. [Originally presented as the author's thesis, University of Chicago, 1951.]

1982　Art Worlds. Berkeley: University of California Press.

1986　Writing for Social Scientists. Chicago: University of Chicago Press.

1993　Theory: The Necessary Evil. *In* Theory and Concepts in Qualitative Research. David J. Flinders and Geoffrey E. Mills, eds. Pp. 218–229. New York: Teachers College Press.

1996　The Epistemology of Qualitative Research. *In* Ethnography and Human Development. Richard Jessor, Anne Colby, and Richard A. Shweder, eds. Pp. 53–71. Chicago: University of Chicago Press.

Beebe, James
1995　Basic Concepts and Techniques of Rapid Appraisal. Human Organization 54(1):42–51.

2001　Rapid Assessment Process: An Introduction. Walnut Creek, CA: AltaMira Press.

Beer, C. G.
1973　A View of Birds. *In* Minnesota Symposia of Child Psychology, Vol. 7. Anne Pick, ed. Pp. 47–86. Minneapolis: University of Minnesota Press.

Benedict, Ruth
1934　Patterns of Culture. Boston: Houghton Mifflin.

Bernard, H. Russell
1994a Methods Belong to All of Us. *In* Assessing Cultural Anthropology. Robert Borofsky, ed. Pp. 168–179. New York: McGraw-Hill.
1994b Research Methods in Anthropology: Qualitative and Quantitative Approaches. 2nd ed. Thousand Oaks, CA: Sage.
2000 Social Research Methods: Qualitative and Quantitative Approaches. Thousand Oaks, CA: Sage.
2001 Research Methods in Anthropology: Qualitative and Quantitative Approaches. 3rd ed. Walnut Creek, CA: AltaMira Press.

Bernard, H. Russell, ed.
1998 Handbook of Methods in Cultural Anthropology. Walnut Creek, CA: AltaMira Press.

Berreman, Gerald D.
1968 Ethnography: Method and Product. *In* Introduction to Cultural Anthropology. James A. Clifton, ed. Pp. 336–373. Boston: Houghton Mifflin.

Bidney, David
1953 Theoretical Anthropology. New York: Columbia University Press.

Boas, Franz
1897 Social Organization and the Secret Societies of the Kwakiutl Indians. Washington, DC: Government Printing Office.

Bochner, Arthur P., and Carolyn Ellis, eds.
2002 Ethnographically Speaking: Autoethnography, Literature, and Aesthetics. Walnut Creek, CA: AltaMira Press.

Bohannan, Paul
1995 How Culture Works. New York: The Free Press.

Borofsky, Robert, ed.
1994 Assessing Cultural Anthropology. New York: McGraw-Hill.

Bosk, Charles L.
1979 Forgive and Remember: Managing Medical Failure. Chicago: University of Chicago Press.

Brandes, Stanley
1982 Ethnographic Autobiographies in American Anthropology. *In* Crisis in Anthropology: View from Spring Hill, 1980. E. Adamson Hoebel,

Richard Currier, and Susan Kaiser, eds. Pp. 187–202. New York: Garland Press.

Bruner, Edward M.
1993 The Ethnographic Self and the Personal Self. *In* Anthropology and Literature. Paul Benson, ed. Pp. 1–26. Urbana: University of Illinois Press.

Burgess, Robert G., ed.
1995 Howard Becker on Education. Buckingham, England: Open University Press.

Burke, Kenneth
1935 Permanence and Change. New York: New Republic.

Burns, Allan F.
1993 Everybody's a Critic: Video Programming with Guatemalan Refugees in the United States. *In* Anthropological Film and Video in the 1990s. Jack R. Rollwagen, ed. Pp. 105–129. Brockport, NY: The Institute, Inc.

Carpenter, Edmund
1971 The Eskimo Artist. *In* Anthropology and Art. Charlotte M. Otten, ed. Pp. 163–171. Garden City, NY: Natural History Press. [Originally published as Comment to H. Haselberger, Method of Studying Ethnographic Art. Current Anthropology 2(4):361–363, 1961.]

Chagnon, Napoleon A.
1968 Yanomamö: The Fierce People. New York: Holt, Rinehart and Winston.

Childress, Herb
1998 Kinder Ethnographic Writing. Qualitative Inquiry 4(2):249–264.

Christensen, Garry
1993 Sensitive Information: Collecting Data on Livestock and Informal Credit. *In* Fieldwork in Developing Countries. Stephen Devereux and John Hoddinott, eds. Pp. 124–137. Boulder, CO: Lynne Rienner Publishers.

Clifford, James
1988 The Predicament of Culture. Cambridge, MA: Harvard University Press.

Clifford, James, and George E. Marcus
1986   Writing Culture: The Poetics and Politics of Ethnography. Berkeley: University of California Press.

Coffey, Amanda
1999   The Ethnographic Self: Fieldwork and the Representation of Identity. London: Sage.

Cooper, Patricia, and Norma Bradley Allen
1989   The Quilters: Women and Domestic Art. 2nd ed. New York: Anchor Press, Doubleday. [Originally published 1978.]

Crapanzano, Vincent
1980   Tuhami: Portrait of a Moroccan. Chicago: University of Chicago Press.

Creswell, John W.
1998   Qualitative Inquiry and Research Design: Choosing among Five Traditions. Thousand Oaks, CA: Sage.
2003   Research Design: Qualitative, Quantitative, and Mixed Methods Approaches. 2nd ed. Thousand Oaks, CA: Sage.

Crocker, William H., and Jean Crocker
1994   The Canela. Fort Worth, TX: Harcourt, Brace.

Darwin, Charles
1969   The Autobiography of Charles Darwin. Nora Barlow, ed. New York: W. W. Norton. [Orig. published 1887]

Demerath, Peter
2001   The Social Cost of Acting "Extra": Students' Moral Judgments of Self, Social Relations, and Academic Success in Papua New Guinea. American Journal of Education 108:196–235.

Denzin, Norman K.
1994a   The Art and Politics of Interpretation. *In* Handbook of Qualitative Research. Norman K. Denzin and Yvonna S. Lincoln, eds. Pp. 500–515. Thousand Oaks, CA: Sage.
1994b   Review Essay: Messy Methods for Communication Research. Journal of Communication. September.

Denzin, Norman K., and Yvonna S. Lincoln, eds.
1994   Handbook of Qualitative Research. Thousand Oaks, CA: Sage.

2000   Handbook of Qualitative Research. 2nd ed. Thousand Oaks, CA: Sage.

Descola, Philippe
1996   The Spears of Twilight: Life and Death in the Amazon Jungle. (Translated by Janet Lloyd.) New York: The New Press/Harper-Collins. [Originally published 1993 in French by Librairie Plon as Lances du crepuscule.]

Devereux, George
1968   From Anxiety to Method in the Behavioral Sciences. The Hague: Mouton.

DeWalt, Kathleen M., and Billie R. DeWalt
2002   Participant Observation: A Guide for Fieldworkers. Walnut Creek, CA: AltaMira.

Douglas, Jack
1976   Investigative Social Research. Beverly Hills, CA: Sage.
1985   Creative Interviewing. Beverly Hills, CA: Sage.

Eisenberg, Merrill
1994   Translating Research into Policy: What More Does It Take? Practicing Anthropology 16(4):35–39.

Eisner, Elliot
1985   On the Differences between Artistic and Scientific Approaches to Qualitative Research. In The Art of Educational Evaluation: A Personal View. Elliot Eisner, ed. Pp. 189–200. Philadelphia: Falmer Press.

Eliot, T. S.
1950   Selected Essays. New York: Harcourt, Brace and Co.

Ellis, Carolyn
1991   Emotional Sociology. In Studies in Symbolic Interaction 12. Norman Denzin, ed. Pp. 123–145. Greenwich, CT: JAI Press.

Ellis, Carolyn, and Arthur P. Bochner, eds.
1996   Composing Ethnography: Alternative Forms of Qualitative Writing. Walnut Creek, CA: AltaMira Press.

Emerson, Robert M., Rachel I. Fretz, and Linda L. Shaw
1995   Writing Ethnographic Fieldnotes. Chicago: University of Chicago Press.

Epstein, A. L., ed.
1967   The Craft of Social Anthropology. London: Tavistock.

Erickson, Frederick
1984   What Makes School Ethnography "Ethnographic"? Anthropology and Education Quarterly 15(1):51–66.

Erickson, Kai
1967   A Comment on Disguised Observation in Sociology. Social Problems 14:366–373.

Evans-Pritchard, E. E.
1952   Social Anthropology. Glencoe, IL: Free Press.

Feinberg, E. L.
1987   Art in the Science Dominated World. (Translated by J. A. Cooper.) New York: Gordon and Breach.

Fernandez, James W.
1994   Time on Our Hands. *In* Others Knowing Others. Don D. Fowler and Donald L. Hardesty, eds. Pp. 119–144. Washington, DC: Smithsonian Institution Press.

Fetterman, David M.
1989   Ethnography Step by Step. Newbury Park, CA: Sage.

Fine, Gary Alan
1993   Ten Lies of Ethnography. Journal of Contemporary Ethnography 22(3):267–294.

Firth, Raymond
1951   Elements of Social Organization. New York: Philosophical Library.

Fleck, Ludwik
1979   Genesis and Development of a Scientific Fact. Chicago: University of Chicago Press. [Translated by F. Bradley and T. Trenn from the text originally published in German in 1935.]

Flick, Uwe
1998   An Introduction to Qualitative Research. London: Sage.

Flinders, David J., and Geoffrey E. Mills, eds.
1993   Theory and Concepts in Qualitative Research: Perspectives from the Field. New York: Teachers College Press.

Flyvbjerg, Bent
　　2001　Making Social Science Matter: Why Social Inquiry Fails and How It Can Succeed Again. (Translated by Steven Sampson.) New York: Cambridge University Press.

Foster, George
　　1969　Applied Anthropology. Boston: Little, Brown.

Fowler, Don D., and Donald L. Hardesty
　　1994　Others Knowing Others: Perspectives on Ethnographic Careers. Washington, DC: Smithsonian Institution Press.

Fox, Richard G., ed.
　　1991　Recapturing Anthropology: Working in the Present. Santa Fe, NM: School of American Research.

Freeman, Mark
　　1993　Finding the Muse: A Sociopsychological Inquiry into the Conditions of Artistic Creativity. New York: Cambridge University Press.

Galtung, Johan
　　1990　Theory Formation in Social Research: A Plea for Pluralism. *In* Comparative Methodology. Else Øyen, ed. Pp. 96–112. Newbury Park, CA: Sage.

Gearing, Frederick O.
　　1970　The Face of the Fox. Chicago: Aldine.

Geertz, Clifford
　　1973　The Interpretation of Cultures. New York: Basic Books.
　　1983　Local Knowledge. New York: Basic Books.
　　1988　Works and Lives. Stanford, CA: Stanford University Press.

Getzels, Jacob W., and Mihaly Csikszentmihalyi
　　1976　The Creative Vision: A Longitudinal Study of Problem Finding in Art. New York: John Wiley and Sons.

Gluckman, Max
　　1967　Introduction. *In* The Craft of Social Anthropology. A. L. Epstein, ed. Pp. vii–xx. London: Tavistock.

Goldschmidt, Walter, ed.
　　1954　Ways of Mankind: Thirteen Dramas of Peoples of the World and How They Live. Boston: Beacon Press. [Produced by the National Association of Educational Broadcasters.]

Green, Jesse, ed.
1979   Zuni: Selected Writings of Frank Hamilton Cushing. Lincoln: University of Nebraska Press.

Grinker, Roy Richard
2000   In the Arms of Africa: The Life of Colin M. Turnbull. Chicago: University of Chicago Press.

Guba, Egon
1981   Criteria for Assessing the Trustworthiness of Naturalistic Inquiries. Educational Communication and Technology Journal 29(2):75–91.

Gubrium, Jaber F., and James A. Holstein, eds.
2002   Handbook of Interview Research: Context and Method. Thousand Oaks, CA: Sage.

Handwerker, W. Penn
2001   Quick Ethnography: A Guide to Rapid Multi-method Research. Walnut Creek, CA: AltaMira Press.

Harrington, Walt
2003   What Journalism Can Offer Ethnography. Qualitative Inquiry 9(1):90–104.

Harrison, Barbara
2001   Collaborative Programs in Indigenous Communities: From Fieldwork to Practice. Walnut Creek, CA: AltaMira Press.

Hatcher, Evelyn Payne
1985   Art as Culture: An Introduction to the Anthropology of Art. Lanham, MD: University Press of America.

Hawthorn, Harry B.
1961   The Artist in Tribal Society: The Northwest Coast. In The Artist in Tribal Society. Marian W. Smith, ed. Pp. 58–70. New York: Free Press.

Henry, Jules
1955   Culture, Education, and Communications Theory. In Education and Anthropology. George D. Spindler, ed. Pp. 188–207. Stanford, CA: Stanford University Press.
1963   Culture against Man. New York: Random House.

Henry, Jules, and Melford E. Spiro
1953   Psychological Techniques: Projective Techniques in Field Work. In Anthropology Today. Alfred L. Kroeber, ed. Pp. 417–429. Chicago: University of Chicago Press.

REFERENCES AND SELECT BIBLIOGRAPHY

HFW (See Wolcott, Harry F.)

Hilbert, Richard A.
1980   Covert Participant Observation. Urban Life 9:51–78.

Hill, Michael R.
1993   Archival Strategies and Techniques. Newbury Park, CA: Sage.

Homans, George
1962   Sentiments and Activities: Essays in Social Science. New York: Free Press of Glencoe.

Howell, Nancy
1990   Surviving Fieldwork. Special Publication No. 26. Washington, DC: American Anthropological Association.

Humphreys, Laud
1989   The Sociologist as Voyeur. In In the Field: Readings on the Field Research Experience. Carolyn D. Smith and William Kornblum, eds. Pp. 128–133. New York: Praeger. [Adapted from Tearoom Trade: Impersonal Sex in Public Places, 2nd ed. New York: Aldine de Gruyter, 1975.]

Jackson, Bruce
1987   Fieldwork. Urbana: University of Illinois Press.

Jackson, Jean E.
1990   "I Am A Fieldnote": Fieldnotes as a Symbol of Professional Identity. In Fieldnotes: The Makings of Anthropology. Roger Sanjek, ed. Pp. 3–33. Ithaca, NY: Cornell University Press.

Johnson, John
1976   Doing Field Research. New York: Free Press.

Jorgensen, Danny L.
1989   Participant Observation. Newbury Park, CA: Sage.

Keesing, Felix
1958   Cultural Anthropology: The Science of Custom. New York: Rinehart and Company.

Keesing, Roger M., and Felix M. Keesing
1971   New Perspectives in Cultural Anthropology. New York: Holt, Rinehart and Winston.

Kemper, Robert V., and Anya Peterson Royce, eds.
2002   Chronicling Cultures: Long-Term Field Research in Anthropology. Walnut Creek, CA: AltaMira Press.

Kimball, Solon T., and William L. Partridge
1979   The Craft of Community Study: Fieldwork Dialogues. Gainesville: University of Florida Press.

Kincheloe, Joe L., and Peter L. McLaren
1994   Rethinking Critical Theory and Qualitative Research. *In* Handbook of Qualitative Research. Norman Denzin and Yvonna S. Lincoln, eds. Pp. 138–157. Thousand Oaks, CA: Sage.

Kinsey, Alfred C., Wardell B. Pomeroy, and Clyde E. Martin
1948   Sexual Behavior in the Human Male. Philadelphia: W. B. Saunders Company.

Kirk, Jerome, and Marc L. Miller
1986   Reliability and Validity in Qualitative Research. Beverly Hills, CA: Sage.

Kleinman, Sherryl, and Martha A. Copp
1993   Emotions and Fieldwork. Newbury Park, CA: Sage.

Kluckhohn, Clyde
1949   Mirror for Man: The Relation of Anthropology to Modern Life. New York: Whittlesey House, McGraw Hill.

Kluckhohn, Clyde, and Henry A. Murray, eds.
1948   Personality in Nature, Society, and Culture. New York: Alfred A. Knopf.

Kluckhohn, Florence
1940   The Participant Observer Technique in Small Communities. American Journal of Sociology 46(3):331–344.

Kottak, Conrad P.
1994   Teaching in the Postmodern Classroom. Bulletin of the General Anthropology Division, American Anthropological Association 1:10–12.

Kulick, Don
2004   Review of *Sneaky Kid and Its Aftermath*. Sexualities 7(1):117–118.

Kulick, Don, and Margaret Willson, eds.
1995   Taboo: Sex, Identity and Erotic Subjectivity in Anthropological Fieldwork. New York: Routledge.

Kutsche, Paul
1998   Field Ethnography: A Manual for Doing Cultural Anthropology. Upper Saddle River, NJ: Prentice Hall.

REFERENCES AND SELECT BIBLIOGRAPHY

Lakatos, Imre
1978   The Methodology of Scientific Research Programmes: Philosophical Papers, Vol. l. London: Cambridge University Press.

Langer, Susanne K.
1953   Feeling and Form: A Theory of Art Developed from Philosophy in a New Key. London: Routledge & Kegan Paul.

Langness, L. L., and Gelya Frank
1981   Lives: An Anthropological Approach to Biography. Novato, CA: Chandler and Sharp.

Latour, Bruno
1987   Science in Action: How to Follow Scientists and Engineers Through Society. Milton Keynes, England: Open University Press.

Latour, Bruno, and Steve Woolgar
1986   Laboratory Life: The Construction of Scientific Facts. 2nd ed. Princeton, NJ: Princeton University Press.

Lave, Jean, and Steinar Kvale
1995   What Is Anthropological Research? An Interview with Jean Lave by Steinar Kvale. International Journal of Qualitative Studies in Education 8(3):219–228.

Lawless, Robert, Vinson Sutlive Jr., and Mario Zamora, eds.
1983   Fieldwork: The Human Experience. New York: Gordon and Breach.

Layton, Robert
1981   The Anthropology of Art. London: Granada.

Leach, Edmund
1957   The Epistemological Background to Malinowski's Empiricism. In Man and Culture: An Evaluation of the Work of Bronislaw Malinowski. Raymond Firth, ed. Pp. 119–137. New York: Harper Torchbooks.

LeCompte, Margaret, Wendy L. Millroy, and Judith Preissle, eds.
1992   Handbook of Qualitative Research in Education. San Diego, CA: Academic Press.

Lee, Raymond M.
1995   Dangerous Fieldwork. Thousand Oaks, CA: Sage.

Lévi-Strauss, Claude, and Didier Eribon
1991   Conversations with Claude Lévi-Strauss. (Translated by Paula Wissing.) Chicago: University of Chicago Press.

Lewin, Ellen, and William L. Leap, eds.
1996   Out in the Field: Reflections of Lesbian and Gay Anthropologists. Urbana: University of Illinois Press.
2002   Out in Theory: The Emergence of Lesbian and Gay Anthropology. Urbana: University of Illinois Press.

Lewis, Oscar
1961   The Children of Sanchez: Autobiography of a Mexican Family. New York: Random House.
1965   La Vida: A Puerto Rican Family in the Culture of Poverty—San Juan and New York. New York: Random House.

Lincoln, Yvonna, and Egon G. Guba
1985   Naturalistic Inquiry. Beverly Hills, CA: Sage.

Lindeman, E. C.
1924   Social Discovery: An Approach to the Study of Functional Groups. New York: Republic.

Lorenz, Konrad B.
1950   The Comparative Method in Studying Innate Behaviour Patterns. Symposia for the Society for Experimental Biology 4:221–268.

Maines, David R., William Shaffir, and Allan Turowetz
1980   Leaving the Field in Ethnographic Research: Reflections on the Entrance-Exit Hypothesis. In Fieldwork Experience. W. B. Shaffir, R. A. Stebbins, and A. Turowetz, eds. Pp. 261–281. New York: St. Martin's.

Malinowski, Bronislaw
1922   Argonauts of the Western Pacific. London: Routledge.
1929   The Sexual Life of Savages. New York: Halcyon House.
1967   A Diary in the Strict Sense of the Term. New York: Harcourt, Brace, and World.

Mead, Margaret
1953   National Character. In Anthropology Today. A. L. Kroeber, ed. Pp. 642–667. Chicago: University of Chicago Press.
1970   The Art and Technology of Fieldwork. In Handbook of Method in Cultural Anthropology. Raoul Naroll and Ronald Cohen, eds. Pp. 246–265. Garden City, NY: Natural History Press.

Medawar, Peter Brian
1969   The Art of the Soluble. Hammondworth, England: Penguin.

REFERENCES AND SELECT BIBLIOGRAPHY

Metcalf, Peter
2002   They Lie, We Lie: Getting on with Anthropology. London: Routledge.

Miles, Matthew B., and A. Michael Huberman
1984   Qualitative Data Analysis: A Sourcebook of New Methods. Beverly Hills, CA: Sage.
1994   Qualitative Data Analysis: An Expanded Sourcebook. 2nd ed. Thousand Oaks, CA: Sage.

Mintz, Sidney W.
1974   Worker in the Cane: A Puerto Rican Life History. New York: W. W. Norton. [Originally published 1960 by Yale University Press.]

Mitchell, Richard G., Jr.
1993   Secrecy and Fieldwork. Newbury Park, CA: Sage.

Moerman, Michael
1988   Talking Culture: Ethnography and Conversation Analysis. Philadelphia: University of Pennsylvania Press.

Moffatt, Michael
1989   Coming of Age in New Jersey: College and American Culture. New Brunswick, NJ: Rutgers University Press.

Moustakas, Clark
1994   Phenomenological Research Methods. Thousand Oaks, CA: Sage.

Murdock, George Peter
1971   Anthropology's Mythology. Proceedings of the Royal Anthropological Institute of Great Britain and Ireland for 1971:17–24.

Nisbet, Robert
1976   Sociology as an Art Form. New York: Oxford University Press.

Nyberg, David
1993   The Varnished Truth: Truth Telling and Deceiving in Ordinary Life. Chicago: University of Chicago Press.

Ottenberg, Simon
1990   Thirty Years of Fieldnotes: Changing Relationships to the Text. In Fieldnotes: The Makings of Anthropology. Roger Sanjek, ed. Pp. 139–160. Ithaca, NY: Cornell University Press.
1994   Changes over Time in an African Culture and in an Anthropologist. In Others Knowing Others. Don D. Fowler and Donald L. Hardesty, eds. Pp. 91–118. Washington, DC: Smithsonian Institution Press.

Paul, Benjamin D.
   1953   Interview Techniques and Field Relationships. *In* Anthropology To-
          day. A. L. Kroeber, ed. Pp. 430–451. Chicago: University of Chicago
          Press.

Peacock, James L.
   1986   The Anthropological Lens: Harsh Light, Soft Focus. New York:
          Cambridge University Press.

Pelto, Pertti J., and Gretel H. Pelto
   1978   Anthropological Fieldwork: The Structure of Inquiry. 2nd ed. New
          York: Cambridge University Press.

Plattner, Stuart
   1989   Commentary: Ethnographic Method. Anthropology Newsletter
          32:21, 30. Washington, DC: American Anthropological Association.

Poewe, Karla [pseudonym Manda Cesara]
   1982   Reflections of a Woman Anthropologist: No Hiding Place. New
          York: Academic Press.

Powdermaker, Hortense
   1950   Hollywood: The Dream Factory: An Anthropological Look at the
          Movie-makers. Boston: Little, Brown.
   1966   Stranger and Friend: The Way of an Anthropologist. New York:
          W. W. Norton.

Price, Sally
   1989   Primitive Art in Civilized Places. Chicago: University of Chicago
          Press.

Punch, Maurice
   1986   Politics and Ethics of Fieldwork: Beverly Hills, CA: Sage.

Rabinow, Paul
   1977   Reflections on Fieldwork in Morocco. Berkeley: University of Cali-
          fornia Press (Quantum Books).

Rappaport, Roy A.
   1994   Comment on "Cultural Anthropology's Future Agenda." Anthropol-
          ogy Newsletter 35(6):76.

Richards, Audrey I.
   1939   The Development of Field Work Methods in Social Anthropology.
          In The Study of Society. F. C. Bartlett, M. Ginsberg, E. J. Lindgren,

and R. H. Thouless, eds. Pp. 272–316. London: Kegan Paul, Trench, Trubner.

Richardson, Laurel
2000 Writing: A Method of Inquiry. *In* Handbook of Qualitative Research. 2nd ed. Norman K. Denzin and Yvonna S. Lincoln, eds. Pp. 923–948. Thousand Oaks, CA: Sage.

Romney, A. K., Susan Weller, and W. H. Batchelder
1986 Culture as Consensus: A Theory of Culture and Informant Accuracy. American Anthropologist 88:313–338.

Roth, Julius A.
1962 Comments on *Secret Observations*. Social Problems 9:283–284.

Rubin, Herbert J., and Irene S. Rubin
1995 Qualitative Interviewing: The Art of Hearing Data. Thousand Oaks, CA: Sage.

Rubinstein, Robert A., ed.
1991 Fieldwork: The Correspondence of Robert Redfield and Sol Tax. Boulder, CO: Westview Press.

Saldaña, Johnny
2002 Finding My Place: The Brad Trilogy. *In* Sneaky Kid and Its Aftermath: Ethics and Intimacy in Fieldwork, by Harry F. Wolcott. Pp. 167–210. Walnut Creek, CA: AltaMira Press.
2003 Dramatizing Data: A Primer. Qualitative Inquiry 9(2):218–236.

Sanjek, Roger
1990 On Ethnographic Validity. *In* Fieldnotes: The Makings of Anthropology. Roger Sanjek, ed. Pp. 385–418. Ithaca, NY: Cornell University Press.
1991 The Ethnographic Present. Man: The Journal of the Royal Anthropological Institute 26:609–628.

Sanjek, Roger, ed.
1990 Fieldnotes: The Makings of Anthropology. Ithaca, NY: Cornell University Press.

Sartwell, Crispin
1995 The Art of Living: Aesthetics of the Ordinary in World Spiritual Traditions. Albany, NY: State University of New York Press.

Schlechty, Phillip, and George W. Noblit
1982　Some Uses of Sociological Theory in Educational Evaluation. *In* Research in Sociology of Education and Socialization, Vol. 3. Pp. 283–306. Greenwich, CT: JAI Press.

Schram, Thomas H.
2003　Conceptualizing Qualitative Inquiry: Mindwork for Fieldwork in Education and the Social Sciences. Upper Saddle River, NJ: Pearson Education.

Seidel, John
1992　Method and Madness in the Application of Computer Technology to Qualitative Data Analysis. *In* Using Computers in Qualitative Research. Nigel G. Fielding and Raymond M. Lee, eds. Pp. 107–116. Newbury Park, CA: Sage.

Seidman, I. E.
1991　Interviewing as Qualitative Research: A Guide for Researchers in the Social Sciences. New York: Teachers College Press.

Shaffir, William B., and Robert A. Stebbins, eds.
1991　Experiencing Fieldwork: An Inside View of Qualitative Research. Newbury Park, CA: Sage.

Shweder, Richard A.
1996　True Ethnography: The Lore, the Law, and the Lure. *In* Ethnography and Human Development. Richard Jessor, Anne Colby, and Richard A. Shweder, eds. Pp. 15–52. Chicago: University of Chicago Press.

Silverman, David
1993　Interpreting Qualitative Data: Methods for Analyzing Talk, Text and Interaction. London: Sage.

Siu, Paul C. P.
1987　The Chinese Laundryman: A Study of Social Isolation. New York: New York University Press.

Slater, Mariam
1976　African Odyssey: An Anthropological Adventure. Garden City, NY: Anchor Press/Doubleday.

Smith, Alfred G.
1964　The Dionysian Innovation. American Anthropologist 66:251–265.

Smith, Robert J.
    1990   Hearing Voices, Joining the Chorus: Appropriating Someone Else's Fieldnotes. *In* Fieldnotes: The Makings of Anthropology. Roger Sanjek, ed. Pp. 356–370. Ithaca, NY: Cornell University Press.

Sparkes, Andrew C.
    2002   Telling Tales in Sport and Physical Activity: A Qualitative Journey. Champaign, IL: Human Kinetics.

Spicer, Edward H., ed.
    1952   Human Problems in Technological Change. New York: Russell Sage.

Spindler, George, ed.
    1955   Education and Anthropology. Stanford, CA: Stanford University Press.
    1970   Being an Anthropologist: Fieldwork in Eleven Cultures. New York: Holt, Rinehart and Winston.

Spindler, George, and Louise Spindler
    1965   The Instrumental Activities Inventory: A Technique for the Study of the Psychology of Acculturation. Southwestern Journal of Anthropology 21(1):1–23.

Spiro, Melford E.
    1990   On the Strange and the Familiar in Recent Anthropological Thought. *In* Cultural Psychology. J. W. Stigler, R. A. Shweder, and Gilbert Herdt, eds. Pp. 47–61. New York: Cambridge University Press.

Spradley, James P.
    1979   The Ethnographic Interview. New York: Holt, Rinehart and Winston.
    1980   Participant Observation. New York: Holt, Rinehart and Winston.

Stake, Robert E.
    1995   The Art of Case Study Research. Thousand Oaks, CA: Sage.

Stoller, Paul, and Cheryl Olkes
    1987   In Sorcery's Shadow: A Memoir of Apprenticeship among the Songhay of Niger. Chicago: University of Chicago Press.

Strickland, Donald A., and Lester E. Schlesinger
    1969   "Lurking" as a Research Method. Human Organization 28(3):248–251.

Tedlock, Barbara
1991　From Participant Observation to the Observation of Participation: The Emergence of Narrative Ethnography. Journal of Anthropological Research 47(1):69–94.

Turnbull, Colin M.
1961　The Forest People. New York: Simon and Schuster.
1965　Wayward Servants. Garden City, NY: Natural History Press.
1972　The Mountain People. New York: Simon and Schuster.

VanderStaay, Steven L.
2003　Believing Clayboy. Qualitative Inquiry 9(3):374–394.

Van Maanen, John
1978　On Watching the Watchers. In Policing: A View from the Street. P. K. Manning and J. Van Maanen, eds. Pp. 309–349. Santa Monica, CA: Goodyear.
1988　Tales of the Field: On Writing Ethnography. Chicago: University of Chicago Press.
1995　An End to Innocence: The Ethnography of Ethnography. In Representation in Ethnography. John Van Maanen, ed. Pp. 1–35. Thousand Oaks, CA: Sage.

van Willigen, John, and Timothy L. Finan
1991　Soundings: Rapid and Reliable Research Methods for Practicing Anthropologists. NAPA Bulletin #10. Washington, DC: American Anthropological Association.

van Willigen, John, Barbara Rylko-Bauer, and Ann McElroy, eds.
1989　Making Our Research Useful: Case Studies in the Utilization of Anthropological Knowledge. Boulder, CO: Westview Press.

Wagley, Charles
1983　Learning Fieldwork: Guatemala. In Fieldwork: The Human Experience. Robert Lawless, Vinson H. Sutlive Jr., and Mario D. Zamora, eds. Pp. 1–17. New York: Gordon and Breach.

Wax, Rosalie
1971　Doing Fieldwork: Warnings and Advice. Chicago: University of Chicago Press.

Wengle, John L.
1988　Ethnographers in the Field: The Psychology of Research. Tuscaloosa: University of Alabama Press.

Werner, Oswald, and G. Mark Schoepfle
    1987a Systematic Fieldwork. Vol. 1, Foundations of Ethnography and Interviewing. Newbury Park, CA: Sage.
    1987b Systematic Fieldwork. Vol. 2, Ethnographic Analysis and Data Management. Newbury Park, CA: Sage.

Whyte, William F.
    1943 Street Corner Society. Chicago: University of Chicago Press.
    1955 Street Corner Society, 2nd ed. Chicago: University of Chicago Press.
    1984 Learning from the Field: A Guide from Experience. Beverly Hills, CA: Sage.
    1994 Participant Observer: An Autobiography. Ithaca, NY: ILR Press, Cornell University.

Williams, Joseph M.
    1990 Style: Toward Clarity and Grace. Chicago: University of Chicago Press.

Wolcott, Harry F.
    1967 A Kwakiutl Village and School. New York: Holt, Rinehart and Winston.
    1973 The Man in the Principal's Office: An Ethnography. New York: Holt, Rinehart and Winston.
    1974 The African Beer Gardens of Bulawayo: Integrated Drinking in a Segregated Society. New Brunswick, NJ: Rutgers Center of Alcohol Studies. Monograph Number 10.
    1975 Feedback Influences on Fieldwork, Or: A Funny Thing Happened on the Way to the Beer Garden. *In* Urban Man in Southern Africa. Clive Kileff and Wade Pendleton, eds. Pp. 99–125. Gwelo, Rhodesia: Mambo Press.
    1977 Teachers versus Technocrats: An Educational Innovation in Anthropological Perspective. Eugene: Center for Educational Policy and Management, University of Oregon.
    1981 Home and Away: Personal Contrasts in Ethnographic Style. *In* Anthropologists at Home in North America: Methods and Issues in the Study of One's Own Society. Donald A. Messerschmidt, ed. Pp. 255–265. New York: Cambridge University Press.
    1982 Mirrors, Models, and Monitors: Educator Adaptations of the Ethnographic Innovation. *In* Doing the Ethnography of Schooling. George D. Spindler, ed. Pp. 68–95. New York: Holt, Rinehart and Winston.
    1983a Adequate Schools and Inadequate Education: The Life History of a Sneaky Kid. Anthropology and Education Quarterly 14:3–32.

1983b A Malay Village that Progress Chose: Sungai Lui and the Institute of Cultural Affairs. Human Organization 42:72–81.

1987 Life's Not Working: Cultural Alternatives to Career Alternatives. *In* Schooling in Social Context: Qualitative Studies. G. W. Noblit and W. T. Pink, eds. Pp. 303–325. Norwood, NJ: Ablex.

1988 Ethnographic Research in Education. *In* Complementary Methods for Research in Education. Richard M. Jaeger, ed. Pp. 187–249. Washington, DC: American Educational Research Association. [Also reprinted in the second edition, 1997, pp. 327–398.]

1990 On Seeking—and Rejecting—Validity in Qualitative Research. *In* Qualitative Inquiry in Education: The Continuing Debate. Elliot W. Eisner and Alan Peshkin, eds. Pp. 121–152. New York: Teachers College.

1994a Confessions of a "Trained" Observer. *In* Transforming Qualitative Data: Description, Analysis, and Interpretation. Pp. 149–172. Thousand Oaks, CA: Sage.

1994b Transforming Qualitative Data: Description, Analysis, and Interpretation. Thousand Oaks, CA: Sage.

1997 The Teacher as an Enemy. *In* Education and Cultural Process: Anthropological Approaches. 3rd ed. George D. Spindler, ed. Pp. 77–92. Prospect Heights, IL: Waveland Press.

2001 Writing Up Qualitative Research. 2nd ed. Thousand Oaks, CA: Sage.

2002 Sneaky Kid and Its Aftermath: Ethics and Intimacy in Fieldwork. Walnut Creek, CA: AltaMira Press.

2003a A Kwakiutl Village and School. Updated Edition. Walnut Creek, CA: AltaMira Press.

2003b The Man in the Principal's Office: An Ethnography. Updated Edition. Walnut Creek, CA: AltaMira Press.

2003c A "Natural" Writer. Anthropology and Education Quarterly 34(3):324–338.

2003d Teachers versus Technocrats: Updated Edition. Walnut Creek, CA: AltaMira Press.

2004 The Ethnographic Autobiography. Auto/Biography 12(2): 93–106.

Wolf, Eric
1964 Anthropology. Englewood Cliffs, NJ: Prentice Hall.

Woolgar, Steven
1983 Irony in the Social Study of Science. *In* Science Observed: Perspectives on the Social Study of Science. K. D. Knorr-Cetina and M. J. Mulkay, eds. Beverly Hills, CA: Sage.

Young, David E., and Jean-Guy Goulet, eds.
1994 Being Changed: The Anthropology of Extraordinary Experience. Peterborough, Ontario: Broadview Press.

Zelditch, Morris
1962 Some Methodological Problems of Field Studies. American Journal of Sociology 67:566–576.

NAME INDEX

SUBJECT INDEX

ABOUT THE AUTHOR/ABOUT THE BOOK

Harry Wolcott began doing fieldwork in 1962, began writing up fieldwork in 1963, began lecturing about fieldwork in 1967, and began writing about the doing of fieldwork in 1970. He has been engaged in these pursuits ever since. On completing doctoral studies at Stanford University in 1964, he accepted a position at the University of Oregon as a research associate in its newly funded Research and Development Center in Educational Administration. Having survived four decades of administrative changes, he is still at Oregon. He has served on the faculties of education and anthropology and is now professor emeritus in the Department of Anthropology.

This second edition of *The Art of Fieldwork* incorporates more than fifteen years of his publishing history in association with Mitch Allen, publisher of AltaMira Press, now a division of Rowman & Littlefield. That association began in 1988 when Mitch approached him about writing a monograph for the Sage series on qualitative research. Following that, Mitch asked then, as he has asked ever since, "What are you going to do for us next?" The answer on that occasion was a proposed collection of several chapter-length pieces to be combined with some new material and published as *Transforming Qualitative Data*. Before Mitch could ask his perennial question again, he had his own imprimatur, AltaMira Press. Wolcott was given the option of publishing *The Art of Fieldwork* under Mitch's aegis or staying with the parent firm. He opted to go with AltaMira Press.

By the time Wolcott completed *Ethnography: A Way of Seeing*, Mitch and AltaMira Press had joined forces with Rowman & Littlefield. At Mitch's urging, Wolcott next developed the story of the Sneaky Kid from a life story that began in 1980. After *Sneaky Kid and Its Aftermath: Ethics and Intimacy in Fieldwork* was completed in 2002, a revision of *The Art of Fieldwork* seemed overdue, and here it is.

* * *

The Art of Fieldwork was something of a complement to those two earliest Sage publications, giving attention both to fieldwork and to the essential mindwork that must accompany it. Its focus is on the distinction between the orderly activities of data gathering and whatever else is involved that makes fieldwork more than just that. This is not to insist that fieldwork is art, but rather to suggest that the doing of fieldwork calls for qualities we associate with the imaginative and creative work of the artist as much as it calls for the systematic efforts of the scientist. That remains the book's purpose and focus.

The success of the first edition of *The Art of Fieldwork* left its author cautious about editing it for a second. His goal was to leave what worked, to improve what didn't, and to update the text to include current sources as well as to preserve the original ones. While Wolcott's own orientation is ethnographic, the book deals with fieldwork in general.

A number of people helped with the first edition and are acknowledged there. For this revision the author once again asked Mark Wohl to cast a sharp editorial eye over the entire manuscript, the earlier material as well as the new. Subsequently, Jen Kelland did a masterful job of copyediting. Thanks are due also to Johnny Saldaña and, as always, to Mitch Allen for timely suggestions.